ONTARIO'S AFRICAN-CANADIAN HERITAGE

Collected Writings by Fred Landon, 1918–1967

Fred Landon. *Courtesy of Hilary Bates Neary.*

ONTARIO'S AFRICAN-CANADIAN HERITAGE

Collected Writings by Fred Landon, 1918–1967

edited by

Karolyn
Smardz Frost
Bryan
Walls
Hilary
Bates Neary
Frederick H.
Armstrong

on behalf of The Ontario Historical Society

NATURAL HERITAGE BOOKS
A MEMBER OF THE DUNDURN GROUP
TORONTO

Copy-edited by Chad Fraser
Proofreader: Allison Hirst
Designed by Courtney Horner
Printed and bound in Canada by Webcom

Library and Archives Canada Cataloguing in Publication

Landon, Fred, 1880-1969.
    Ontario's African-Canadian heritage : collected writings by Fred Landon, 1918-1967 / edited by Frederick Armstrong, Bryan Walls, Karolyn Smardz Frost and Hilary Bates Neary.

Includes bibliographical references and index.
ISBN 978-1-55002-814-0

    1. Blacks--Ontario--History. 2. Black Canadians--Ontario--History. 3. Landon, Fred, 1880-1969. I. Armstrong, F. H. (Frederick Henry), 1926- II. Walls, Bryan E. III. Smardz Frost, Karolyn, 1956- IV. Title.

FC3100.B6L36 2008   971.3'00496   C2008-900712-3

1   2   3   4   5   13   12   11   10   09

We acknowledge the support of **The Canada Council for the Arts** and the **Ontario Arts Council** for our publishing program. We also acknowledge the financial support of the **Government of Canada** through the **Book Publishing Industry Development Program** and **The Association for the Export of Canadian Books**, and the **Government of Ontario** through the **Ontario Book Publishers Tax Credit** program, and the **Ontario Media Development Corporation**.

Care has been taken to trace the ownership of copyright material used in this book. The author and the publisher welcome any information enabling them to rectify any references or credits in subsequent editions.

J. Kirk Howard, President

Printed and bound in Canada.
www.dundurn.com
Published by Natural Heritage Books
A Member of The Dundurn Group

Front Cover: Horace Pippin, artist. Interior, oil on canvas. Gift of Mr. and Mrs. Meyer P. Potamkin, in honour of the 50th anniversary of the National Gallery of Art, 1991.42.1/PA. Courtesy of the Board of Trustees, National Gallery of Art, Washington, 1944.
Back Cover: The Travis family settled in the Queen's Bush, Normanby Township, before moving on to Buxton. Courtesy of Buxton Historic Site and Museum.

Dundurn Press	Gazelle Book Services Limited	Dundurn Press
3 Church Street, Suite 500	White Cross Mills	2250 Military Road
Toronto, Ontario, Canada	High Town, Lancaster, England	Tonawanda, NY
M5E 1M2	LA1 4XS	U.S.A. 14150

Table of Contents

Letter from the Honourable Jean Augustine, P.C.

 The Ontario Historical Society is to be congratulated on the publication of this lovely retrospective volume on the writings of Dr. Fred Landon.

As Chair of the Bicentenary Commemorative Committee on the Abolition of the Atlantic Slave Trade Act, I am proud that a Roots of Freedom Grant helped support the project to reprint Dr. Landon's landmark scholarship relating to Ontario's African-Canadian past.

Ontario's African-Canadian Heritage: The Collected Writings by Fred Landon 1918–1967, edited by Karolyn Smardz Frost, Bryan Walls, Hilary Bates Neary, and Fred Armstrong, is a remarkable contribution. It makes accessible to teachers and students, as well as scholars and the general public, articles that shed light on many aspects of Black history in this province.

Most of the articles in this volume were first printed in the pages of *Ontario History* and in the then-new publication, the *Journal of Negro History*. This was produced at Washington D.C. by Carter G. Woodson. Dr. Woodson was founder of both the Association for the Study of African American Life and History and of Negro History Week, now celebrated as Black History Month. I am proud to have been the Member of Parliament for Etobicoke-Lakeshore who sponsored the 1995 all-party bill to make Black History Month a national celebration in Canada.

It is vitally important that every schoolchild in Canada understand the role played by peoples of African descent in building the nation as we know it today. This book, which both celebrates and illuminates Ontario's proud African-Canadian heritage, will assist in meeting that goal.

Sincerely,

Augustine

Hon. Jean Augustine, P.C.

11

Foreword

A Tribute to Fred Landon

As a proud past president of The Ontario Historical Society, I thank the society for asking me to share my deeper thoughts about the prolific writer Fred Landon. I would also like to thank my colleagues, Karolyn Smardz Frost, Hilary Bates Neary, and Fred Armstrong, for making this literary project so enjoyable. I never had the privilege of meeting Dr. Landon, but having read his wonderful writings, contained within the pages of this book, I feel that I understand where his inspiration came from. I am reminded of a poem written by the great writer Langston Hughes, who wrote these words:

> The Night is Beautiful, so are the faces of my people,
> The Stars are Beautiful, so are the eyes of my people,
> Beautiful also is the Sun, Beautiful also are the Souls
> of my people!

And, if I may paraphrase, Beautiful also was the Soul of Fred Landon.

The capacity to care is the thing that gives life its greatest significance, and Fred Landon cared about the souls of, as Langston Hughes would say, my people. I am a direct descendant of the people Landon wrote about. As a descendant, writer, and founder of the John Freeman Walls Historic Site and Underground Railroad Museum, I feel that I understand the deeper reasons why Landon was so captivated and inspired to write about African-Canadian history. Allow me to go off on a tangent for a moment and share a bit of my own family history, to more fully explain my thoughts regarding Fred Landon.

At the entrance to the John Freeman Walls Historic Site and Underground Railroad Museum there is a historic plaque that reads:

In 1846, John Freeman Walls, a fugitive enslaved from North Carolina, built a log cabin on land purchased from the Refugee Home Society, an organization founded by the abolitionist Henry Bibb, publisher of the *Voice of the Fugitive* and the famous Josiah Henson. The cabin, subsequently, served as a terminal of the Underground Railroad and the first meeting place of the First Baptist Church, Puce. Although many former slaves returned to the United States following the American Civil War, Walls and his family chose to remain in Canada; the story of their struggles forms the basis of the book, *The Road That Led To Somewhere*.

When I was doing research for my book, *The Road That Led to Somewhere*, I was fortunate to have the opportunity to interview my aunt, Stella Butler. Aunt Stella was a third-generation Canadian and the Griot of my family. *Griot* is the African term for "keeper of the oral history," and she told me many fascinating stories of, as she would describe them, "old-time days." Subsequent to the interviews, she encouraged me to take on her role and become the modern-day Griot of my family, and to write down the story for future generations to enjoy. Her wisdom traversed many decades, as she was born in 1884 and passed away in 1986, at 102 years of age. She did not have, as she would have described it, "a lot of book learning." However, she had a steely determination, the wisdom that comes with age, and the experience to know how to inspire people to listen to her and take her stories seriously. I remember her kind, yet resolute, stare that went through your eyes, past your intellect, and settled forever in your soul. You simply could not disobey Aunt Stella, or marginalize her requests. Thus, building on the oral African tradition, I researched and verified the truth of the legends that she told me and I enthusiastically wrote them down in documented narrative book form. Her mind was keen right up until the end of her life. During her one-hundredth year, I had a lawyer, Mr. Robert Baksi, carefully go over, sentence by sentence, the oral history that she told to me, and she signed, for posterity, a statutory declaration of truth. After signing the document, to let the young lawyer know that her mind was not given to exaggeration or feebleness, she recited a five-minute poem that she had learned in primary school. While interviewing Aunt Stella on another occasion, I directly asked what, to her knowledge, had caused slavery. She was 23 years old when our ancestors, John and Jane, who had escaped the slave South, died. Aunt Stella had talked to them on many occasions around an old kerosene lantern in their tiny log cabin. She looked at me and slowly shook her head. Then she rubbed her thumb and index finger together as if counting money, and said, "Greed."

She told me that my ancestors thirsted for freedom so much that they would literally run through the woods at night and hide by day; they thirsted for freedom so much that at times they would even kneel down and drink rainwater out of the hoofprints of cattle in order to quench their thirst and continue their perilous journey on the Underground Railroad to the heaven that they sang about in their songs, namely Canada.

I share this personal story of my aunt to partially explain why Fred Landon was inspired to write prolifically about African-Canadian people. Although many were from a time of oppression, and often of meagre means, nevertheless they were, like Aunt Stella, proud, intelligent, charming, and full of a passion for life and freedom. As a writer, Landon must have been touched by the souls of these ordinary people who thirsted to tell their extraordinary tales, and who thirsted to feel important, appreciated, and to make a contribution to their new, cold, and distant land called Canada.

I also intuitively feel, after reading his writings, that another reason why Fred Landon was inspired to do such groundbreaking writing is because he had the compassionate soul of a nineteenth-century abolitionist freedom fighter. I am certain that if he had been born at another time and place, he would have risked his life to help my ancestors and others to freedom. Fred knew that the Underground Railroad was the first great freedom movement in the Americas, and the first time that good people, Black and white, and of different races and faiths, worked together in harmony for freedom and justice. His friendship, and support of the work of Carter G. Woodson, founder of the Association for the Study of African-American Life and History, further underscores his celebration of multiculturalism.

Fred Landon's writings speak to me with deep significance on a humanitarian level. He understood the essence of the people he wrote about. He understood that you cannot take freedom for granted. Through their stories and his writings, we must all, on a daily basis, continue to develop the fruits of the spirit, the fruits of love, joy, peace, patience, kindness, gentleness, and self-control, against which there is no argument. He does not diminish the role of faith in giving strength and courage to the freedom seekers ennobled in his writings. In fact, he writes that Ontario churches were friends to the panic-stricken fugitives fleeing from drastic slave laws. The first thing these desperate pioneers did was kneel down, kiss the ground, and thank the good Lord that they were free. Then, they immediately built churches where they could sing their praises. Symbolized by the words of that old spiritual, "Swing low, sweet chariot, coming for to carry me home ..." that home became places like Amherstburg, Chatham, St. Catharines, Windsor, Sandwich, the Buxton Settlement, Dresden, Wilberforce, and the Refugee Home Society (in the Town of Lakeshore, near Windsor). And some were places with less familiar names, like: New Canaan, Matthew Settlement, Haiti Village, Shrewsbury, Gilgal, and others. Like the uncovering of an Egyptian tomb in terms of historical wealth, Landon entered into the kings' chamber of Canadian and American history.

Landon's writings applaud Canadian and American historic notables such as Henry Bibb, Samuel Ringgold Ward, John Brown, Dr. Alexander Milton Ross, Reverend William King, Abraham Lincoln, and many more. However, he does not forget lesser-known freedom fighters and pioneer Canadians who make up the bulk of his literary work. His writings underscore the fact that we must remain committed to celebrating diversity and promoting mutual respect, reconciliation, and co-operation. There is innate goodness in humanity; however, we still face the same challenges today that existed during the time that Landon was writing. The age-old challenge is to follow the Golden Rule and to do unto others as we would have them do unto us. Fred Landon's writings give us hope, especially in our post 9/11 world.

History tells us that there are always good people who are willing to help and tell the stories of those who are oppressed; Landon was one of these people. The motto of the Order of Canada is *"Desiderantes Meliorem Patriam,"* translated, "They Desire a Better Country." This book helps us get to that better place, that better country. It celebrates the importance of freedom of mind, body, and soul. Writers of, as Aunt Stella would describe, "old-time days," must celebrate the fact that we stand on the shoulders of the great women and men who have gone before and paved the way. None are more deserving of our respect and praise than Dr. Fred Landon.

Dr. Bryan E. Walls, C.M. O.Ont.

Introduction

This book, *Ontario's African-Canadian Heritage: Collected Writings by Fred Landon, 1918–1967*, is the culminating project for The Ontario Historical Society's (OHS) commemoration of the Bicentenary of the Abolition of the Atlantic Slave Trade within the British Empire, celebrated in 2007. It is expected that the volume will find a very broad audience, for not only is there tremendous and rising interest in African-Canadian history, but Fred Landon's writing is both engaging and informative. Many of his articles stand to this day as authoritative resources for the study of several aspects of Ontario's Black history.

Ontario's African-Canadian Heritage: Collected Writings by Fred Landon, 1918–1967 is comprised of a series of articles about Ontario's rich African-Canadian past written by Fred Landon over the course of his long life. It is the first attempt to publish the collected results of Landon's groundbreaking research into this crucial aspect of our provincial history. Many of his papers were first published in the pages of *Ontario History* and its predecessor journal, *Ontario Historical Society, Papers and Records*. Landon was a long-time member of the OHS Board of Directors, and from 1926–28 he chaired the society.

To celebrate the 2007 bicentenary of the abolition of the Atlantic slave trade within the British Empire, Canada joined with many other nations in support of the United Nations resolution of November 20, 2006, to commemorate this important landmark in the struggle for human liberty.

The UN Secretary-General was asked, in collaboration with the United Nations Educational, Scientific and Cultural Organization (UNESCO), to establish an outreach program to mobilize educational institutions and civil society so that future generations will learn the lessons of the transatlantic slave trade, and to highlight the dangers posed by racism and discrimination in today's global community. March 25 has been designated the International Day of Remembrance for the Victims of Slavery and the Transatlantic Slave Trade.

Participating nations were challenged to develop their own information and education programs. The Province of Ontario announced, on March 21, 2007, the allocation of one million dollars in grant funding. This was to be distributed by the newly struck Committee for the Commemoration of the Abolition of the Atlantic Slave Trade Act, chaired by Ontario's fairness commissioner, former federal member of Parliament, and long-time professional educator, the Honourable Dr. Jean Augustine. Dr. Karolyn Smardz Frost, then executive director of The Ontario Historical Society and a scholar of African-Canadian history, was among the fifteen people appointed to the committee.

The committee's granting program was entitled "The Roots of Freedom." All allocations were made based on staff recommendations, with strict adherence to all conflict-of-interest guidelines.

A proposal from The Ontario Historical Society was accepted. The plan was twofold: the first phase involved the development of an educational website to publish the scholarly papers delivered at the OHS Annual Conference of 2007. The conference was entitled "Forging Freedom: A Conference in Honour of the Abolition of the Atlantic Slave Trade." The website was to include a series of lesson plans based on the papers, so that teachers could introduce this cutting-edge scholarship to students of elementary, middle, and secondary schools. The second phase of the project was to be the publication of a book highlighting The Ontario Historical Society's long-time commitment to publishing in the field of African-Canadian heritage. It was decided that, since Fred Landon published much of the earliest work on African-Canadian history in the pages of *Ontario History*, a collected volume of his work would be a most appropriate memorial, and would meet the terms of the UN resolution.

Fred Landon was an exceptional man. A journalist, librarian, and eventually the chief librarian at the University of Western Ontario, as well as a much-loved history professor at that institution, Landon was also a community historian of unparalleled stature. Remarkable for a Canadian scholar of his era in his appreciation of the centrality of the African-Canadian experience to Ontario's growth as a province, Fred

Landon and his colleague, Justice William Renwick Riddell, also an OHS board member, began their investigations into the Ontario Black experience just after the First World War. It was a time when academic historians gave but glancing mention, if any at all, to the Black presence in Canada. As a result, the works of Landon and Riddell stand forth as almost the only early-twentieth-century examples of research into this uniquely important aspect of our provincial history.

Fred Landon, a white historian from London, Ontario, was also exemplary among the scholars of his generation in his personal support for Black activism, both in Ontario and abroad. He was an admirer of Dr. Carter G. Woodson, who had just convinced the American government to acknowledge Negro History Week, the precursor of Black History Month on both sides of the border. Landon supported the efforts of Dr. Woodson and the newly formed Association for the Study of African American Life and History to publish the results of fresh research illuminating the North American Black experience. Starting in 1918, Fred Landon published a long series of truly seminal articles in the *Journal of Negro History*, he and William Renwick Riddell being the first Canadians to do so.

Landon was also engaged in African-Canadian issues closer to home: in 1924, he and Sir Adam Beck (who established the Hydro-Electric Power Commission of Ontario and who, in 1924, was the member of provincial parliament for the London district), worked with the Georgia-born African-American James Jenkins of London and J.W. Montgomery of Toronto to found the Canadian League for the Advancement of Coloured People (CLACP). Jenkins, later appointed a London District youth court judge, had established a Black newspaper in that city just a year earlier. The *Dawn of Tomorrow* became the vehicle for the CLACP. The Canadian government chartered the league in 1925 as the equivalent to the American NAACP, established at the instigation of W.E.B. DuBois in 1909. Branches of the CLACP were also founded at Dresden, Brantford, Niagara Falls, Toronto, and Hamilton, Ontario.

Beginning in 1918 with "The Buxton Settlement in Canada," published in the Washington-based *Journal of Negro History*, Fred Landon wrote a long succession of both scholarly and popular articles on

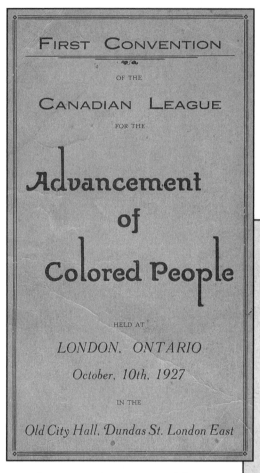

Below: Fred Landon, seventh on the list, was a member of the executive board. *Courtesy of Manuscripts, Archives and Rare Books Division, Schomburg Center for Research in Black Culture, The New York Public Library, Astor, Lenox and Tilden Foundations, 1259968.*

CHAIRMAN A. E. SILVERWOOD

AND MEMBERS OF EXECUTIVE BOARD

DAVID ROSS, Treasurer
J. F. JENKINS, Secretary
G. A. WENIGE
JAMES GRAY
JOHN GUNN
REV. G. Q. WARNER
PROF. FRED LANDON
HARRY WRAY
E. R. DENNIS
E. J. CARTY
R. H. WADE
A. J. E. BUTLER
PAUL LEWIS
MAX LERNER
DEAN TUCKER
REV. F. O. STEWART
J. M. MONTGOMERY
REV. W. F. SEAY
REV. THOMAS WOODCOCK
COL. W. G. COLES
C. H. BROWN

The Advisory Board

HON. WM. R. RIDDELL, L.L.B.
W. T. SAMPSON, ESQ.
C. L. BURTON, ESQ.
PROF. J. A. DALE
PRES. W. SHERWOOD FOX
DR. H. W. HILL
J. A. SLEMIN, ESQ.
C. L. MESSACER, ESQ.

Above: First Convention of the Canadian League for the Advancement of Coloured People held at London, Ontario, October 10, 1927, in the Old City Hall, Dundas Street, London East. *Courtesy of Manuscripts, Archives and Rare Books Division, Schomburg Center for Research in Black Culture, The New York Public Library, Astor, Lenox and Tilden Foundations, 1259960.*

Below: James Jenkins, born in Atlanta, Georgia, and his wife Christina published the *Dawn of Tomorrow* weekly newspaper. Jenkins was a founding member of the Canadian League for the Advancement of Coloured People and a Juvenile Court judge in London, Ontario. *Courtesy of Manuscripts, Archives and Rare Books Division, Schomberg Center for Research in Black Culture, The New York Public Library, Astor, Lenox and Tilden Foundations, 1259963.*

Above: John Montgomery of Toronto worked with James Jenkins and Fred Landon to establish the Canadian Association for the Advancement of Coloured People, a branch of the United States-based National Association for the Advancement of Colored People (NAACP). During the First World War, he founded the Home Service Association that entertained and assisted African-Canadian enlisted men, and after the war provided community services to families and youth. *Courtesy of Manuscripts, Archives and Rare Books Division, Schomburg Center for Research in Black Culture, The New York Public Library, Astor, Lenox and Tilden Foundations, 1259961.*

the subject of Black Ontarians and their legacy. Fred Landon's impact on what was then a much-neglected field was profound. In fact, his research into many aspects of African-Canadian heritage in this province has not been surpassed to this day, hence this book.

Ontario's African-Canadian Heritage: Collected Writings by Fred Landon, 1918–1967 is a combined effort by four editors, two of whom, Dr. Bryan Walls and Dr. Frederick H. Armstrong, are former presidents of The Ontario Historical Society. Dr. Walls is a noted author, playwright, and anti-racism activist as well as the owner and operator of the John Freeman Walls Historic Site in Puce, Ontario, where his own ancestors settled after arriving in Canada on the Underground Railroad. He has been honoured with both the Order of Ontario and the Order of Canada for his work in anti-racism education with the Metropolitan Toronto Police Department. Historian Frederick H. Armstrong, who knew Fred Landon personally, is professor emeritus of the University of Western Ontario. A well-known author of books and articles mainly dealing with Toronto's urban history, his most notable work on African-Canadians is his landmark "The Toronto Directories and the Negro Community in the Late 1840s," *Ontario History*, vol. 61 (1969).

Hilary Bates Neary is a respected community historian from London, Ontario, who completed her master's degree on the life and works of William Renwick Riddell under Dr. Armstrong. In 1970, she published a bibliography of Landon's academic publications in *Ontario History*, after his death in 1969, and also frequently contributed to the "Book Notes" section of that journal.

Dr. Karolyn Smardz Frost was executive director of The Ontario Historical Society at the time this project was initiated. She edited the first *Ontario History* issue on the subject of Ontario Black history to commemorate the bicentenary in the spring of 2007, and initiated "Forging Freedom: A Conference in Honour of the Bicentenary of the Abolition of the Atlantic Slave Trade," which took place in St. Catharines, Ontario, in June 2007. Dr. Frost's book, *I've Got a Home in Glory Land: A Lost Tale of the Underground Railroad*, the biography of fugitive slaves Lucie and Thornton Blackburn was some twenty years in the making, and won the 2007 Governor General's Award for Non-Fiction.

Introduction

Ontario's African-Canadian Heritage: Collected Writings by Fred Landon, 1918–1967, stands as both a memorial to Fred Landon's prodigious scholarship and a tribute to the lives and experiences of the more than 35,000 people of African descent who chose to make their homes here in Ontario during the tumultuous years before the American Civil War. The editors have made very few changes to the original articles; they stand almost entirely as Fred Landon wrote and published them over the course of his long life. In the interests of historical authenticity, we have chosen to leave the terminology he used as it stood. Consequently, readers will note the use of the terms "Negro," "race," and "coloured" in the pages of the book, reflecting common usage at the time of Landon's writing. There are also quotations from nineteenth-century newspapers. These Fred Landon used to demonstrate the degree of racial discrimination in Canada faced by incoming "passengers" on the Underground Railroad. For the same reason, the original wording has been retained in this book. Readers should take note that some contain offensive language, and that Fred Landon's turns of phrase and references to racial and other issues are at times antiquated.

In order to enhance access to resources, the editors have added publication and other information to works cited in the notes. In a few cases we have also added annotations of our own, indicated by the use of square brackets to include more modern resource material not available in Fred Landon's day, to identify some personalities perhaps not readily recognizable to today's readers, or to make minor corrections based on more recent scholarship. Where such corrections or additions are associated directly with his articles, we have used an asterisk to mark the annotation. Otherwise, the changes are those needed for the sake of consistency: numbers over ten have shown as numerals, the word "Black" is capitalized to reflect modern usage, minor alterations have been made to punctuation and wording for the sake of clarity, and once an interesting endnote was moved into the body of a chapter (Chapter 3, note 19).

In closing, the editors would like to thank the editors of the *Journal of Negro History* at the Association for the Study of African American Life and History, the *Transactions of the London & Middlesex Historical*

Society, and the *London Free Press* for their kind permission to reproduce articles by Fred Landon originally published in their pages. Kirk Howard of the Dundurn Group has been a long-time friend and supporter of The Ontario Historical Society, as have Barry Penhale and Jane Gibson, of Natural Heritage Books, a member of the Dundurn Group. They deserve our sincere gratitude for their encouragement and generosity throughout the development of this book. Drs. Jean Augustine and Afua Cooper, and all the members of the Bicentenary Committee for the Commemoration of the Abolition of the Slave Trade Act were enthusiastic about this project's possibilities from the very beginning. We thank them, as well as the former minister of citizenship and immigration, Mike Colle, and the current minister of citizenship and immigration, Michael Chan, for their financial assistance in helping make this volume of work possible. Finally, our thanks to the Board of Directors of The Ontario Historical Society, to Executive Director Robert Leverty, and to past chair Chris Oslund for seeing the value in *Ontario's African-Canadian Heritage: Collected Writings by Fred Landon, 1918–1967,* and for helping make this book a reality.

Dr. Karolyn Smardz Frost

Life of Fred Landon (1880-1969)

While writing this piece on Fred Landon, a person I knew, some forty years after his death, I often asked myself, "why did I not think to ask him what influenced his action on this occasion?" This is particularly the case for Fred Landon's early career. Sources of information on Landon during that period are frequently inaccurate, and there is little certain information on his background and early years.

For one who grew up in a very conservative city, in a family that was reasonably comfortable, Fred Landon's liberal outlook and interest in the lives of common people seem a bit surprising, and, as suggested below, it was probably his rather brief exposure to the wider world through working on Great Lakes ships that was a major factor in his later writing.

Landon was born in London, Ontario, on August 1, 1880, the son of Abram Landon, a mason from Kent County, Ontario, who moved to London toward the end of the 1870s. Abram and his wife, Hannah Helen Landon (née Smith), had two children, Fred, and his sister, Florence, who died at the age of sixteen in 1900. Abram died in May 1904, aged about fifty-two; but his wife, like her son, had a long life, dying at the age of eighty in 1940.

Landon was educated in the city schools and afterwards, from about 1898 on, was employed in the wholesale dry-goods business of R.C. Struthers & Co. As noted, the sources for his early career are not clear, but, about the spring of 1901, he joined the Northern Navigation Company of Sarnia and became a Great Lakes sailor. Landon worked on *The United Empire* and the passenger-freighter *Majestic*, where he was the assistant purser. He returned to London in December 1903.

The reason for the occupational change to the lake ships was probably a need to raise sufficient funds to attend university, for he enrolled at the Western University of London, Ontario, as the University of Western Ontario was then called, upon his return.

As noted, this nautical recess from a lifetime residence in an inland city, though brief, was probably very influential in forming his future interests in both his teaching and writing. Although social history was pretty well ignored by most writers of his day, who tended to concentrate on political and constitutional issues, Landon's writing would focus on social conditions.

Working on the ships, visiting the diverse Great Lakes cities, and mingling with their peoples, he would have met a wide variety of individuals, an experience that must have been a major factor in developing his interest in the working classes, their outlook, and their living conditions. As well, it would have given him a much broader picture of life in the United States.

To categorize his academic writings, some naturally dealt with library issues, or political/constitutional history. His interests, however, as noted, were particularly directed to the study of social history, often with an emphasis on the lives of the oppressed. As he himself expressed in the title of one of his articles, he concentrated on the life of the "common man." His last book, *An Exile from Canada to Van Dieman's Land* (1960), recounts the difficulties of a rebel prisoner exiled to Tasmania after the 1837 rebellions.

Two categories particularly stand out in his many articles: Great Lakes studies and Black history. Regarding the first, from 1943–69 he devoted some forty publications to the Great Lakes and their shipping. Also, when the journal *Inland Seas* was established in 1945, he became both a frequent contributor and a lifelong member of the editorial board. His most extensive work in this field was *Lake Huron* (1944), a work of history for the American Lakes Series. At that time, an American war bond committee was raising money by having authors donate manuscripts, which were then auctioned off for bond purchases. Landon donated the Lake Huron manuscript for the auction, and it was then given to the Detroit Public Library.

Growing up in London, Landon would naturally have been familiar with the city's flourishing Black community, and during his lake voyages he probably witnessed the more stringent conditions under which Blacks lived in the American border centres. Certainly, the subject that engaged his scholarly interest the most was the history of Blacks in Ontario. When

Hilary Bates Neary compiled a general bibliography of Fred Landon's writings in 1970, fifty-four were indexed in the category of "The Negro in Canada, Colonization, Settlement, Abolition Movements and the Underground Railway." Many of these were scholarly articles published between 1918 and 1960 in the *Journal of Negro History* and in the publications of The Ontario Historical Society. For this book, Neary has produced a bibliography of Landon's publications in Black history that includes his newspaper articles. This bibliography numbers 153 titles.

To return to his career, at the time he enrolled at university in 1903, after working on the ships, Western University was a fledgling institution in very strapped financial circumstances. Struggling to survive, it had no money to expand, or to assist students with scholarships. It was, however, attracting some very able students. Landon's seven-member class included two other future scholars: Norman S.B. Grass, later a professor of business history at Harvard, who was one of the first academic writers to study the development of cities, and Ray Palmer Baker, who had a prominent career at the Rensselaer Polytechnic Institute at Troy, New York.

While studying at Western, Landon also worked for a time as assistant secretary of the local YMCA. He received his Bachelor of Arts degree in 1906, and although he was not able to continue his studies at that time, he maintained his connections to the university. Immediately, he worked at the *London Free Press* for a decade, where his varied, deadline-hastened assignments must have sharpened his writing abilities. During these years he was mostly stationed in London, but had two stints in the Press Gallery at Ottawa in 1906–07 and 1912–14. Before the first, in 1905, he held the title of news editor and, in 1900–10, he was the city editor.

While at the *Free Press*, Landon formed what would become a lifelong friendship with Arthur R. Ford, who would become editor-in-chief of the newspaper and chancellor of the University of Western Ontario. Later, and for many years, both Ford and Landon would frequently contribute to the *Free Press*'s historical column, "Looking Over Western Ontario," where some of Landon's articles dealt with Black history.

Landon married during his journalism years, but unfortunately there were tragedies in his life. His first wife, Lena Rowntree, died in 1912, and in 1914 he married Margaret Smith, of Ivan, Middlesex County, who outlived him, dying at the age of ninety-three in 1982. They had three children, a daughter Mary, a son Alan Frederick, who was killed in a sleighing accident in 1930, and an adopted son Robert.

Family life would have dictated a more settled career than journalism, and in 1916 he accepted an offer to become chief librarian of the London Public Library, then another fledgling institution, a post he held for seven years. His particular monument at the library is the excellent collection of research material on the city, which he began, and which has developed into the collections now kept in the library's Ivey Family London Room.

He maintained his library connections in later life, becoming a member of the library board from 1950–66 and chairman of the board of trustees of its associated art gallery. In 1955, the library showed its appreciation for his work by naming its Wortley Road branch, in Old South London, in his honour.

During these years there was a duality in his efforts, for he concurrently held a lectureship in history and English at the university. There, in 1917, Fred Landon introduced Canada's first American history course, entitled "The Constitutional and Diplomatic History of The United States."

He was also simultaneously working on his master's degree in history, which he completed in 1919. His thesis topic, "The Relation of Canada to the Anti-Slavery and Abolition Movements in the United States," foreshadowed the many articles that appear in this book.

As well as being a journalist and an academic, Landon also had talents as an entrepreneur, a quality that was a major asset in building up a first-class library. Like his student and chosen successor, James J. Talman, he was always on the lookout for opportunities to enhance the public library's collections, and whenever possible he expanded the university's holdings, as well.

Western's university library only possessed 5,000 volumes when, in 1918, Landon persuaded John Davis Barnett, a wealthy Stratford book and pamphlet collector, to give the university his library of some 40,000 books, which was especially rich in all fields of history and nineteenth-century English literature. The gift included a huge pamphlet collection that was later transferred to the National Library at Ottawa. The physical task of housing this munificent gift in a small institution, without a library building, must have been immense. Some years later, Arthur Ford noted that "[Landon] found the library a tiny affair housed in an old house near Huron College." His appointment as librarian was a joint one, for he also became an associate professor in the history department, where he continued to teach both Canadian and American history as long as the increasing pressures of library work allowed it. Not surprisingly, when the university found the funds to appoint a full-time librarian in 1923, Fred Landon was appointed to the post.

For more than two decades, Landon oversaw development of the collections, and the transfer of the library to first University College, and finally, in 1939, to an especially built library building. In 1934, James J. Talman, a former pupil who was then archivist of Ontario, joined Western as his deputy. By the time Landon retired from the librarianship in 1947, there were over 150,000 volumes.

With his special interest in local history, Landon also began what became the regional collection of books and documents relating to western Ontario — or as we would say now, southwestern Ontario — history. He also acquired many important document collections, such as the papers of the Honourable David Mills, and the Reverend James Evans.

To support research and make the library's collections available to more distant scholars, Landon started two series of publications: *Western Ontario Historical Notes* for short articles and *Western Ontario Historical Nuggets* for longer papers. He also began the publication of the *Library Bulletin* in 1941. His particular interest, both in his own region and more broadly in Canadian-American relations, can be seen in his 1941 book, *Western Ontario and the American Frontier*.

Landon and Talman, and their contemporary, W. Stewart Wallace of the University of Toronto library, strongly believed that university librarians should also be publishing scholars. Landon's most extensive work, written with Jesse E. Middleton in 1928, was the five-volume *History of Ontario*, long the only overview of the province's growth.

Landon's other contributions to the development of libraries and library science in Canada were equally considerable. In 1934, Landon and George H. Locke, chief librarian of the Toronto Public Library, surveyed Canadian university and college libraries from coast to coast to arrange the distribution of Carnegie grants up to the then-princely sum of $15,000 per library. He was also president of the Ontario Library Association, beginning in 1927, and in the field of bibliographical research was a founder of the Bibliographical Society of Canada, and its president from 1948–50.

With the post-Second World War boom came new duties in university administration despite the fact that he had by then reached retirement age. In 1946, he was the first appointee to the new post of vice-president of the university, and, a year later, as graduate work also expanded, he became the first dean of Graduate Studies. The librarianship then passed to Jim Talman, who enthusiastically carried on his work.

In his memoirs, President W. Sherwood Fox of Western stated that "without Dr. Landon's help I could not have pulled through 1946 and 1947, the last two years before my retirement." After helping bridge the transition to the new regime of President G. Edward Hall, Landon himself retired in 1950 at the age of sixty-nine. At that time he was honoured with the degrees of Doctor of Letters from Western and Doctor of Laws from McMaster.

Such, briefly, is the outline of Fred Landon's administrative and scholarly career at Western. However, some mention must be made of his contributions to and recognition by many historical and community organizations, and finally of his influence as a teacher.

Landon held office in, and was honoured by, a wide variety of organizations. In London he was active in the Metropolitan United Church, the Community Concert Association, the Western Fair Board, and the Council of Social Organizations. He was also chairman of the board of the Victorian Order of Nurses (1924–38), and president of the Canadian Club in 1925. In 1924 he established a London branch of the National Association for the Advancement of Coloured People. Finally, in 1948, he became Western's first representative on the board of directors of the Royal Ontario Museum.

Naturally, he was active in historical organizations and was successively president of the London & Middlesex Historical Society in 1918–20, The Ontario Historical Society in 1926–28, and the Canadian Historical Association in 1941–42. In 1929, he was elected a fellow of the Royal Society of Canada, and he was the Ontario representative on the Historical Sites and Monuments Board of Canada in 1932–58, and its chairman from 1950–58. In 1945, he was awarded the Tyrrell Medal of the Royal Society of Canada, and he received The Ontario Historical Society's Cruikshank Medal in 1967.

As a teacher, Landon was noted for both the clarity of his lectures and his willingness to devote time to his students and their problems. Many of these students went on to careers in the field of history. Talman was one, and others with a later Western connection were Wallace K. Ferguson and Fred. H. Hitchins, who both taught at New York University before coming back to Western. Other former students included John T. Cooper of McGill and several who taught in the United States.

For those of us who only had the pleasure of knowing him during his last years, Landon will be most clearly remembered in the setting of his comfortable, book-lined study on St. James Street. There, he was said to talk about historical problems, give his advice on an article, or help a student in the preparation of a thesis. When I first came to Western, in 1963, I found him always ready to discuss historical problems with a new lecturer.

He was fortunate in retaining his faculties to the last, and though quite frail, even well into his eighties he was able to continue his walks with his wife. He also continued writing, and his remarkable memory was most impressive. After his death, a new article appeared in the *Dictionary of Canadian Biography* and two historical columns in the *London Free Press*.

The last time I visited him, shortly before his death in 1969, I found him reading a new issue of the *Canadian Historical Review*, with an article related to Charles H. Hyman, London's colourful member of Parliament at the beginning of the twentieth century. He commented that, when he was a young journalist in Ottawa, Hyman — once Canada's tennis champion — opened the lawns of his public works ministry for civil servants' tennis courts. He also recalled Hyman's son, who had died in 1892.

A small, amiable, and unassuming man, Landon's career exemplifies the large amount of good work a conscientious scholar can accomplish.

Dr. Frederick H. Armstrong, Professor Emeritus
University of Western Ontario

The Course of Events in the Abolition of American Slavery with Special Reference to Upper Canada

Background to the Sequence of Events

While the articles in this volume concentrate on the flight of fugitive slaves to Upper Canada (today's southern Ontario), and on their settlements here, to place them in the international picture this chronology includes both the major dates in Upper Canadian Black settlement and the major stages and incidents in the long campaign to abolish slavery, particularly in the United States.

Some comment may be helpful by way of a background for these events. In the late eighteenth century, American political power was fairly well-balanced between the Northern and Southern states. As time passed, however, the North's burgeoning population and growing economic power caused increasing concern in the South, which saw both its political power and its way of life as being threatened.

In America's early years, there were abolitionists in both sections of the nation. However, industrial changes in the South's economy — particularly following Eli Whitney's 1792 invention of the cotton gin — gradually transformed the Southern economy, making it much more dependent on slave labour. As well, there was an ongoing fear of a loss of social control if slavery was abolished.

Thus, the South came to feel that not only its economic prosperity, but also its very way of life, depended on the survival of the institution of slavery. At the same time, however, there was a growing demand in the North for the abolition of slavery, a demand that was also found in the western European countries.

Inflaming these underlying differences was an ongoing controversy over whether slavery should be permitted to expand into America's newly acquired western territories — the Louisiana Purchase acquired in 1803 and the land seized from Mexico in the 1845–48 war. Thus, many of the subsequent major clashes arose from the settlement of these new regions. The South wanted its way of life expanded; the North increasingly demanded that slavery be prohibited. War, the almost inevitable end, finally came in 1861.

Chronology of the Slavery Issue

Events affecting Upper Canada (today's southern Ontario) are preceded with "UC":

1780   Abolition of slavery in the northern states, beginning with Vermont in 1777, Massachusetts and Pennsylvania in 1780, New Hampshire in 1783, and Rhode Island in 1784. Some of this legislation only provided for gradual emancipation.

1787   UC: Ordinance of Congress prohibited slavery in the territories north of the Ohio River and east of the Mississippi. This included the lands of the future states of Ohio and Michigan, which would be adjacent to what would soon become western Upper Canada.

1791   UC: Upper Canada established as a separate British colony. Its southwestern peninsula, jutting down into the United States, would provide easy river crossings and would become the major terminus for escaping slaves.

1793   UC: Lieutenant-Governor John Graves Simcoe of Upper Canada ordered the colonial legislature to prohibit the importation of slaves and provide for the gradual emancipation of children of slaves already in the colony.

1793   The United States Congress passed the first Fugitive Slave Law, an ineffectual law governing the return of runaway slaves.

1803 The United States purchased the vast Louisiana territory to the west from France. The South soon focused on spreading slavery westward into this territory.

1807 Abolition of the Atlantic slave trade in the British Empire.

1808 United States Congress prohibited the African slave trade (effective January 1, 1809).

1812–14 UC: The War of 1812 saw hundreds of Black men volunteer for British military and Upper Canadian militia service against the American threat. Returning Kentucky soldiers carried the news back to the South that they had fought "Black men in red coats" on the borders of Upper Canada, and that in Canada African-American refugees from slavery were free.

1814–30s The first formal organization of what would come to be called the "Underground Railroad" emerged as more and more enslaved Americans sought freedom in Upper Canada.

1820 The Compromise of 1820 provided for the admission of Missouri as a slave state over Northern objections (1821); but prohibited further slavery in the Louisiana territory, north of latitude 36° 30'. To balance Senate representation, Maine was admitted as a free state in 1820.

1829 UC: Lieutenant-Governor Sir John Colborne assured visiting abolitionists that slaves would be both free and welcome in the colony.

1830 UC: The Wilberforce Settlement was begun in Biddulph Township, just north of London. The first Black national anti-slavery convention was held in Philadelphia the same year.

1831 William Lloyd Garrison published the first issue of *The Liberator* at Boston on January 1.

1832 UC: The Reverend Nathaniel Paul of the Wilberforce Settlement addressed a select committee of the British House of Commons on the migration of escaped slaves to Upper Canada.
UC: Abolitionist Benjamin Lundy visited Upper Canada.

1833 The British Empire passed the Act to Abolish Slavery, effective 1834, with compensation allowed. Several other European states also passed abolition legislation about the same time.

1833 Civil War.

1834 UC: Increasing numbers of slaves began fleeing into Upper Canada from the adjoining American states.

1837 UC: The Upper Canadian Rebellion of 1837 broke out; Black men flocked to enlist to defend the borders against American incursions, and to demonstrate their loyalty to Queen Victoria.

1838 UC: The "Underground Railroad" became more organized. The name is confusing, for it was neither a railroad nor underground, but rather a network of abolitionist sympathizers who aided and hid escaping slaves as they fled north to Upper Canada. Important termini in Upper Canada included Amherstburg, across from Detroit, Sandwich, Niagara, Fort Erie, St. Catharines, Toronto, Collingwood, and Owen Sound.
UC: The African Methodist Episcopal Church began its work in Canada.

1845–48 The United States went to war with Mexico, winning western territory stretching to the Pacific.

1848 France abolished slavery, later than most western European countries, leaving the United States essentially isolated.

1848–64 UC: American Missionary Society began missionary work based at Amherstburg, near Windsor-Detroit.

1849 UC: The Elgin Association settlement was established at Buxton in Kent County, near Chatham.

1850 The Compromise of 1850 in the United States cooled down immediate tensions over the west and gave new states the right to decide on the issue of slavery themselves. Under a new, stronger Fugitive Slave Law, however, escaped slaves in the North could now be reclaimed by Southern owners and forcibly returned to their owners. Some dreadful incidents inevitably followed.

1850   UC: Naturally, with sanctuary in the North denied, the number of slaves fleeing to Canada West greatly increased in the last decade before the American Civil War.

1851   UC: The Anti-Slavery Society of Canada was founded.

1851   UC: Henry Bibb began publishing the *Voice of the Fugitive* in Sandwich, near Windsor.

1852   UC: Harriet Beecher Stowe's *Uncle Tom's Cabin*, the most influential book attacking slavery, was widely read in Canada West immediately upon its publication.

1853   UC: The *Provincial Freeman*, edited by Mary Ann Shadd, began publication at Windsor, and then in Toronto. It later moved to Chatham.

1850s   The Kansas-Nebraska Act of 1854 repealed the Compromise of 1820 (also known as the Missouri Compromise) and left the question of whether a state would be slave or free up to local residents. Settlers from both sides streamed into what is now Kansas, setting off a virtual civil war. Kansas finally became a free state in 1861 with the outbreak of the Civil War.

1856   The long-established Whig party, which tried to compromise over slavery, split up, and the new, anti-slavery Republican party was formed in its place.

1858   UC: John Brown held a convention in Chatham to plan an assault on slavery in the United States. This began the planning of his raid at Harper's Ferry, Virginia, which he carried out in October 1859. The raid failed and John Brown was executed, but he became a martyr to the abolitionist cause.

1860   UC: The case for the return of John Anderson, a fugitive slave and accused murderer who had fled to Canada West, was tried at Toronto and he was freed on a technicality.
Republican Abraham Lincoln was elected president.

1861   The Southern states began seceding from the Union before Lincoln assumed office on March 4 and the Civil War soon broke out. Eleven Southern states seceded in all, and formed the Confederate States of America under their own president, Jefferson Davis.

1863   January 1, Lincoln's Emancipation Proclamation. African-American soldiers were permitted to enlist in the Union forces, and thousands of Black Canadians joined them in the ranks.

1864   UC: Dr. Samuel G. Howe visited Canada on behalf of the Freedmen's Inquiry Commission, which Lincoln had established to investigate the condition of Blacks who had settled here.

1865   With the South defeated, the 13th Amendment abolished slavery, effective December 18.

Post-1865 UC: With slavery ended, former slaves, particularly those who had left family members behind when they fled, began to return to the United States. Most stayed on, however, to help build the new Dominion of Canada after the confederation of the provinces in 1867.

In summary, while the flight of slaves to Upper Canada involved only a very small portion of those locked in servitude, the very existence of an escape route provided a promise of freedom to many who were enslaved.

Dr. Frederick H. Armstrong, Professor Emeritus
University of Western Ontario

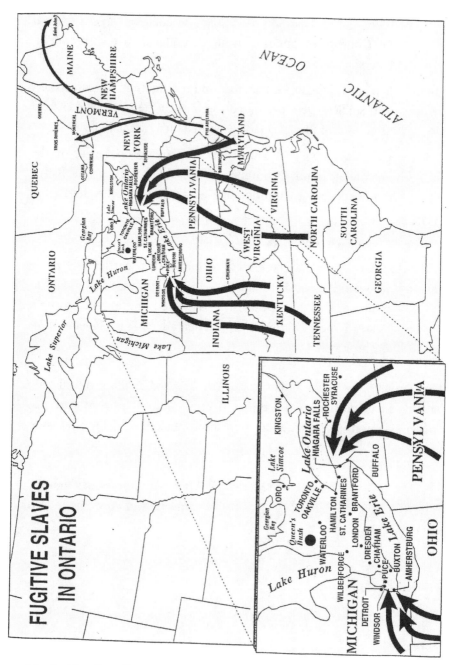

Map by Tim C. Walker. *Courtesy of James W. St.G. Walker.*

1

Canada's Part in Freeing the Slave

Ontario Historical Society, Papers and Records, *vol. 17 (1919)*, *74–84*

Historians of the anti-slavery movement in the United States have for the most part overlooked the very great measure of assistance that came to that cause from the geographical location of the free British provinces to the north, and from the attitude of the people of those provinces with regard to the Blacks escaping out of bondage. To those in this country [Canada] who lived during the years immediately preceding the Civil War, or who since that period have had anything to do with older coloured people, the term "Underground Railroad" is not the mysterious term that it is to a younger generation. When Professor Wilbur Siebert, of Ohio State University, one of the eminent historians of the United States, can make the statement that "the Underground Railroad was one of the greatest forces which brought on the Civil War and destroyed slavery," we on this side of the border may properly add that during a large part of the period of its activity, Canada was practically essential to the success of the underground system.

Though slavery was legal in all of the 13 original states of the Union at some time or another, it was natural that in the group of northern states it should die out quickly. It was excluded by Congress from the old northwest territory by the ordinance of 1787, thus creating a group of states around the Great Lakes that were never to know slavery. By 1820, the republic had been divided by a more or less irregular geographical line, north of which were the free states and south of which were the slave states. It was in that year that the first state was created west of the Mississippi River, Missouri, and though lying as far north as southern Illinois, which was free, Missouri came in as a slave state. From that time until the end of the Civil War, one of the great issues in the nation's politics was the control of the new West: should it be free or slave? Prior to 1830 or 1835 there had been many in the South to whom the evils of slavery were something to be rid of, and abolition societies actually existed in the South before they did in the North. But from 1830 on there came a new teaching in the South, the doctrine that slavery is a positive good, ordained by God, for the benefit of the Black race. Economic conditions were changed, too, by the spread of cotton growing. The old domestic slavery, bad though it might be, was a mild evil compared with the conditions that came when huge cotton plantations demanded vast hordes of slaves, and there grew up the domestic slave trade. Virginia, the mother of presidents, became a vast breeding ground, and her aristocratic families made fortunes in the selling of men, women, and children to the far southern plantations.

From the very earliest days, slaveowners had experienced severe losses because of their slaves running away. As early as the first half of the seventeenth century there were found laws and regulations for the return, from one colony to another, of fugitives. In the federal constitution, adopted at Philadelphia in 1787, there is a clause that reads: "No person held to service or labor in one state under the laws thereof, escaping into another, shall, in consequence of any law or regulation therein, be discharged from such service or labor, but shall be delivered up on claim of the party to whom such service or labor may be due."

The first federal law providing for the return of a runaway slave was passed in 1793. The law was none too effective from the southern standpoint, and was amended at various times until the passage of the famous Fugitive Slave Law of 1850, which proved a powerful influence in creating anti-slavery sentiment in the North. Under this act, the question of ownership was determined by the simple affidavit of the person claiming the slave. The testimony of the slave himself was not to be received. There were heavy penalties for harbouring or interfering with the arrest of a runaway. Federal commissioners were paid $10 for every slave returned and only $5 if the fugitive was discharged. Thus, a direct premium was paid to convict fugitives. But the clause that particularly irritated the North was that which declared that the federal commissioners might call "all good citizens" to aid and assist in the execution of the law. It was at once pointed out that this made every northern citizen liable to be a slave-catcher. Added were such other injustices as denying jury trial, resting liberty on *ex parte* evidence, making habeas corpus ineffective, and offering a bribe to the federal commissioner to return the fugitive to slavery.

"The passage of the new law," says one writer, "probably increased the number of anti-slavery people more than anything else that had occurred during the whole agitation."

The period from 1850–61 is filled with incidents arising out of this Fugitive Slave Law. The most famous is probably the case of Anthony Burns, who was arrested in Boston on May 24, 1854. Boston blazed with indignation, and a riot broke out in which blood was shed. On June 2, Burns was formally remanded to slavery.

The authorities felt it was necessary to line the streets with troops and place cannons in the squares on the day that Burns was taken from jail to the boat that was to carry him south. Fifty-thousand people, standing with bared heads, watched the grim military procession pass. Business houses were draped with black cloth for blocks, and at one prominent corner a coffin hung suspended over the street. It is not to be wondered at that the *Richmond Examiner* commented: "A few more such victories and the South is undone."

The later life of Burns has a Canadian interest. His stay in the South was brief, money being subscribed to purchase his freedom and provide him with an education. He became a clergyman, came to Canada, and lived for many years at St. Catharines as a missionary among his own people.

Canada had known slavery at an earlier date, but had long since cleared herself of the blot. The French introduced slavery into Canada in an effort to meet the ever-prevalent shortage of labour. It existed all through the old regime, and was not changed by the passing of the country into the hands of the English. Indeed, it was not until the beginning of the nineteenth century that slavery disappeared, though at no time and in no locality was it ever existent on a large scale.* The early disappearance of slavery in Canada had the effect of creating an anti-slavery sentiment at an early date. In 1829, when the Negroes of Cincinnati were threatened with ruin by the enforcement of the Black Laws, they sent a deputation to York to interview the lieutenant-governor, Sir John Colborne, and find out if they would be allowed to take refuge in Canada. "Tell the Republicans on your side of the line," replied the lieutenant-governor, "that we Royalists do not know men by their colour. Should you come to us, you will be entitled to all the privileges of the rest of His Majesty's subjects." [1]

This position was taken by all of the later governors, and on the very eve of the Civil War, Sir Edmund Walker Head declared that "Canada could still afford homes to the fugitives."[2]

From a very early period, there had been those in the northern free states who felt it their duty to give aid and comfort to the Blacks making their way north. This was particularly true of the Quakers, who at all times were friends of freedom. Gradually, there grew up a strangely organized system of aiding the fugitives, and to this was given the name "Underground Railroad." As the slaveowners remarked, the slave disappeared at some point in the South and reappeared only in Canada, as if he had gone through a long tunnel. The underground is the most romantic highway this new world has known. It followed certain definite routes that have been charted by Professor Siebert, and the small army of people that were engaged in its operations formed a sort of freemasonry of freedom that brings them the tributes of all who love liberty and hate oppression. A railroad "jargon" grew up. The places where fugitives making their way north could obtain temporary shelter, food, and clothing were known as the "stations." Those living there and aiding the

---

* Editors' Note: There are no reliable figures for the number of people, both of African and of First Nations descent, who were enslaved in Upper Canada. Certainly, slavery was a far more important component of both the economy and the society of what is now Ontario than early historians like Landon were aware. The United Empire Loyalists were permitted to bring their slaves, as well as other movable property, into what is now Ontario when they migrated. Several members of Lieutenant-Governor Simcoe's first Executive Council were slaveholders.

runaways were "station agents." More daring individuals travelling with the runaways and guiding them to freedom were "conductors," while in Canada, ready to receive the newcomers were "freight agents." A code for messages was used. An innocent telegram stating that two cases of hardware were being forwarded meant to the recipient that two slave men were on the way, while references to cases of dry goods referred to women. Sometimes these phrases had very special meaning, for there are instances where men and women were actually boxed up and shipped in freight cars to the north.[3]

With a fugitive slave law that made freedom impossible, even in Boston, there was danger for the fugitive after 1850, except in Canada. From 1850 to 1860, therefore, the Negro immigration that had been a trickling stream ever since the War of 1812 became a regular torrent and thousands of coloured people crossed the border every year. Professor Siebert has charted the main routes by which the fugitives made their way to Canada, and his map shows most clearly the important influence that the free British provinces exerted upon slavery through their geographical location. Along the northern boundaries of the states of New York and Pennsylvania there were ten main points from which the runaways crossed into Canada, the more important of these being on the Niagara frontier. On Lake Erie and the Detroit River, there were eight points at which entry was made into Canada, the Detroit River, of course, taking first place. At Fort Malden (Amherstburg), as many as 30 fugitives a day entered in the period after 1850.[4] On Lake Erie proper, a considerable number seem to have come in by Kettle Creek (Port Stanley), thence making their way to London or Ingersoll.

Slavery had scarcely disappeared in Canada before runaways from the southern states began to make their appearance, and that in considerable numbers. Isolated instances of Negroes reaching Canada can be found, of course, at a very early date. As early as 1705 an act was passed in New York, and renewed in 1715, to prevent slaves running away to Canada from frontier towns like Albany,[5] and there was also frequent trouble between the French and the English or the French and the Dutch over the runaways who came to Canada. It was not, however, until the beginning of the nineteenth century that Canada began to be known to any degree among the Negroes in the southern states. This was really the period of the discovery of Canada to the Negro mind. The War of 1812 exercised a powerful influence in directing Negro thought to the free country to the north. Kentuckians and others who fought in the War of 1812 must have been surprised to encounter Negroes among the Canadian forces who opposed them. But back in the South, when the news of the war began to penetrate there, the Negro might fairly conclude that his master's enemy was likely to be his friend, and it was not long before the fact that Canada offered real asylum to the runaway had permeated the slave population throughout the border states, at least. As early as 1815, Negroes were reported crossing the western reserve in Ohio in large numbers, and one group of Underground Railroad workers in southern Ohio is stated to have passed on more than 1,000 fugitives before 1817.[6] Dr. Samuel G. Howe, who made one of the best investigations of the condition of the refugees in Canada, states that the arrivals, few in number at the start, increased rapidly early in the century, with special activity between 1830 and 1840 and the greatest activity of all between 1850 and 1860, when the drastic Fugitive Slave Law was in operation.[7]

There were many ways in which the reputation of Canada was spread abroad among the Negroes. The effect of the War of 1812 has already been noted. In this connection, the slaveholders themselves probably helped to make Canada known by spreading the most foolish stories with regard to its cold climate and the hardships that were endured by the people there.[8] The shrewd Negro mind saw through this, and was even more determined to reach this place that his master derided. Black men from Canada were a second influence in making the country known. Many a refugee slave, successful in his break for liberty, would afterwards return to the slave states to assist relatives or friends to freedom. Such a one would serve to plant the germ of freedom in the minds of those with whom he came in contact, and thereby increase the number of runaways. White men, too, went from Canada to spread the news of freedom and to aid slaves in reaching their Canaan. James Redpath, the biographer of John Brown, writing in 1860, said that 500 men went south from Canada annually to assist others in securing their freedom.[9] Slaves who were sent from the South into the border states to work would likely hear of Canada there. And so, in many and devious ways, there was a certain amount of acquaintance with Canada all through the slavery area.

By 1826, the South was feeling the loss of its human property to such an extent an effort was made to reach an agreement with Great Britain on the subject. But Britain was not responsive. In the troubles of 1837–38, the citizens of the United States who tried to create trouble along the border received another shock like that of their compatriots of 1812, for again Negroes were found defending their new home. All through the 1840s there was a steady influx of Negroes into Canada, the *Western Citizen* of Chicago stating in its issue of September 23, 1842, that "there are over $400,000 worth of southern slaves in a town near Malden, Canada."

"It (slave abduction) threatens to subvert the institution in this state," said a Missouri newspaper of the period,[10] while another authority estimated that between 1810 and 1850 no less than 100,000 slaves, valued at $30,000,000, were abducted from the South.[11] After 1850 the situation, from the southern standpoint, grew worse and worse. Senator Polk of Missouri said in 1861: "Underground railroads are established stretching from the remotest slaveholding states clear up to Canada."[12] The New Orleans *Commercial Bulletin* of December 19, 1860, estimated that 1,500 slaves had escaped annually for 50 years past, a loss to the slaveholders of $40,000,000.[13] A vigilance committee at Detroit is stated to have assisted 1,200 Negroes to freedom in one year.[14] A similar committee at Cleveland is stated to have assisted over 100 a month.

Estimates of the number of refugees in Canada on the eve of the Civil War vary greatly. The Canadian census figures have been shown to be quite unreliable, and the estimates made by contemporary observers range all the way from 20,000 to 75,000. The bulk of the refugee population in Canada was located in the western part of the province of Upper Canada, where many of their descendants are to be found today.

The fugitives who came into Canada during the half-century before the Civil War were a continual object lesson to the people of Canada of what slavery meant in the degradation of the Black race. Homeless, friendless, destitute, their bodies marked by the lash and the still more brutal punishment of the "paddle," their feet torn, bleeding, frozen, often as the result of a flight north in the dead of winter, these products of the slavery system made their own mute appeal to the compassion of a free people. Older people in Canada today still speak with emotion of the impression that was made upon their minds 60 years ago by the coming into their communities of Negro fugitives. The escaped Negro was himself one of the powerful influences operating to create, in Canada, as in the free states of the North, a sentiment hostile to slavery. The Canadian newspapers of the 1850s contain many narratives of fugitives reaching Canada, so that those who did not come into actual contact with the Negroes were made acquainted with their condition. The Negroes themselves also published newspapers at Chatham and at Sandwich that were agencies in creating anti-slavery sentiment in Canada.

Another influence that was powerful in creating anti-slavery sentiment in Canada, and on a tremendous scale in the northern states, was the publication of Mrs. [Harriet Beecher] Stowe's famous novel *Uncle Tom's Cabin*. First published serially in the *National Era*, an anti-slavery paper printed at Washington, it was issued in book form in March 1852, with the first Canadian edition appearing in the same year and having a large sale. Above all else, the book brought home the conviction that slavery was an injustice, opposed both to the law of God and the best interests of mankind. Many who were careless of the issue were brought to a consciousness of the evils of the slavery system by the reading of this book, or by the dramatic presentations of it that soon followed its first publication. Even today, with the issue it presented settled a half a century ago, *Uncle Tom's Cabin* remains one of the most widely read books in Canada, as it is also one of the most widely read books in the United States.

Towards the enslaved race the Canadian people performed a remarkable service during the years 1815–60. The Canadian hatred of slavery found its most spectacular outlet in the abduction of slaves from the South, both by native Canadians and by Negroes who had settled in the country. Dr. Alexander Milton Ross tells in his memoirs[15] of more than 30 Blacks he assisted to freedom. Josiah Henson, himself a fugitive, claims that he brought out 118 slaves.[16] William Wells Brown says he took 69 over Lake Erie in six months;[17] and the famous woman, Harriet Tubman, is credited with having assisted more than 300 fugitives to liberty, making repeated trips into the slave states for that purpose.[18]

Sandwich Baptist Church. The first church on this site was built of logs by freed slaves in 1820. The current church was constructed in 1851 from bricks made by hand by members of the community, many formerly enslaved African Americans. The Reverend Madison Lightfoot, a founder of the Amherstburg Baptist Association, was minister at the time. *Photo by Karolyn Smardz Frost.*

A second work performed by Canadians was that of receiving the fugitives at the end of their flight and assisting them to get on their feet in the new country. Missions were established at Malden, Sandwich, Toronto, and elsewhere, and the material, as well as the moral, side of the Negro was cared for. Reverend Isaac Rice, a graduate of Hamilton College, laboured for many years at Malden. He had been well-situated in Ohio as the pastor of a Presbyterian church, and with fine prospects, but he gave it up in order to aid the helpless Blacks who crowded over the Canadian border. At his missionary house in Malden, he sheltered hundreds of the fugitives until homes could be found for them elsewhere.[19]

Of another character was the work done by men like Reverend William King, Henry Bibb, and Josiah Henson in the founding of distinctly Negro colonies with schools and churches, with effort directed to improving the whole social status of the race. Interesting observations have been recorded in connection with these colonies. The constant violation of domestic relations under a slave system was bound to react on home life and take away the incentive to constancy, yet one of the first things married slaves did upon arriving in Canada was to have their plantation union reaffirmed by the form of marriage legal in Canada. It was observed that the refugees tended to settle in families and to hallow marriage, and that sensuality lessened in freedom. Their religious instincts were manifested in charity to the sick and to newcomers, and in their attitude toward women. The general improvement was well summed up by one competent observer, who wrote: "The refugees in Canada earn a living and gather property; they build churches and send their children to school; they improve in manners and morals — not because they are picked men, but because they are free men."[20]

Here, then, was a most important truth that Canada was showing forth to the people of the United States, namely that slavery was not necessary to the welfare of the Black race, as the South claimed.* Canada was also showing that, though brutalized by slavery, the best instincts of the Negro race were reasserted in freedom, and the degraded bondsmen developed morality and intelligence. In short, Canada steadily gave the lie to the plea that slavery was the state best suited to the Negro, and the one best calculated to raise him intellectually and morally.

But Canadians were not satisfied to be merely passive agents in the larger phases of the long struggle against slavery. Early in 1851, there was organized in the City of Toronto the Anti-Slavery Society of Canada, which continued to be active until the Emancipation Proclamation had been made effective, and the United States had itself removed the blot [of slavery] from its fair name. The objects of the Anti-Slavery Society of Canada were declared to be "to aid in the extinction of slavery all over the world by means exclusively lawful and peaceable, moral and religious." Reverend Dr. [Michael] Willis, principal of Knox College, Toronto, was president of the society all through its history, and among others who associated themselves with its work were George Brown, the editor of the *Globe*, and Oliver Mowat, afterwards premier of the Province of Ontario. From Toronto, the work of the society was spread out to the leading centres of Negro population, branches being formed and a steady campaign carried on. The *Globe*, under Brown, proved a stout ally, and gave much attention to the society's work. Working relations were entered into with anti-slavery societies in Great Britain and the United States, and a large amount of the relief work was looked after by the Women's Auxiliaries. Though the churches generally, with the exception of the Presbyterians,

---

* Editors' Note: Landon is referring to the "positive good" argument that slave-holders promoted by the 1830s. That is, those who benefited most from slavery suggested that enslaved African Americans were morally and intellectually incapable of self-management, and therefore should never be freed. Abolitionists, Black and white, knew that this self-serving propaganda was most effectively refuted by the success of the formerly enslaved in establishing new lives, acquiring farms and homes, and raising families in freedom in the American North and in Canada.

held somewhat aloof from the work of the society, recruits in plenty were drawn from the clergy. It was a Presbyterian clergyman who was president of the society all through its history; the first secretary was a Methodist minister, and on the committees appointed from year to year there was always to be found a good representation of the clergy.[21]

Canadian law gave the Negro fugitive all the rights of citizenship and protected him in their enjoyment. The Negro was encouraged to take up land, and the law gave him the franchise, the same as his white neighbour. Negroes were enrolled in the Canadian militia and bore their share of service during the troubles of 1837–38. "The coloured men," says Josiah Henson, "were willing to defend the Government that had given them a home when they had fled from slavery."[22] Under Canadian law, the fugitives were allowed to send their children to the common schools or to have separate schools provided for them out of their share of the school funds.[23] Separate schools were established in some places where prejudice existed, and religious agencies also established schools at a number of points. Visitors noted that a surprisingly large number of the Negroes learned to read and write after coming to Canada, and in the University of Toronto a number of prizes were taken by coloured youth. Principal McCullum of the Hamilton Collegiate Institute was quoted as saying that his teachers agreed that the Blacks were the equal of the whites in mentality. The best educational work seems to have been done by the schools that were established by the Negroes themselves, the mission schools and those located in the Negro colonies.[24] Government interest was shown by the incorporation in 1859 of the Association for the Education of the Coloured People in Canada, the object of which was to secure educational advantages for the younger people of the race.[25]

The attempts at planting distinctly Negro settlements in western Ontario form one of the interesting phases of Canada's relation to the slavery issue. Most interesting of all, probably, was the work of Reverend William King, who was the founder of the Elgin Association or Buxton Settlement. King was an Irishman, a graduate of Glasgow College who came to America and was made rector of a college in the State of Louisiana. There, by marriage, he became the owner of 15 slaves worth an estimated value of $9,000. For a time, he placed them on a neighbouring plantation and gave them the proceeds of their labour, but that did not satisfy his conscience, and in 1848 he brought them to Canada, thereby giving them their freedom. But his work did not end there, for he felt it was his duty to look after them, to educate them, and to make them useful citizens. With some prominent Canadians, King organized what was known as the Elgin Association, which was legally incorporated "for the settlement and moral improvement of the coloured population of Canada, for the purpose of purchasing crown or clergy reserve lands in the township of Raleigh and settling the same with coloured families resident in Canada of approved moral character."

The aims were met with decided opposition from certain elements in Kent County, but this did not impede the progress of the association, a tract of about 9,000 acres south of Chatham being purchased. This was surveyed into small farms of 50 acres each, which were sold to the colonists at $2.50 an acre, payable in ten annual instalments. Each settler bound himself, within a certain period, to build a house at least as good as the model house set up by the association, to provide himself with necessary implements, and to proceed with the work of clearing land. Roads were soon cut through the forest, and the work of clearing up the country began. The slaves who had been freed by Reverend Mr. King formed the nucleus of the colony, but others came as soon as the land was offered, so that within four years there were 400 people located, and in 1857 it had a population of 800. Dr. Samuel Howe gave the warmest praise to what he saw at the Elgin Settlement: "Buxton is certainly a very interesting place," he wrote:

> Sixteen years ago it was a wilderness. Now good highways are laid out in all directions through the forest and by their side, standing back 33 feet from the road, are about 200 cottages, all built in the same pattern, all looking neat and comfortable; around each one is a cleared place of several acres which is well cultivated. The fences are in good order, the barns seem well filled, and cattle and horses, and pigs and poultry, abound. There are signs of industry and thrift and comfort everywhere; signs of

intemperance, of idleness, of want, nowhere. There is no tavern and no groggery: but there is a chapel and a schoolhouse. Most interesting of all are the inhabitants. Twenty years ago most of them were slaves, who owned nothing, not even their children. Now they own themselves; they own their houses and farms; and they have their wives and children about them. They are enfranchised citizens of a government which protects their rights. The present condition of all these colonists, as compared with their former one, is remarkable. The settlement is a perfect success. Here are men who were bred in slavery, who came here and purchased land at the government price, cleared it, bought their own implements, built their own houses after a model and have supported themselves in all material circumstances and now support their schools in part. I consider that this settlement has done as well as a white settlement would have done under the same circumstances.[26]

Interchange of effort between the abolitionists of Canada and those of the United States was noticeable all through the course of the movement. The Canadian Negroes did their part, of course, chiefly by going south and helping relatives and friends to escape to freedom. In this, they were given the active assistance of a few white Canadians, Dr. Alexander Milton Ross being the most noteworthy example of this daring kind of work. From the United States, there came workers on behalf of the fugitives whose efforts deserve every tribute that has ever been paid to them. Hiram Wilson and Isaac Rice, missionaries to the Negroes, are names that should never be forgotten by the coloured race, and like tribute might be paid to the work of such Black men as Reverend Samuel Ringgold Ward, Austin Steward, Reverend Jermain W. Loguen, Frederick Douglass, and Henry Bibb. Bibb was a worker on both sides of the line, putting in several years as a speaker for the anti-slavery forces in Michigan before coming to Canada to attempt a colonization venture in what is now Essex County. Benjamin Lundy, the most prominent of the pioneer abolitionists, was an early visitor to Canada and wrote an account of his trip in *The Genius of Universal Emancipation*. Noticeable, too, is the fact that the American abolitionists took a deep interest in the condition of the fugitives in Canada. Men like Levi Coffin, and more particularly Benjamin Drew, made careful investigations of the results that had attended emancipation by coming to Canada.

Abolition was a common cause for Canadians and their neighbours. Boundary lines did not separate in this fight for the freedom of a race, which went on during half a century. The Anti-Slavery Society of Canada entered into working relations with the American Anti-Slavery Society at its inception. Newspaper comment interpreted the movement in the United States to Canadian readers, and few American editors had a surer grasp of the direction in which events were heading after 1850 than did George Brown of the *Globe*. His paper not only reported on the activities of the Canadian abolitionists, but as well kept them in close touch with what was going on across the line. Perusal of *Globe* files, particularly in the 1850s, shows that the newspaper was always aggressive in its support of the cause of the slave. It is quite true that not all of the Canadian press was of like mind, but a pro-slavery attitude, or scornful indifference, was never quite so marked as Brown's ceaseless anti-slavery agitation through the columns of his newspaper. The actual attitude of the Canadian parties was quite clearly indicated by their newspapers. The Tory press was usually scornful of the abolitionist movement in the United States, and treated the Canadian effort with more or less contempt. The Reformer in Canada naturally fitted abolition into his program, and gave to it some of the same enthusiasm that he directed to the curing of distinctly Canadian abuses. Professor Albert B. Hart has drawn attention to the fact that the 1830s and 1840s in the United States were a period in which religious life had as its characteristic the sincere effort to make religion effective, "to make individual and community correspond to the principles of Christianity."

This ideal led to the organization of various reform movements, "causes," each of which took the form of a national society, with newspaper organs, frequent meetings, and appeals to the public. Some of this same spirit was manifest in Canada at the same period, and the anti-slavery cause gathered to its support a few people who practically devoted their whole lives to its ends, while many others contributed their time and money as opportunity afforded. The anti-slavery movement had about it an atmosphere of crusade that gave it a spiritual power with many people. Nor must it be overlooked that to some Canadians of the time there was a secret pleasure in striking a blow at the institution that seemed to be the chief power in Washington. Not that the average Canadian loved the Northerner or despised the Southern slaver. The opposite would be nearer the truth, but, when the North permitted its laws to be used to arrest runaways in the streets of Northern cities and to drag them back to slavery, the Canadian of the time was not far out when he associated the North with South in the guilt of slavery. That belief was nurtured by the constant attempts at compromise, and it was not until toward the end of the 1850s that there was a clear understanding in Canada as to where sympathies should lie. To Thomas D'Arcy McGee is due in part the credit for setting Canadian opinion aright in this respect. He saw and described the southern Confederacy as a "pagan oligarchy" and strongly championed the cause of the North.

John Quincy Adams wrote in his diary in 1820: "If slavery be the destined sword in the hand of the destroying angel, which is to sever the ties of this Union, the same sword will cut in sunder the bonds of slavery itself." It took 40 years for that prophetic utterance to be fulfilled, and there were many agencies at work during that long period working to the one end of destroying the system of human bondage that had been planted in the new lands of the western hemisphere, and that had sapped its life for so many years. Not all these agencies working for the destruction of slavery were apparent on the surface. A contrast of conditions as between 1830 and 1860 might have seemed to indicate that the future of the Negro was darker than ever before on the eve of the Civil War. The area given up to slavery in 1860 was larger than at any previous time, the slaves were more numerous, and the slave codes and Fugitive Slave Law the most rigorous the country had ever known. Steps were even being taken to revive the African slave trade.

All this existed after 30 years of debate on the issue. It is doubtful if either side made converts to its own particular views. Indeed, by 1860, the South had reached the point where denunciation of slavery had ceased, when no further efforts were being made to ameliorate the slave's condition, when justification of slavery had become praise of the system, and to speak ill of the institution was regarded as treason. Naturally, the South desired to see the area of slave territory increased, and never ceased its demands for expansion; but as individuals, the slaveholders were more powerfully affected by two other considerations, both related to their property, namely, the constant fear that the slaves would rise up and murder them, and the constant loss suffered by the slaves running away or being spirited away. In a sense, the Civil War began when the first Negro slave was abducted, and every loss added to the steadily growing division in the country. The climax came when the people of the North rebelled against being made slave-catchers by the Fugitive Slave Law, and instead gave assistance, as never before, to aiding the slaves to gain their liberty. There was a war raging between North and South for ten years before the first gun was fired at [Fort] Sumter, and in that conflict Canada had become an ally of the free states. With the opening of the Civil War, the Canadian government assumed an attitude of neutrality, but of her citizens at least 35,000 joined the Northern armies and played their part in war as they had already played it in peace, to the end of making the Negro race free.

2

A Pioneer Abolitionist in Upper Canada[1]

Ontario History, *vol. 52, no. 2 (June 1960), 77–83*

When Benjamin Lundy, pioneer American abolitionist, visited Upper Canada in January 1832, it was with a definite purpose in mind, namely, "to obtain correct information respecting the situation, climate, soil, the present prospects of the coloured settlers, etc., etc., with a view of publishing an accurate statement thereof, as extensively as possible, for the benefit of that oppressed and persecuted race in the United States."[2] This publicity he at once provided in subsequent issues of his little newspaper, *The Genius of Universal Emancipation*, where an account of his Canadian journey appeared in the numbers for March, April, and May 1832.[3] An announcement had been made in an earlier issue that one Hezekiah Grice, a Baltimore coloured man, was preparing for early publication a map of Upper Canada that would distinctly mark "the location and particular boundaries of the extensive tract which is offered for the settlement of the coloured people and also designate the

American Quaker abolitionist, Benjamin Lundy, visited Upper Canada in February 1832 and reported on the conditions under which fugitive slaves were living. He heartily endorsed their future prospects in the pages of his newspaper, *The Genius of Universal Emancipation. Courtesy of Ohio Historical Society, SC-296.*

various routes that lead to it from the United States." This map was to be sold for 25 cents a copy.

That Lundy should undertake such a journey, in the middle of a Canadian winter and entirely at his own expense, indicates the measure of his devotion to the cause to which he was giving the best years of his life. That a map should be in preparation showing to the Negro fugitives the routes to this promised land of freedom indicates that Upper Canada, lying just over the international boundary, was already in the minds of many who had known slavery and had escaped, or hoped to escape, from its degradation.

Migration to Canada of escaped slaves from the South had been going on for some years before Lundy visited the British province. American soldiers returning from service during the War of 1812 told of this country to the north, of its well-watered lands, its forests and other resources, and, what was of greatest interest to the Negro, that in this land there was no slavery. Soon runaway slaves were heading for that happy country, and by the time Lundy came there were already in the province several scattered communities of coloured folk. In his narrative, Lundy speaks of such settlements as situated near Lake Simcoe, on the Grand River above Brantford, on the Thames River around Chatham, and at [Fort] Malden (Amherstburg) on the Detroit River. He apparently knew about these colonies when he entered Upper Canada, but limited his visit on this occasion to one that had been established to the north of the present City of London, and to which had been given the name of the great English humanitarian William Wilberforce. The Wilberforce colonists were themselves not runaway slaves but mostly freedmen from the vicinity of Cincinnati, Ohio, who had left the state because of threatened enforcement of repressive Black Laws.

Ohio legislation of 1804 and 1807 had required from all Negroes residing in the state, a certificate of freedom issued by a United States court. No one might employ a Negro lacking such a certificate, and harbouring or hiring such a one was punishable by a fine. In 1807, it was ordained that no Negro might settle in the state without providing a bond of $500 for his good behaviour. The fine for concealing a Negro, which had earlier been $50, was now doubled. No Negro might give evidence against a white man. Later legislation in 1830 made the Negro ineligible to serve in the militia, and in

1831 it was ordained that no person of colour might serve on a jury.[4]

When possible enforcement of unjust laws made their whole future uncertain, the people of colour, already knowing something of the freedom accorded their race in Upper Canada, sent two men, James C. Brown and Stephen Dutton, to the provincial capital at York (Toronto) to interview the British authorities and find out if they could receive asylum. Brown has left an account of the favourable reception the men received when they met Sir John Colborne, the lieutenant-governor. Tradition has it that his reply was: "Tell the Republicans on your side of the line that we Royalists do not know men by their colour. Should you come to us you will be entitled to all the privileges of the rest of His Majesty's subjects."[5]

Following upon the favourable report of their agents, the Ohio freedmen entered into negotiations with the Canada Company, an English concern that had bought a large acreage in Upper Canada for speculative purposes. These lands included a large area in the western section of the province in which are today the populous counties of Perth and Huron. The purchase made by the migrants from Ohio was in the present Township of Biddulph, on the border of Huron County, though today a part of Middlesex County. The labour that they gave in the opening of roads through the company's holdings was to be credited in partial payment for the lands they received. Brown and Dutton, the men who had met with the authorities at York, were among the first to receive deeds to land in Biddulph Township.

There is evidence that the earlier settlers were aided financially by Quaker sympathizers in the United States, and had help from other sources. Lundy had been acquainted with the migration as early as 1830, for in *The Genius of Universal Emancipation* of May of that year he makes reference to the visit of the two representatives to York and records the satisfactory reception they received. It was natural, therefore, that he should later visit this colony and gain his own impressions of its prospects.

Benjamin Lundy was 43 years of age when he entered Upper Canada, and had already been active in the anti-slavery movement since 1815, so that he ranks as one of the pioneers in the crusade. He was born in Hardwick, Sussex County, New Jersey, in 1789, the son of Quaker parents, and when 19 years old removed to Wheeling, Virginia. There he had his first view of slavery, as he saw coffles of slaves being taken through the streets of the town. Later, he removed to St. Clairsville, Ohio, where he founded an anti-slavery society known locally as the Union Humanitarian Society. Beginning with a mere handful of members, it grew within a few months to have a membership of nearly five hundred. In 1816, Lundy issued a small circular signed "Philo Justicia," which Horace Greeley speaks of in his [book], *American Conflict*, as "containing the germ of the entire anti-slavery movement."

A more ambitious effort was the beginning of publication by Lundy of his little paper, *The Genius of Universal Emancipation*. The first issue appeared at Mount Pleasant, Ohio, in January 1821, but was shortly transferred to Greeneville in Tennessee. Three years later it was moved to Baltimore, Maryland, the first issue of volume IV appearing there in October 1824. Hitherto, *The Genius* had been a monthly, but from 1825 to 1830 it was issued weekly. In 1830 the monthly issue was resumed, Washington then being the nominal place of publication until 1834, when Philadelphia became its headquarters and continued as such until 1836, being the last year of issues from an eastern source. The paper did not disappear, however, for when Lundy removed to Illinois in 1837 he resumed publication, with 11 numbers of volume XIV appearing before his death at Lowell, Illinois, on August 22, 1839.[6] He was then in his 51st year. The final issue, appearing after his death and numbered 316, contained a simple but eloquent tribute to the man. It bore the signature "The Printer."

Lundy's journey to Upper Canada in 1832 was not the first he had made in his search for a land where the people of colour might find home, freedom, and protection. During his residence in Baltimore he had twice visited Haiti, being interested in the possibilities of the island as a place to which manumitted [freed] slaves might be sent. On his return from the island in 1825, he found that his wife had died during his absence and that his family was scattered.

"I collected my children together," he wrote. "Placed them with friends in whom I could confide and renewed my vow to devote my energies to the cause of the slave ... I relinquished every prospect of the future enjoyment of an earthly home until this object should be accomplished."

There is no more pathetic incident in Lundy's career than this return to a broken home, and no more noble passage in his writings than this prompt rededication of himself to the "unfinished work" that lay before him. In carrying out his vow he journeyed again to Haiti in 1829, to Texas in 1831, to Upper Canada in 1832, to Texas once more in 1833, and for a third time in 1834.[7]

Lundy crossed the Niagara River from Lewiston to Queenston, Upper Canada, on the morning of Friday, January 13, 1832, and began the journey westward to Wilberforce, which would be made by stage as far as London. To observe more closely the country through which he would pass, Lundy took his stand with the driver on the front of the vehicle, which, because of the snow, was on runners. He arrived at Hamilton in the evening and spent the night there. He noted, among other things, the considerable number of Americans among the settlers in the country through which he had passed on his first day in Canada, but he makes no mention of seeing any Negroes.

There was opportunity to walk about the Village of Hamilton before the hour for departure arrived the next morning. A few hours' ride, as before, on the outside of the coach with the driver, brought Lundy to the Village of Brantford. Here, he observed the presence of numerous Indians and also some Negroes, the first he had seen since entering Canada. And here, as elsewhere, Americans were numerous, and he noted that they had the familiar prejudice of their countrymen against the coloured race. He learned that there was a settlement of coloured people north of the village bearing the name Woolwich [Woolwich Township in the Queen's Bush]. Lundy spent the night in Brantford, disturbed but little, he says, by the noise of the tavern barroom beneath his room where, he learned later, there had been quite a "fracas" during the evening. The next day being Sunday, he was delayed in his journey.

The stage set out early on Monday morning, January 16, "in the direction of Detroit." The weather, which until now had been mild, had turned cold and frosty, but the snow was light and the sleighing poor. The country was now more thinly settled. After 30 miles of travelling, a short halt was made at the Beachville post-house [roadside inn]. Here, Lundy noted better farms and dwellings. He was nearing the Thames River, with its beautiful stands of pine and other trees. In the evening, the stage arrived at a tavern kept by Hiram Martin, 60 miles from Brantford and three miles southwest of the Village of London. Lundy had spent the whole day outside with the driver, observing the character of the country through which he passed. The weather had warmed up during the day, and by evening the snow was melting.

London village was as far as the stage would carry Lundy toward his destination. From London he would have to walk to the edge of the Wilberforce Colony, a distance of 12 to 15 miles, since there was no conveyance. He was early on his way to the village after a night's rest at the Martin tavern, and by mid-morning was headed north through the heavy, soft snow covering the primitive roads. By mid-afternoon he had arrived at the home of Elder Benjamin Paul, a coloured preacher of the Baptist faith who sometimes also served white Welsh settlers living in London Township to the south. Lundy stayed overnight with Paul, and in the morning went further north to the cabin of Austin Steward, where he remained for the next two days, visiting and interviewing various settlers and gaining all possible information about the prospects of the colony. Steward, whose autobiography is the best source of information on the settlement, was from Rochester and had left his home and business to render what guidance and assistance he could to the newcomers from Ohio. He had made a considerable sacrifice in coming to Wilberforce, and continued his residence there until January 1837, when he returned, a much poorer man, to Rochester. At Wilberforce, he had been the president of the Board of Managers, providing the local government of the colony. His narrative was first published at Rochester in 1856, and went into a second edition three years later.[8] The book contains an interesting account of Lundy's visit.

In January 1832, when Lundy was there, the Wilberforce Settlement numbered about 32 families, with an average of five individuals each. Many more had visited the place, but had gone elsewhere seeking work. Twenty-five families had purchased land from the Canada Company, and most of them had done some clearing and built log cabins. There were about 200 acres cleared, and some 60 acres sown with wheat. There was also some livestock, cattle, pigs, and horses, and sawmills and a gristmill within a reasonable distance. Two schools had been opened, one of which was taught by a daughter of Elder Benjamin Paul and some white children in attendance. Religious services of both the Baptist and Methodist faiths were held, and a Sunday school was conducted during the warmer months. Local administration was in the hands of the Board of Managers.

Plans had been made for the establishment at Wilberforce of a seminary where more advanced education might be provided, and to this end agents had been sent to both England and the United States to solicit funds. Reverend Nathaniel Paul, a brother of Elder Benjamin Paul, had already gone to England, while the American canvass was in the hands of one Israel Lewis. The results were unfortunate: Nathaniel Paul collected about $600 for education, and also other sums from interested individuals, but none of it reached Wilberforce. Though not dishonest, Paul lacked any business sense. Israel Lewis, on the other hand, appears from all the accounts to have been both dishonest and a troublemaker. The most interesting experience of Nathaniel Paul while in England was his appearance in June 1832 before a select committee of the House of Commons to give evidence with respect to the coloured inhabitants of Upper Canada. The committee, which was presided over by the Right Honourable Sir James Graham, had been set up to consider measures, which were to be considered by Parliament, for the extinction of slavery in British possessions overseas, and included some of the foremost Parliamentary figures of the day.

Before his departure from Wilberforce on January 20, Lundy met with most of the male adults of the community in a public meeting, where he added further to his knowledge of the settlement. Then he set out for London, but had only gone four miles when night approached, and he sought shelter with an Irish settler named Henry O'Neal. Lundy says that his host was friendly to the coloured people and warmly approved of the object of his visit. O'Neal had a coloured man named Williams working for him with whom Lundy had had acquaintance in Baltimore. He was treated, says Lundy "precisely as though he were white."

On the following morning, O'Neal insisted on driving Lundy about ten miles toward London, so he arrived in the village before noon. He spent the afternoon looking about the village and taking note of its inhabitants and their occupations. His notes were included in the printed record of his journey, and provide us today with the earliest description we have of the village. At night, he went back to the Hiram Martin tavern to await the morning stage. This he boarded once more on the morning of January 22, taking his place, as before, on the outside with the driver. He arrived in Detroit on the evening of January 23, his journey having occupied ten days. Summing up his experiences and observations, Lundy had this to say about the Wilberforce experiment in Negro colonization:

> From every investigation I have been able to make and all the information I could obtain by frequent conversation and inquiry among many intelligent persons, both those who were friendly and those who were inimical to our coloured people, that the country in question will be very suitable for them, particularly those north of the Carolinas, if they choose to locate themselves therein. The same rights and privileges will be guaranteed to them as to other British subjects and many of the white inhabitants of the republic have voluntarily exchanged their citizenship here for the immunities they may there enjoy. I would not urge, I would not ask a single free man to go, who is not so disposed. My business is to give him information. If he can profit by it I shall rejoice. If he neglects to pay attention to it he does but exercise a perfect right which it would be highly improper for me to question him about. Believing, however, that there are many among the persecuted coloured people south of the Delaware who are extremely desirous to change their situation, and would be glad of such information as I have collected, I shall be amply rewarded for the hardship and expense of my cold and toilsome journey, if I can be successful in laying it, generally before them.

Any reader of the original narrative of the journey in Upper Canada will recognize the practical character of the report Lundy made and published. His observations on the climate, soil, timber, and other features of a country that he was visiting for the first time are remarkably accurate, and answer such questions as might be asked by a prospective settler. Knowing that coloured settlers would come from a warmer climate, he had much to say about weather conditions as he himself experienced them, and he included in his report a statement of temperatures at Wilberforce during the month of December 1831, compiled by Austin Steward. During the month there had been but one real drop below zero, while on moist days the temperature had ranged between 15 and 25°F with winds from the south and west.

Lundy has had but one published biography, which appeared from the pen of Thomas Earle in 1847 and has never been republished. Most of Lundy's correspondence and papers were lost in the fire that destroyed Pennsylvania Hall on the night of May 8, 1838.

> Well, [he wrote after this event] my papers, books, clothes — everything of value (except my journal in Mexico, etc.) are all gone — a total sacrifice on the altar of Universal Emancipation. They have not yet my conscience, they have not taken my heart, and until they rob me of these they cannot prevent me from pleading the cause of the suffering slave.... I am not disheartened, though everything of earthy value (in the shape of property) is lost. Let us persevere in the good cause. We shall assuredly triumph yet.

Lundy had one more year of life. He removed to Illinois early in 1839, and there resumed publication of *The Genius,* of which 12 issues appeared prior to his death on August 22, 1839.[9]

When the centenary of Lundy's death came in the summer of 1939, suitable observance was made at the grave by members of the Society of Friends, and the State of Illinois placed a bronze pillow, suitably inscribed, beside the plain little marble stone at the head of the grave.

Herman Von Holst [1841–1904], the historian, has said of Lundy that he was the immediate precursor, and in a certain sense the founder of abolitionism, and he adds the tribute that "the 19th century can scarcely point to another instance in which the command of Christ to 'leave all things and follow Him' was so literally fulfilled."

3

Amherstburg, Terminus of
the Underground Railroad

Journal of Negro History, *vol. 10, no. 1 (January 1925), 1–9*

The little Canadian town of Amherstburg is situated on the east bank of the Detroit River, not far from the mouth of that beautiful stream. From the later years of the eighteenth century, it has figured in the history of Canada and today proudly holds its place as one of the most historic spots in Ontario. Throughout the earlier period of the War of 1812 it was the headquarters of the British commander, [Isaac] Brock, and it was here that the first meeting took place between Brock and the great Indian chief Tecumseh. Later, during the troubles of 1837–38, there were important happenings at this point, particularly the capture of the schooner *Anne,* in which Negro volunteers from the district had a hand. But apart entirely from its military importance, Amherstburg, or Fort Malden as it was called in earlier days, has special interest as being the chief place of entry for the large number of fugitives who made their way here from the slave states of the South by way of the Underground Railroad to Canada, and freedom.

Even today, there are many coloured families resident in Amherstburg, descendants of those who came in the days before the Civil War and who did not leave their adopted home when the abolition of slavery and the downfall of the Confederacy made it possible for them to return in safety to the South. In other towns and cities of western Ontario there are similar groups of people, whose colour is a constant reminder of the movement of the fugitives into Canada in the first half of the last century.

The Negro population of Amherstburg on the eve of the Civil War was placed by one observer[1] at 800 out of a total population of 2,000, a rather large percentage, it will be noted. In 1855, another visitor to the place[2] had estimated the Negro population at between 400 and 500, which would indicate that the population had doubled in the late 1850s. This might well be accounted for by the large number of Negroes who came into Canada between 1850 and 1860, consequent upon the operations of the Fugitive Slave Act of 1850. It does not necessarily follow that either of the figures given above represent the actual Negro population resident in Amherstburg, since there must always, due to its nature as a place of entry, have been many transients in the town. Probably most Negroes preferred a permanent location further back from the international boundary, where there was less risk of kidnapping and forcible return to the American jurisdiction. This would account for the colonies in such towns as London, Ingersoll, and Chatham, each of which, even to this day, has its Negro population.

The number of transients in Amherstburg must always have been somewhat of a problem for those engaged in any religious or philanthropic work at this place. The missionaries placed here by the American Missionary Society were driven to the greatest extremities at times when some unusually large incursion of fugitives made demands upon them for food, for shelter, for clothing, and all other forms of assistance that could be rendered. In 1849, Isaac J. Rice, who had been located at Amherstburg since 1838, wrote to *The Liberator*:[3]*

> Whole families reach us, needing clothing, provisions, a home for a few days, until arrangements can be made for life, and all this amid strangers, the prejudiced.
>
> They are driven from schools in the States, they are no better here. If they go in schools by themselves, their portion of public money is allowed; but Canadians will

---

* Editors' Note: *The Liberator* was the newspaper founded by abolitionist William Lloyd Garrison at Boston on January 1, 1831. His first edition was uncompromising on the need for immediate emancipation of America's slave population. Garrison wrote: "I am in earnest — I will not equivocate — will not excuse — I will not retreat a single inch — AND I WILL BE HEARD." The newspaper continued until Congress ratified the Thirteenth Amendment in 1865, and abolished slavery in the United States.

not teach them, so that your teachers from the States must do it and aid them also about getting land and various other ways.

Seven or eight missionaries are here, brought by my influence.... Last month three of us lay sick here and two were not expected for a time to live.... We have received at our house and clothed more than 50 from the South.... We need about $400 this fall. We are $100 in debt. We greatly need better accommodations, a house that will cost $250 or $300.

Less than a year later a letter signed by Milly Morse, of Foxboro, made an appeal through *The Liberator*,[4] on behalf of Isaac Rice and his missionary work. This letter speaks of his efforts as follows: "He has suffered much in silence and given himself up for the good of the slave. He has lived principally on bread and beans and without the means to purchase these."

The letter goes on to state that Rice had divided what he had with the fugitives until he was actually wanting for clothing. He sold his watch and even his beds to buy food. He is quoted as placing the Negro population of Canada at about 20,000, with 3,000 of them located in the district around Amherstburg. He had clothed as many as 300 fugitives in one year, and had 90 pupils in his school at that time. Siebert, in his study of the Underground Railroad,[5] says that after 1850 as many as 30 fugitives would cross in one day at Amherstburg, so that the figures given by Rice as to be the extent of his work are probably not exaggerated. William Wells Brown, himself a fugitive, says that from the first of May to the first of September 1842 he conveyed no less than 69 fugitives across Lake Erie to Canada and that, subsequently, on a visit to Amherstburg, he met no less than 17 of these located there.[6] The Chicago *Western Citizen* estimated in 1842 that there was $400,000 worth of Southern slaves in and around the town.[7] The place was, as Professor Siebert has pointed out, a terminus for several routes of the underground, along which runaways travelled and which converged at Toledo, Sandusky, and Cleveland. From the lake ports, friendly captains of lake vessels brought the fugitives to the Detroit River, the last lap of a journey that had often been begun deep in the South.

The arrivals, all too frequently, were in pitiable state. Usually they were without money, food, or clothing suited to the rigours of a Canadian winter. Children arrived with scarcely enough to cover them, and that of thin cotton. There was probably reason for some of the appeals that were broadcasted in the United States for clothing, food, and money, though some of the more ambitious Negroes strongly condemned this practice as leading to imposture and fraud. Doubtless there was fraud at times, with money and supplies destined for needy fugitives getting into other hands, but such things have ever been where need exists, and charity is more open-handed than sharp-eyed.

There are many romantic tales that have come down of the reunion at Amherstburg of families separated in the South. Miss Martineau says she was told by a gentleman that the sublimest sight in America was not Niagara or Quebec, or the Great Lakes, but the leap of a slave from a boat to the freedom of the Canadian shore. Fort Malden must have seen many touching incidents of this character. Reverend William M. Mitchell, in his book on the Underground Railroad, tells of a Negro named Hedgman who had been sold south from Kentucky but escaped and made his way to Canada, locating in Amherstburg. His wife had been separated from him, and of her and his family he had lost all trace. Twelve years after he had arrived in Canada, the wife also escaped from her owner and eventually arrived at the very town where her husband was located. Friendless and alone, she wandered about the streets seeking shelter, and was attracted by the singing in a little chapel. Opening the door timidly, the first person she saw was the husband from whom she had been so long separated, and of whose whereabouts she had had no knowledge.[8]

Church and school occupied an important place in the lives of a majority of the fugitives. Old and young seemed seized with the desire to go to school, and the churches were the meeting place of all. There was a surprising keenness about the desire of many of these people to better themselves. Canadian law drew no distinction between Black and white in matters of citizenship, of which education was one. In practice, however, there were not infrequently some distinctions likely to be drawn, the whites preferring that Negroes should have schools of their own.[9] As might be expected under such circumstances, there were some Negroes ready, occasionally, to test the principle of their right to share the benefits of the public schools. When Benjamin Drew visited the place [Amherstburg] in 1854, he found the Negro separate school a small, low building, having neither blackboard nor chairs. Long, rough benches were placed against the walls with desks before them. The whole interior was comfortless and repulsive. The teacher was a coloured woman, apparently doing the best she could under the discouragement of poor surroundings and the frequent absences of her pupils.[10] The situation was improved shortly after this, however, by the Colonial Church and School Society of England, opening a school,[11] and when Dr. Samuel G. Howe visited Amherstburg in the summer of 1863, he found 90 coloured children enrolled in the school with an average attendance of 60.[12]

Main Street, Amherstburg, 1865. Amherstburg on the Detroit River was a favourite place of settlement for refugees from American slavery. By the time this picture was taken there was a substantial Black community in the town, and many more African Canadians owned prosperous farms in the area. *Courtesy of the Archives of Ontario, F2076-16-6-2-44.*

Levi Coffin, the abolitionist, visited the town in 1844 and stayed at the mission school. He was much impressed with the work that was being done then, and in his reminiscences pays tribute to the self-sacrifice of Isaac Rice, who, he says, had given up fine prospects in Ohio to take up this work, to which he felt himself called. Coffin describes Fort Malden as "the great landing place, the principal terminus of the underground railroad of the west."[13]

An educational movement among the Negroes, quite apart from the schools, had its origin at Amherstburg in 1854, when the first True Band was formed, similar organizations springing up in other communities where Negroes were located. The True Bands were open to both sexes, and a small monthly fee was charged. The aims of the bands were to improve the schools, increase attendance, abate race prejudice, arbitrate disputes between members of the Negro race, to assist the destitute, suppress begging, etc.

The coming of so many people of another race and colour into southwestern Ontario was not pleasing to all the white inhabitants. Deep prejudice manifested itself at times, and an occasional outburst in some newspaper reflected the feelings of an element of the population. The *Amherstburg Courier* of October 27, 1849 printed a resolution of the district council, passed on October 8 of that year, protesting vigorously against the proposed Elgin Settlement, which was planned by Reverend William King as a home for the fugitives from slavery. This resolution, which appears to have been instigated by a local politician, [Edwin] Larwill, resident in Chatham, declared that "there is but one feeling, and that is disgust and hatred, that they (the Negroes) should be allowed to settle in any township where there is a white settlement." The resolution proceeded to ask for a disallowance and a requirement that Negroes shall furnish good security that they will not become a burden. It was also suggested that it would be well to ascertain whether it would be politic to allow them the suffrage.[14]

Amherstburg itself does not seem to have been the scene of any unusual manifestations of racial prejudice, despite the presence there of so many Negroes.

Dr. Samuel G. Howe, who visited the place in 1863 to investigate conditions there, has left us some interesting data. The town clerk said of the Negroes that "a portion of them are well behaved, and another portion not.... A great many of these coloured people go and sail in the summer time and in the winter lie around and don't do much. We have to help a great many of them, more than any other class of people we have.... I think the Council have given more to the coloured people than to others." But he added that they were no worse than the French.[15]

A Mr. Park, resident in Amherstburg, told Dr. Howe that the Negroes were part of them indolent and part industrious. They tended to neglect their own poor, and begged more than the whites. A Captain Averill who was interviewed said that the Negroes were satisfactory as sailors, "the best men we have," but they were never made mates and none owned ships of their own.[16]

Benjamin Drew, when he visited the place, found Negro mechanics and shopkeepers, while one of the best hotels in the place was also kept by a man of colour.

Those whom he interviewed said that they were able to make a living. He mentions one James Smith, who had been driven into Canada by the operation of the Fugitive Slave Act. He was making a comfortable living from a small grocery business, owned a lot worth $200, and had some other property.[17]

Howe gives some interesting figures of taxation, which he obtained from the town authorities. At the time of his visit in 1863, one in three whites was a taxpayer and one in 11 Negroes. The average tax paid by a white was $9.52, as compared with $5.12 paid by a Black. There is not as great a difference here as might be expected. There were 500 taxpayers in all, and 71 of these were coloured.[18] Howe found the home conditions superior to those of other foreigners, and much superior to slave quarters in the South. The houses were tidy, in good repair, and had gardens adjoining. He found carpets and curtains, pictures on the walls, tables decently spread, and other indications of a proper family life. The exceptions were chiefly among newcomers who had not yet had the opportunity to better themselves.[19] He wrote:

> The refugees for the most part live in small, tidy houses;
> not shanties, with old hats sticking out of broken

windows. Their habitations are not filthy huts, in filthy grounds, but comfortable dwellings, in good repair. Many are owned by the occupants. They have little gardens, which seem well cared for. This is the case not only in the Colonies, as they are called, where the form and dimensions of the houses are prescribed by the Company, but in those places where the refugees are entirely free to live as they choose. In the outskirts of Chatham and other large places are scores of small two-story [sic] houses, with garden lots, owned and inhabited by refugees who came to the country penniless.

We visited many of these houses, and found that the decencies of life are well observed, and that the comforts of life are not wanting. Cooking, eating and sleeping are not done in the same room, but in separate ones. They are tidily furnished; and some have carpets on the floors; and curtains at the windows. It is pleasant to see the feeble dawnings of taste in rude pictures, and simple attempts at ornament.

The tables are decently spread, and plentifully supplied. It is evident that they spend more money upon their households than foreign emigrants do. They live better; and they clothe their children better. They say, indeed, that this is the reason they do not lay up so much money as many Irish and Germans do.

Beyond the town limits there were Negroes located on the land, and Dr. Howe speaks of one Buckner, a coloured man who had his place in good cultivation, with a number of fine cattle and signs of thrift and care about the place. The soil around Amherstburg was of good quality, and rewarded any refugees who were resourceful and industrious enough to undertake farming.[20] One family group from Virginia, fine-looking mulattoes of unusual intelligence, formed what was known as the McCurdy Settlement in the Township of Malden, and had their own school and teacher.

How many fugitives passed through this "terminal station" of the Underground Railroad in the period before 1860 can never be computed. Immigration agents were not there in those days to register newcomers or determine their fitness for entry to the country. Had they been there, they would probably have been evaded. Only by the casual references of travellers and others, or by the scanty records of missionary workers, may be obtained an idea of the steady stream of people fleeing from slavery who came in by this doorway. Amherstburg, living on today chiefly in the reflection of its historic past, may well attract the interest of a citizen of the United States, as it does that of a Canadian, for it played an international role in days gone by.

4

The History of the Wilberforce Refugee Colony in Middlesex County

Transactions of London & Middlesex Historical Society, *vol. 19* (1918), 30–44

The history of the coloured refugee settlements in western Ontario is a chapter of our provincial history that does us credit. To the Black men in bondage, Canada was always the haven of refuge. With the Fugitive Slave Law and other repressive measures in force, they were not safe, even in Boston. In some states, supposedly free, they were subject to fierce persecution, but in Canada they always found protection and the fullest freedom. They were given a welcome and an opportunity to show themselves worthy of citizenship. Hundreds who made their escape from slave plantations in the South never halted until they had crossed the boundary, and, to use their own very expressive phrase, "had shaken hands with the lion." Out of the free states of the North there came, too, a steady stream of coloured folk who had found their dreams of security and peace rudely disturbed by pro-slavery interests and pro-slavery sentiment.

The Wilberforce coloured colony does not rank as one of the larger settlements of this kind in Canada. Neither was it as long-lived as some others. It was a failure almost from the start. Yet its story is not without interest, and it is rather remarkable that after nearly a century there are descendants of the little group of original settlers still in the locality.

For the beginnings of the Wilberforce Colony we go to Cincinnati, Ohio. Here, on the border line between the free North and the slave South, was a city that profited largely by trade with the South, and was influenced accordingly in its attitude to the slavery issue. In Cincinnati, there was a constant turmoil over the race question and the abolition movement. At one time, the Lane Theological Seminary, famous for

Lyman Beecher,* was threatened with fire and its faculty with lynching if the students were not prohibited from discussing slavery. Twice, James G. Birney's Philanthropist Press was wrecked by mobs. Coloured people were subject to persecution on trivial excuses.

The climax came when, in 1829, the law of 1804, known as the Ohio Black Law, was revived in the state and enforced. By this law, every coloured man was to give bonds of $500 not to become a town charge, and to find bonds for his heirs. No one could employ a coloured man or coloured woman to do any kind of labour under penalty of $100.

There were about 3,000 coloured people in Cincinnati at the time, and they were all thrown out of work. Moreover, there were threats that if they remained they would be sold back into slavery. A meeting was called, and there was talk of an appeal. The uselessness of this was apparent. There was talk of going to Texas, then Canada was proposed, and a colonization society was formed, with James C. Brown as president. Brown wrote for the society to Sir John Colborne, the lieutenant-governor, to ask if the coloured people would be admitted. Two members of their Board, one of them being Israel Lewis, took the letter to York and laid the case before the lieutenant-governor.

"Tell the Republicans on your side of the line," said Sir John, "that we Royalists do not know men by their colour. Should you come to us you will be entitled to all the privileges of the rest of His Majesty's subjects."

The lieutenant-governor's official reply to the Cincinnati Colonization Society, which was in similar terms, was published in the Cincinnati press and created much excitement, since it offered a refuge for all escaped

---

* Editors' Note: Lyman Beecher (1775–1863) was a noted New England Presbyterian clergyman and principal of the Lane Academy from 1832–50. The Lane Academy students had become involved in educating Black children in Cincinnati, and were becoming progressively more anti-slavery in their views. They held a famous debate on the subject of abolition in 1834. The trustees of the academy ordered them to end their anti-slavery activism, and some 50 students left the school. Hiram Wilson, who was a missionary to the fugitive slaves living in Canada for many years, was one of the best known of these students. Lyman Beecher was also father of the famous abolitionist author, Harriet Beecher Stowe. Her *Uncle Tom's Cabin* published in 1852 inflamed anti-slavery sentiment on both sides of the Atlantic and continues in print to this day.

slaves under British protection. The day after publication the mayor of Cincinnati sent for Brown and two other members of the Board and asked them to delay action on sending any people to Canada, as steps were being taken to have the law repealed.

Some of the refugees were assured by the promise that the law would be repealed, but Brown and some others decided to set out for the land of freedom. Inside of a month they were in Canada, and a contract was entered into with the Canada Company for a township of land for which $60,000 a year for ten years was to be paid. The intention was to bring as many as possible of the Cincinnati people to this township and settle them as a colony. But with the Black Law having really become inoperative in Cincinnati, of the 2,700 or more who were affected, only 460 left their home, and of these only five or six families actually settled in Biddulph. The rest of the Cincinnati refugees settled promiscuously in the province. Almost at the same time, however, there was an immigration of refugees from Boston, and 15 families came to Biddulph and settled. As a matter of fact, the colony only paid for about 1,200 acres, which was divided into plots of from 25 to 50 acres per family. The site was the present Village of Lucan.

The founders of the colony had two objects in view. First of all, they sought freedom and security for themselves and their families. But, in the second place, they had the idea that such a colony would furnish homes for future refugees who might be stirred to greater exertions for their freedom by the knowledge that at the end of their long journey a home awaited them. The failure of the colony came through two main causes: First of all, the persecutions in the State of Ohio moderated almost as soon as the first refugees left, reducing the number of emigrants to a handful. In the second place, the Canada Company's agents, fearing that the coloured colony would tend to keep away white settlers, suddenly refused to sell more land to the colonists, and thus prevented any expansion. Then, while this rule was in force, there came the Irish immigration of the 1830s, and Biddulph, instead of becoming a coloured colony, was in a very few years turned into an Irish colony, and has so remained to this day. The old coloured families who had settled there remained, and prospered in a measure, but few new ones came, and by the middle of the

1840s Wilberforce as a colony was practically non-existent. Henceforth, it was but a small coloured settlement in the midst of the Irish.

The chief record of the Wilberforce Colony has been left by Austin Steward, who resided there from 1830 to 1837, and during a large part of that time was president of the council that administered its affairs. His autobiography was published at Rochester, New York, in 1857, and is valuable for the information it gives concerning the lives of Negro refugees in Upper Canada in the 1830s and later.

Austin Steward was born a slave in Prince William County, Virginia, on the plantation of a Captain William Helm. While Steward was but a youth, Helm sold out in Virginia and removed, first to Sodus Bay, New York, and later to Bath, Steuben County, New York. At Bath, Steward was hired out to a man named Joseph Robinson. Thoughts of freedom entered his head, and as a preliminary step he obtained permission from his master to visit Geneva. There he called on James Moore, one of the directors of the Manumission Society, organized to aid those who were illegally in bondage. To Mr. Moore he told his story, and was advised to return to Bath and go on with his work until March. Before that time came around, however, the desire for freedom became so strong that he ran off in company with a slave girl who had also formerly been in the possession of Helm.

Austin Steward, a successful grocer in Rochester, New York, gave up his business and moved his family to Canada so he could assist in the management of the Wilberforce colony. From *Twenty-Two Years a Slave and Forty Years a Freeman: Embracing a Correspondence of Several Years, While President of Wilberforce Colony, London, Canada West (Rochester, NY: 1859).*

They were pursued, but made their escape, and Steward took refuge in the home of Dennis Comstock, who was president of the Manumission Society. Later, he entered the home of Otis Comstock, a brother, and stayed with him for four years.

"When I arrived there," he says, "I was about 22 years of age, and I felt for the first time in my life that I was my own master. I cannot describe to a free man what a proud feeling came over me when I hired to Mr. Comstock and made my first bargain, nor when I assumed the dignity of collecting my own earnings."

When his first wages were received, he went to a neighbouring town and bought some schoolbooks. Determined to get some education, he attended school for three winters in the Village of Farmington. It could scarcely be expected that his new-found freedom would not be challenged in that time. Helm soon appeared and demanded that Otis Comstock give Steward over. The latter refused and declared that he would carry the case into the courts. Helm then tried to kidnap not only Steward, but others of his slaves who had escaped from him but this plan also failed. Steward's next move was to settle in Rochester, at first peddling the products of the Comstock farm, and later embarking in business for himself as a butcher. At this time, he had a knowledge of the three R's, and had made a start at English grammar. He had considerable success in business, though subjected to some race discrimination and persecution. Eventually he built a two-storey dwelling and store. For his own people, he established a Sunday school, but found little support. Still later, he had so far prospered that he bought another lot and built on it.

In 1830, he attended the convention of coloured people in Philadelphia, and was appointed vice-president of the gathering. It was, in all probability, at this gathering that he first heard of the events in the State of Ohio, which had been responsible for the founding of the Wilberforce Colony in Canada, to which he himself was later to turn. Shortly afterward he heard more of it from Israel Lewis, the agent of the Cincinnati refugees who had gone to Canada on their behalf and returned by way of Rochester. Lewis declared that there were 1,100 coloured people in the woods of Canada and that they were starving. He called upon the humane everywhere to assist them. Steward was deeply impressed with what he heard from Israel Lewis.

"I had at that time," he says, "just made a public profession of my faith in the Christian religion and my determination to be governed by its holy precepts. I felt for the distressed and suffering everywhere, but particularly for those who had fled, poor and destitute, from cruel taskmasters, choosing rather the sufferings of cold and hunger with liberty than the meager necessities of life and slavery. I concluded to go to Canada and try to do some good; to be of some service in the great cause of humanity."

His resolution once made, his action followed. He proceeded from Rochester to Toronto, "which," he says, "I found quite a thriving town and containing some fine brick dwellings, and some I saw were built of mud, dried in the sun, wearing rather a poor than pretty appearance." At Toronto he hired a team and proceeded to Ancaster, stopping there overnight and proceeding on to his destination to find his brethren there in a destitute condition. The country was, of course, an unbroken wilderness, and all the labour of clearing off the heavy timber faced the refugees from slavery.

The day after he arrived at the settlement, a meeting was held in one of the rude log huts to decide on a name for the township, and, at Steward's suggestion, the name Wilberforce was adopted. Describing the settlement he says: "It is situated on what is known as the Huron Tract, Kent [actually Middlesex] County, London District, and is the next north of the Township of London. Our neighbors on the south were a company of Irish people who owned the township, and on the west side were a company of Welshmen, a hardy, industrious and enterprising people." He adds:

> In Wilberforce, there were no white inhabitants. The land appeared level and handsome, with but one stream of any magnitude running through it; this was the 'Oxsable,' [Ausable] which was dry during part of the year. All was one vast forest of heavy timber that would compare well with that of western New York: Beech, maple, ash, elm, oak, whitewood, bass, balm of Gilead, etc. The soil was good for corn, wheat, rye, oats and most kinds of grain and vegetables raised in New York and was

a superior grazing country about 15 miles from London. This was a village containing perhaps 30 dwellings and 200 inhabitants; a courthouse and jail all under one roof, built of stone and plastered; small doors and windows in the style of some of the old English castles. London was built in the forks, or between the east and west branches of the River Thames; hence you would hear people speak of going to 'The Forks' instead of to the village; it is about 200 miles from Buffalo and the nearest port between the two is Port Stanley, 30 miles from London.

Having looked over the condition of the refugees in Canada, Steward decided that he would remove his family to Canada and join in the work of building up the colony. He believed that Wilberforce could be made a haven for those escaping out of the bondage of the South, and that by industry the refugees could make a living there. Consequently, in 1830 he sold out all at Rochester, and, despite the forebodings of his friends, set out with his family for Canada. On a lake boat, they travelled to Port Stanley where there was, he says, a dock, a warehouse, and several farmhouses. The wild and picturesque appearance of the mouth of Kettle Creek attracted his attention, but the family did not tarry long. A farmer was engaged to take them to London. Ten miles on their way they came to the newly laid out Village of St. Thomas, then continued through new country to London, where they arrived tired and hungry and put up for the night with a Mr. Faden. The next day, Steward bought a span of horses for $150 and, putting them before a lumber wagon, the family entered upon the last lap of their journey in good spirits and arrived in due time.

The colony at this time consisted of some 14 or 15 families, numbering over 50 persons in all. The first business done after Steward's arrival was to appoint a Board of Managers to look after the business of the colony. The board consisted of seven members, elected by the settlers, and Steward was chosen president. It was also decided to send out at once two agents for the purpose of soliciting aid for the erection of houses of worship and for the maintenance of schools in the colony. Reverend Nathaniel Paul was chosen to go to Great Britain, while Israel Lewis was to be the agent in the United States. Nothing but ill came from the sending forth of these two men.

To begin with the case of Lewis, it seems certain that he collected considerable sums in the United States, but he would neither pay these over to the Board of Managers, nor give any account of his proceedings. Moreover, while abroad on his mission, he was charged with living in an extravagant fashion. Nothing seemed left to do but expose Lewis, and this was done in several American and Canadian newspapers. This occasioned resentment among friends of Lewis, who possibly shared in his ill-gotten gains, and Steward intimates that Lewis's creditors also supported him when they faced the possibility of his facilities for collecting further money being ended. The worst feature of Lewis's trickery was felt, however, in connection with the land purchases of the colonists. Lewis had dealt extensively with [Thomas Mercer] Jones, the agent of the Canada Company, but Lewis's failure to fulfill his agreement regarding payment so exasperated Jones that he declared he would have nothing to do with any of the coloured people and so, a little later, when Steward wanted to buy some more land, he was unable to make a purchase. This action on the part of the company was one of the main causes of the failure of the colony. The original settlers had secured their farms through the liberality of the Oberlin Society of Friends, who had raised funds sufficient to purchase 800 acres, and had sent Frederick Stover, one of their number, to make the deal. This comprised nearly all of the land possessed by the colony when Steward arrived. The steady refusal of the Canada Company to sell to the coloured people forced Steward into other lines of work. He made his house a sort of tavern for the accommodation of travellers, and also did teaming with his horses. His teaming was cut short by the death of both his horses from some strange disease. Steward's tavern, however, was popular, and had a good name, so that persons travelling from London to Goderich preferred to stay overnight in Wilberforce rather than go further to seek accommodation among their own people.

Steward's book indicates that at no time was there any love lost between Lewis and himself. There appears to have been antagonism between the two men from the time they first met in Rochester, before Steward came to Canada. The climax came when Lewis sold a piece of property to Steward in illegal fashion, then charged Steward with stealing a note for $25 and had him haled into court. The case came before Chief Justice [John Beverly] Robinson, who made his appearance in court with great pomp, dressed in English court style. Lewis gave his evidence. Steward's lawyer then called three respectable white men who said they would not believe Lewis on oath. The jury did not even leave their seats to acquit Steward. A second suit instituted by Lewis also fell flat. Next, he appears to have tried to take Steward's life. The latter, on his way from London, was set upon in McConnell's Dismal Swamp by three men with rifles. Their poor marksmanship probably saved his life.

The rest of the career of Lewis may be briefly dealt with here. His conduct seems to have turned most of the colonists against him. His health gave way and he died in a hospital in Montreal, leaving not enough for his gains to provide a decent burial.

Steward's intense dislike for Lewis shows itself continually throughout his book, but at the same time he is not blind to the ability the man possessed. Lewis was born a slave and raised amid the worst cruelties of the system. He made a bold break for liberty, taking his wife along with him, and though they were tracked with bloodhounds, arrived safely in Cincinnati. His dominant personality made him a leader among his people, so that when they were being forced to leave Ohio he was at once chosen as their agent to spy out the new promised land. Like the agents the Children of Israel sent out, his report was unfavorable, but it did not deter the Cincinnati fugitives from determining to seek liberty under the British government.

Steward says of Lewis that his appearance was prepossessing, and his manner and address easy and commanding. To those unacquainted with his private life he could appear the gentleman, the Christian, and the philanthropist. His education was limited, but he had managed to gather a sufficient amount of knowledge to read and write, together with quite a fund of general information, and his natural shrewdness and tact accomplished all the rest. To strangers he could even appear a scholar if left unquestioned. He was something of an orator, and once spoke with eloquence and marked effect before the New York legislature at Albany. His natural abilities, says Steward, were above mediocrity, but having never had the advantages of a real education or the privileges of a society calculated to refine and cultivate his natural aspiring intellect and ambitions, he had come to manhood with a determined, selfish disposition to accomplish whatever gratified his vanity or administered to his animal nature.

Turning now to Reverend Nathaniel Paul, who had been appointed as the agent of the colony in Great Britain, we find another record of funds collected for a worthy object being appropriated by an individual. In order to pay the expense of his voyage to England, it was found necessary to call upon the generosity of friends in the United States. Everard Peck, of Rochester, New York, signed a note for $700, which was cashed and used to fit out the Wilberforce agent.

Summarizing the work of this agent, Steward says:

> He reached England and collected large sums of money but entirely failed in the remittance of any sums either to Mr. Tappan (a friend of the colony in New York) or to myself. When the note of $700 came due Mr. Peck was obliged to pay it and lose it....
>
> He (Paul) wrote me from time to time and once informed me that he then had $1,200 in hand but not a farthing could we get. We wrote him again and again but all to no purpose. He never paid one dollar.

The failure to get Mr. Paul to make any remittances led to the decision to send somebody else after him, and an Englishman named Nell was appointed for this purpose. Nell left his wife and five children in the colony, and Steward went with him as far as New York, raising among friends in Rochester and New York between $300–$400. Nell arrived in England just as Paul was leaving there, and the colonists never heard from Nell again, at least not during the time that Steward remained with them. Paul arrived in New York in the fall of 1834, bringing with him a white woman whom he had married in England. He and his lady did not come to Wilberforce until the spring of 1835. On sending him forth in the first place, the council of the colony had agreed to allow him $50 a month and expenses. Paul, on his return, charged the board for wages and expenses for a period of four years, three months and twenty days.

Paul's accounts were examined, and showed receipts in England of $8,015.80 and expenses of $7,019.80. But the further bill for wages at $50 a month not only wiped out the balance, but actually left the colony several hundred dollars in debt to him. There was, of course, no money to meet this. In his items of expenditure was an amount of $200 said to have been paid over to William Lloyd Garrison, the famous American abolitionist, while the latter was campaigning in England. Paul had no authority to make any such gift out of funds that had been given to him to assist education and religion at Wilberforce, and Steward took the trouble to write to Garrison asking if he had ever received such an amount. Garrison's reply, given in full in Steward's book, is that he got no money from Paul, though he gives full credit to Paul for assistance rendered to him in his work. "I shall ever remember with gratitude his heartiness and zeal in the cause and on my behalf," he says. "I owe much of the success that so signally crowned my efforts to his presence, testimony and eloquent denunciation of the colonization scheme."

The colonists were excited to fury when they found out how they had been tricked by Paul, and were ready to do him violence. Steward made a careful examination of his accounts and expressed himself as satisfied that Paul had actually spent the money, and had not laid it away for his own future purposes. He said:

> We succeeded at last, after a tedious effort, in satisfying the minds of the colonists to the extent that a violent outbreak was no longer to be feared or dreaded. When all was quiet in the colony I ventured to make my first call on the wife of Reverend Nathaniel Paul who was then stopping with the widow of the late Reverend Benjamin Paul, residing some three miles from us.
>
> The houses of the colonists were generally built of logs, hewn on both sides, the spaces chinked with mortar and the roof constructed of boards. The lower part was generally left in one large room, and when another apartment was desired it was made by drawing a curtain across it. When we arrived at the residence of Mrs. Paul we were immediately

ushered into the presence of Mrs. Nathaniel Paul, whom we found in an inner apartment made by drawn curtains, carpeted in an expensive style, where she was seated like a queen of state — with a veil floating from her head to the floor; a gold chain encircling her neck and attached to a gold watch in her girdle; her fingers and person sparkling with costly jewelry. Her manners were stiff and formal, nor was she handsome but a tolerably fair looking woman of about 30 years of age; and this was the wife of our agent for the poor Wilberforce colony.

Reverend Nathaniel Paul and his white wife evidently found themselves ill at ease in the colony, for they soon departed. Paul gave his promise that he would go to Rochester and pay Everard Peck, who had advanced the money to send him to England, the $700 that was justly due him. But Paul went directly to Albany, where his closing years were darkened by domestic troubles and the serious illness that eventually caused his death.

Considering the financial setbacks that came through the dishonesty of its agents, it is a wonder that the colony made any headway at all. What success was achieved must be attributed to the industry and thrift of the colonists themselves. It was, as Steward points out, never intended by the managers that the agents should collect money to be divided amongst the colonists themselves, but they did feel justified in asking for help with the establishment of education and religion. Most of the settlers were able to work, and did so. They cleared considerable land, sowed grain, planted orchards, raised cattle, and, in short, showed the world that they were not inferior to the whites when given a chance.

While Steward was at Wilberforce, a provincial law was passed allowing each township to elect three commissioners to transact township business. Each township could also elect one township clerk. Three coloured commissioners were elected in the Wilberforce colony, and Steward was appointed clerk.

Five years of unhappy experiences finally led Steward to consider returning to the United States. He gives a pathetic account of his circumstances. He writes:

When I went to Wilberforce, I supposed that the colonists would purchase the whole township of Biddulph and pay for it, which might have been done had they been fortunate enough to put forward better men, when we had a sufficient number of inhabitants, we could have sent a member to Parliament, one of our own race, to represent the interests of the colony. In all this we were disappointed. The Canada Company, in their unjust judgment of a whole people by one dishonest man, had stopped the sale of lands to coloured persons, which, of course, put an end to the emigration of respectable and intelligent coloured men to that place; nor was there any prospect of a favourable change. Moreover, the persecutions which gave rise to the colony had, in a great measure ceased; anti-slavery truth was taking effect on the minds of the people.... These, with other considerations, induced me to leave Canada. As soon as my intentions were made known I was importuned on all sides, both in and out of the settlement, to remain awhile longer at least.

He finally decided to send his family back to the United States but to remain himself until his term as township clerk was terminated. The family was to return by Port Stanley and Buffalo as they had come.

"But what a contrast there was," he said, "between our leaving Rochester five years before and our removing from the colony. Then we had five two-horse wagon loads of goods and furniture and seven in family; now our possessions were only a few articles in a one-horse wagon with an addition of two members to our household."

With affectionate farewells, the colonists said goodbye to the Steward family. At Port Stanley they were entertained in the farmhouse of a Mr. White, a Virginia fugitive who lived on the bank of Kettle Creek. They were detained waiting for a boat, and on the second morning Steward was awakened early to find himself under arrest for a debt of $40. He was taken to London and quickly arranged the matter there but upon returning to Port Stanley found his family gone. They had a rough trip to Buffalo, and one of the children caught a cold that later caused her death. Steward returned to Wilberforce practically penniless, remained there until January 19, 1837, and then left for his old home, arriving in Rochester on January 23. Five old friends quickly offered him a loan of $500 with which he was to re-establish in business. Things did not go well with him, however, and some little time later he joined the conference of the African Methodist Episcopal Church. I have no record that he ever again visited Wilberforce.

It seems clear that the unscrupulous land agents had much to do with the failure of the colony. The refusal to sell land was a blow to the prospect of building a settlement. In some cases, when land had been purchased and money paid, title deeds would be refused, nor would there even be any compensation allowed for the improvements carried out. There was vigorous outcry from the coloured people against this manifest injustice. Steward records one humorous case where a coloured man named Smith followed the land agent to London and demanded compensation for the labour he had put on the land he had been forced to give up. The agent, who was a stout Englishman, met the coloured man in the hall of a tavern and tried to evade him. The coloured man quickly lowered his head and drove like a battering ram into the Englishman's stomach. The latter called for help, but there was little sympathy for him, and that fearful battering ram was again being lowered for action. He quickly capitulated and paid in full amid the jeers of the crowd.

In the library of Mr. J. Davis Barnett, of Stratford, there is a small pamphlet, printed at London, England, in 1832, that contains references to the Wilberforce Colony and to Reverend Nathaniel Paul, then in England as its agent. The credentials of Paul are given, and an appeal made on his behalf. "We shall be opening an asylum," says the appeal, "and a vista of hope, always growing, for all the enslaved people who may succeed in making their escape thither. Canada will be a city of refuge for God's poor. The thousands who might resort thither to us would form one of the most formidable bulwarks of our safety should we ever again be there assailed."

A statement is then given of the amounts received by Reverend Nathaniel Paul up to July 20, 1832, for the establishment of a college, for emigration, and for education in general. The amounts are not large, that for education being credited to the Society of Friends at Leighton.

There is some interest in the proposal for the establishment of a college, since it brings a New England city into the story of Wilberforce. At the first annual convention of free coloured people in the United States, held in Philadelphia, June 6–11, 1831, it was decided to establish a college at New Haven, Connecticut. The people there, however, had no liking for the establishment of a coloured school in their midst, and a strong resolution was passed against it, which was signed by Dennis Kimberley, the mayor, and Elisha Monson, the town clerk. This was in September 1831, and the decision was then made to establish the college at Wilberforce, Upper Canada, and it was on behalf of this, as well as the general education of the colony, that Reverend Nathaniel Paul appealed to the charitable of Great Britain.

The wording of this New Haven resolution, given in the pamphlet mentioned above, shows such a truckling to slavery interests that I quote it in full:

> Whereas endeavours are now making to establish a college in this city for the education of the coloured population of the United States, the West Indies and other countries adjacent; and in connection with this establishment the immediate abolition of slavery in the United States is not only recommended by the advocates of the proposed college, but demanded by right; and, whereas, an omission to notice these measures may be construed as implying either indifference to, or approbation of the same, etc., therefore, resolved by the mayor, aldermen, common council and freemen of the City of New Haven, in city meeting assembled, that we will resent the establishment of the proposed college in this place by every lawful means.

There are a few references to the Wilberforce Colony in the *History of Middlesex County*, which was published in London in 1889. On page 461, reminiscences of William Porte are quoted from the *Lucan Enterprise*, in which he says that lots 5 and 6, north and south of the London-Goderich road in Biddulph, with 600 acres more, were taken up in the name of the Society of Friends of Oberlin, Ohio, the price tag being $1.50 per acre. In 1830, he says, lots 5 north and south were occupied by Peter Butler, J. Wyatt, W. Whitehead, and one Pinkham, who were the original settlers on the land where Lucan village is situated. Of the first buildings, none now exist, he adds, and with the exception of the Butlers, none of the coloured pioneers are to be found. The coloured schoolhouse stood where J.C. Watts' residence now is, and the teacher sent by the Friends vanished with the school, the Friends ceasing their support in 1843. After that, the white settlers hired William Porte to teach the coloured children.

An examination of Austin Steward's book supplies the names of a number of the colonists in the early 1830s. There were the two Pauls, Benjamin and Nathaniel, both preachers. There was also Israel Lewis. A circular issued in March 1836 warning the public against Lewis is signed by Austin Steward, president; Peter Butler, treasurer; John Holmes, secretary; and by four other managers, Philip Harris, William Bell, John Whitehead, and Samuel Peters. Another circular, date not given, bears additional new names of Joseph Taylor and William Brown.

A bundle of manuscript notes in my possession made by William Matheson, of Lucan, who was very interested in the history of the Wilberforce colony, give some details, which, while rather indefinite, may be noted.

He says that he has before him a letter from the Canada Company stating that on September 30, 1830, Messrs. J.C. Brown and Stephen Dutton, both coloured, located certain lots on either side of the London Road and deeded them. These were the first lots deeded in Biddulph.

He also speaks of a coloured man settling on lot 6, concession 11, of London Township as early as 1819. His name is given as Henry Shaw, with the additional information that he was a bachelor, that he was there for 20 years, and that he kept chickens and had a raspberry patch.

Peter Butler, the elder, had a goodly line of descendants, and so something is known of his early life. He was born in Baltimore in 1797, and as a youth became a sailor, following the sea for seven years. He also learned the trade of caulker, and when he came to Canada seems to have followed this trade for a time at Port Stanley and Port Dover. Later, when he went to Biddulph to look over the land, he left his family at St. Thomas, but soon returned, and they all took up their residence on about the present site of Lucan. He was regarded highly in the colony, having some knowledge of simple medicine, which gave him the title of "Dr. Butler" in the district. Settlers came from quite a distance for treatment at times. His farm was later surveyed into village lots and, according to Matheson, he was worth $22,000 at his death in October 1872, his will stipulating that this was to be divided amongst his descendants in the third generation.

Daniel Turner came to Biddulph with Peter Butler. He also was born in Baltimore in 1805, and, like Butler, was a sailor and caulker. He was an elder in the Baptist Church, and, like Paul the Apostle, worked at his trade and preached. There are records of his preaching between Port Stanley and Port Dover, and also in Lobo, London, and Biddulph townships. He died toward the close of 1860. His widow died in 1896, age 90 years.

Philip Harris, mentioned in Austin Steward's book, died March 28, 1857, aged 82 years and 16 days. The gravestones of both Turner and Harris were still to be seen a few years ago on one of the back streets in Lucan. In a field near the Roman Catholic church is the grave of Reverend Benjamin Paul, who died March 31, 1836. This was before Austin Steward had left the colony.

Ephraim Taylor, according to William Matheson's notes, took up the farm on the north and east of the Little Sauble [Au Sauble River] and settled on it in 1830. There are some records of his trading with the people of London Township in 1831. R.H. O'Neil, formerly a banker at Lucan, remembered going with his father to Ephraim's place to get a yoke of steers with which they were to draw in grain. He recalled how rough and full of snags was the road through where Lucan now stands. Ephraim built a log house on his farm in 1843, which was standing some years ago. Later on, he sold out to J.H. Laird and moved over the Goderich and London road, building himself a new house on the pattern of the one in which he had been raised in the southern states. The fireplace was outside the house. It remained standing for a long time, but finally disappeared.

Mr. Matheson has a note of some recollections given him by Mr. B. Stanley in March 1904, in which reference is made to "Irie" Lewis (probably Israel Lewis). The note says that Shaw and Irie Lewis were the first settlers, Lewis being on the Sauble hill. Lewis acted for Stephen Dutton and James C. Brown in blocking out the land for the coloured settlers, 50 acres to each family.

There seems good reason to believe that the population of the colony did not at any time exceed 70. Some who came stayed but a short time, and there was a certain amount of coming and going during the whole period. The colony was visited at various times by travellers who have recorded their impressions. Patrick Shirreff, an East Lothian farmer, who came through about 1834 and published his book, *A Tour Through North America*, in 1835, says on page 178:

> On the boundary of the Huron tract, next to the London district, we passed a Negro settlement. The houses of the coloured people appeared of a particular construction, having the chimney on the outside of the log house, and which stack is composed of thin sawn timber, placed horizontally and mixed with clay. Their chief crop was Indian corn, well cultivated. Before my departure from Britain I had heard this settlement instanced as a complete failure and used as an argument against the emancipation of slaves. The houses, barns, fences and general appearances of this settlement are certainly mean enough but I consider it in most respects equal, and in some respects superior to settlements of whites in the Huron tract of the same standing of three years.

Professor Siebert, in his book on the Underground Railroad, quotes Dr. J. Wilson Moore, of Philadelphia, as stating his observation of the distinct advance made by the settlers at Wilberforce from log cabins to brick-and-frame houses.

Levi Coffin, the reputed president of the Underground Railroad, visited Wilberforce in the 1840s, at a time when he was looking into the condition generally of the Negroes in Canada. He says that Wilberforce was the only settlement he visited that did not contain refugees whom he had personally assisted to liberty.

Reverend William M. Mitchell, who published a book, *The Underground Railway*, at Toronto in 1860, refers to Wilberforce as having good homes and flourishing.

Among those who visited the colony while Austin Steward was there was Benjamin Lundy, the noted American abolitionist. Lundy was in Canada in 1830–31 obtaining subscribers for his paper, *The Genius of Universal Emancipation*, and also making observations on the general condition of the refugees. Steward says that Lundy spent an evening telling them about his journey to Haiti. This journey had been made in 1825 for the purpose of making arrangements for settling emancipated slaves there. Lundy remained in touch with the Wilberforce colonists for some time, a letter written by him to Steward in May 1835 describing a trip to Mexico being quoted. While William Lloyd Garrison did not visit the colony, he knew of its work, both through Steward and Reverend Nathaniel Paul, who was associated with Garrison in his work in Great Britain.

The first annual report of the Canadian Anti-Slavery Society has a brief reference to the Wilberforce colony. This is dated March 1852 and says that the colony then had about 20 families and was not flourishing.

Benjamin Drew's *North-Side View of Slavery*, published in 1856, and which surveys the refugee settlements in Upper Canada, has no reference to the Wilberforce Colony except incidentally in the narrative given by James C. Brown, then living in Chatham. Brown, it will be remembered, was the president of the Colonization Society organized in Cincinnati, and one of the first settlers to come to Wilberforce. His story, given in Drew's book, pages 239–48, is one of the most interesting of the many brought together here. He remained but a very short time at Wilberforce, settling in Toronto for a time and then returning to Cincinnati. He was there for a little over a year, during which time he was subject of further persecution. This induced him to return to Canada, and he settled once more in Toronto, where he was a gunner during the troubles of 1837–38. Later he moved to the

Dawn Settlement, and was elected one of the trustees of the industrial school at that place. From Dawn, he went to Chatham in 1849, and remained there for the rest of his life.

There is no great success to record in connection with the attempt to found in Wilberforce a coloured Utopia. The same idea, in varying form, was attempted at other places in this province, usually with more success. All these attempts are of interest as one phase of the great struggle then under way to end the whole system of slavery.

By giving coloured refugees homes, and land, and an opportunity to make a living, Canada was striking a blow at the whole system of human bondage. That blow, joined with the titanic blows administered by the forces at work in the United States, culminated in the Civil War, with its vast cost of lives and treasure, the outcome of which was the wiping out of the stain that for so long had rested on the land of liberty.

5

Evidence is Found of Race Prejudice in Biddulph, 1848

London Free Press (*July 7, 1951*), 11

Clear evidence of race prejudice against Negro settlers in what is today the Township of Biddulph in Middlesex County is furnished by the *London Times* of May 4, 1849, one of London's early newspapers. In this issue appears an official advertisement issued by Lord Elgin, the governor general, from Montreal, offering a reward of £50 for information that will lead to the apprehension of persons who, on the night of October 19, 1848, set fire to barns and stacks of straw and grain belonging to William Bell, Ephraim Taylor, and the Reverend Daniel A. Furner, coloured inhabitants of the township, which at that time was a part of the District of London.

In the year 1849, there were serious political disturbances in the City of Montreal arising out of the struggle over responsible government. In April, the Parliament buildings had been invaded by a mob and burned, with the consequent destruction of precious records relating to the earlier history of the country. Lord Elgin had himself been insulted by the mob, and for nearly two weeks was virtually a prisoner in his residence on the outskirts of Montreal. Yet, during this time of trouble, he took notice of an outrage [inflicted] on helpless people in Upper Canada and issued the proclamation that was published in the *London Times*.

The Negro settlement in present Biddulph dated back to the late 1820s, when a group of these people were aided by Quakers in coming to Upper Canada from Cincinnati, where they were victims of the notorious "Black Laws." They secured land from the Canada Company, and it was the hope of those who were backing them that this might prove a place of refuge for many refugees escaping from slavery in the southern states.

The settlers were chiefly located near present-day Lucan, and the name Wilberforce was given to the settlement, honouring the great English reformer who did much to end slavery in the British possessions. Though there were never many people in the settlement, and it eventually failed, it is remarkable how much attention it received from philanthropic organizations, as well as from government. Indeed, it was at one time looked into by a committee of the House of Commons at London, who summoned a coloured minister, Reverend Mr. Paul, who happened to be in England, and asked him many questions about the venture. This was at a time when the abolition of slavery in the British West Indies was very much in the public eye, and when information bearing on the problems of the freed slaves was much desired.

We have a good account of Wilberforce as it was in 1832, written by Benjamin Lundy, an American Quaker who came to the place in order to see the working of the experiment in colonization. His visit was made in February 1832, and his observations were published in his little anti-slavery newspaper, *The Genius of Universal Emancipation*.

Lundy entered Upper Canada at Niagara and went out at Windsor. He had to pass through the Village of London on his way to Wilberforce, and left us the first printed account that exists of the little village. Having a day to spare while he waited for his stage to go westward, he made a careful enumeration of the activities in the little village, not overlooking the "Gothic" courthouse, which had been erected just two or three years before he came through. He also noted the fact that the village had a newspaper. This was the *London Sun*, then in its second year, edited by Edward Allen Talbot. Lundy was impressed by the rapid growth that had plainly taken place, and was struck by the variety of the inhabitants, which included a number of coloured people.

A much more voluminous account of Wilberforce was written later by Austin Steward, *Twenty-Two Years a Slave and Forty Years a Freeman*, published at Rochester in 1859. Steward was in business in Rochester when he decided to throw in his lot with the Ohio refugees at Wilberforce. He went to the place and stayed there for several years, guiding and counselling. He ran into a great deal of trouble, however, at the hands of jealous settlers, and the Canada Company in the end decided it would cease to sell land to coloured people. This was the death blow to the settlement, which dwindled and finally disappeared. One or two gravestones in the vicinity of Lucan are all that now remain to record the former existence of the settlement.

Financial difficulties were in part the cause of the failure of the settlement. While the men were able to get work building the road that was linking Goderich with the east, the clearing of the farms was delayed, and it must be remembered that these people, whose earlier occupations had been in the growth of such crops as tobacco and cotton, were brought into a completely different latitude and environment. It could hardly be expected that they would fit easily into the pioneer Upper Canada agriculture of the 1830s and 1840s.

Just what was at the back of the outrage that took place in 1848 is not easy to determine. The population that came in after the Canada Company ceased to encourage the Negroes was predominantly Irish, and it may have been just a racial dislike of the coloured folk and a jealousy of their labour in road-building operations that led to the trouble. This is the only reference that the writer has seen to any racial trouble existing, though there may have been much more that is unrecorded.

Wilberforce was almost the earliest attempt at settling Negro refugees in Upper Canada, but there were others that came later that were much more successful. The Elgin Association Settlement, for example, in Kent County, which began in the late 1840s, had a quite successful record, largely due to the leadership of Reverend William King. It was the subject of investigation by the United States government in the last year of the Civil War, President Lincoln sending a commission to Canada to see how the former slaves from the South had made out in their new environment. This report made very favourable comments on the settlement at Buxton, which to this day is the most distinctively Negro settlement in Canada.

The great migration of Negroes to Upper Canada (or Canada West as it was known after 1841) was the sequel of the passing of the Fugitive Slave Act of 1850, a most unfortunate and highly repressive measure that turned thousands of persons who had formerly been careless or impassive on the slavery issue into ardent opponents of the system. Thus, indirectly it created the sentiment that was needed when war came in 1861.

When the war closed, many of the Negro inhabitants of Upper Canada went back to the United States, greatly lessening the coloured population, which in the middle 1850s was estimated to be at least 30,000. It has never grown by any large immigration since, and it will be interesting to see what the census of 1951 will reveal as to the number of coloured people in Ontario, the province to which they chiefly came in slavery days.

6

The Buxton Settlement in Canada

Journal of Negro History, *vol. 3, no. 4 (October 1918), 360–67*

The Buxton, or Elgin Association Settlement, in Kent County, western Ontario, was in many respects the most important attempt made before the Civil War to found a Negro refugee colony in Canada. In population, material wealth, and general organization it was outstanding, and the firm foundation upon which it was established is shown by the fact that today, more than half a century after emancipation, it is still a prosperous and distinctly Negro settlement.

The western peninsula of Ontario, lying between Lakes Huron and Erie, was long the mecca of the fugitive slave. Bounded on the east by the State of New York, on the west by Michigan, and on the south by Ohio and northwestern Pennsylvania, this was the part of Canada most easily reached by the fugitive; and Niagara, Cleveland, Detroit, and other lake ports saw thousands of refugees cross narrow strips of water to "shake the lion's paw" and find freedom in the British queen's dominions. During the 1840s and 1850s, there was a constant stream of refugees into Canada. As many as 30 a day would cross the Detroit River at Fort Malden alone. Many of these went to the cities and towns, but others found greater happiness in the separate Negro communities that grew up here and there.

The history of the Buxton settlement, one of these, is closely linked with the name of Reverend William King. King was a native of Londonderry, Ireland, a graduate of Glasgow College who had emigrated to the United States and became rector of a college in Louisiana. Later he returned to Scotland, studied theology in the Free Church College, Edinburgh, and, in 1846, was sent out to Canada as a missionary of the Free Church of Scotland. While he was living in Louisiana he became, through marriage, the owner of 15 slaves of an estimated value of $9,000.

For a time he placed them on a neighbouring plantation and gave them the proceeds of their labour, but that did not satisfy his conscience, and in 1848 he brought them to Canada, thereby automatically giving them their freedom. His efforts on their behalf did not end here. Having brought them to this new country, he felt it a duty to look after them, educate them, and make them useful citizens. The same thing, he believed, could be done for others in like circumstances.

The first effort to secure a tract of land for the refugees was made by the Reverend Mr. King as the representative of the Presbyterian Church. This application was before the Executive Council of the Canadian government in September 1848, but was not successful. Steps were at once taken to organize a nonsectarian body to deal with the government, and this new body took the name of the Elgin Association, in honour of the then-governor general of the Canadas, who seems to have been well-disposed toward the refugees. The Elgin Association was legally incorporated "for the settlement and moral improvement of the coloured population of Canada, for the purpose of purchasing crown or clergy reserve lands in the Township of Raleigh and settling the same with coloured families resident in Canada of approved moral character."[1] Reverend Dr. Connor was the first president; Reverend Dr. Michael Willis, of Knox College, Toronto, first vice-president, and Reverend William King second vice-president. J.T. Matthews was the secretary, J.S. Howard, treasurer, while the original directors were E.A.T. McCord, Walter McFarland, Peter Freeland, Charles Berczy, Wilson Ruffin Abbott, John Laidlaw, E.F. Whittesend, and James Brown. These are the names that appear on the petition to the government for lands, the original of which is in the Dominion Archives.

There were difficulties in securing the land. Decided opposition to the whole project made itself manifest in Kent County.[2] In Chatham, the county town, a meeting of protest was held. The plans of the Elgin Association were condemned, and a resolution was passed setting forth objections to selling any of the public domain "to foreigners, the more so when such persons belong to a different branch of the human family and are Black." A vigilance committee was appointed to watch the operations of the Elgin Association, while the various interested township councils were requested to advance the necessary funds for carrying on the campaign. That there was some dissent, however, even in Chatham, is shown by the fact that one Henry Gouins was allowed to speak in favour of the association. The vigilance committee soon issued a small pamphlet, made up chiefly of the speeches and resolutions of the public meeting. The name of Edwin Larwill, member of Parliament for the County of Kent [he was a member for one term only], appears as one of those most active in opposition to the settlement plan. Larwill had a record for hostility to the coloured people, though at election times he was accustomed to parade as their friend. In 1856, he introduced in the House of Assembly a most insulting resolution[3] calling for a report from the government on "all Negro or coloured, male or female quadroon, mulatto, samboes, half-breeds or mules, mongrels or conglomerates" in public institutions. Larwill was at once called to account for his action, and a resolution was introduced calling upon him to retract.

The opposition of Larwill and his supporters failed to impede the progress of the association, and a tract of about 9,000 acres, lying to the south of Chatham and within a mile or two of Lake Erie, was purchased. This was surveyed and divided into small farms of 50 acres each, roads were cut through the dense forest, and the first settlers began the arduous work of clearing. The colonists were allowed to take up 50 acres each at a price of $2.50 per acre, payable in ten annual instalments.[4] Each settler was bound within a certain period to build a house at least as good as the model house set up by the association, to provide himself with necessary implements, and to proceed with the work of clearing land. The model house, after which nearly all the dwellings were copied, was 18 x 24 feet, 12 feet in height, with a stoop running the length of the front. Some of the settlers were ambitious enough to build larger and better houses, but there were none inferior to the model. The tract of country upon which the settlers were located was an almost unbroken forest. The ground was level, heavily timbered with oak, hickory, beech, elm, etc. Part of the soil was rich black loam. Trees two to four feet in diameter were common, and the roads cut through to open up the settlement were hardly more than wide lanes. Reverend King thought that one reason for the colony's success was the fact that so many of the settlers were good axemen. Their industry was remarkable, and some of the more industrious paid for their land in five or six years and took up more to clear.[5]

The prosperity of the Elgin Association Settlement in Raleigh Township, Canada West, made it a model for fugitive slave colonies. *Courtesy of Buxton Historic Site and Museum.*

There are several contemporary references to the sobriety and morality of the colonists. The New York *Tribune* correspondent in 1857 was able to report that liquor was neither made nor sold in the colony, and that drunkenness was unknown. There was no illegitimacy, and there had been but one arrest for violation of the Canadian laws in the seven years of the colony's history. Though the Presbyterian Church gave special attention to the Buxton colony, this did not hinder the growth of other sects — Methodists and Baptists both being numerous, though the best of feeling seems to have prevailed, and many who retained their own connection were fairly regular attendants at Mr. King's services.

The *Tribune* article gives an interesting description of the homes. The cabins, though rough and rude, were covered with vines and creepers, with bright flowers and vegetable gardens round about. Despite the pioneer condition, there abounded comfort and plenty of homemade furniture. Pork, potatoes, and green corn were staple items of the menu. Of King's former slaves, the *Tribune* reports that three had died, nine were at Buxton, one was married and living in Chatham, and two others in Detroit were about to return. The *Tribune* reports on one case as typical of what was being achieved by the colony. A coloured man, 14 years before a slave in Missouri and who had been at Buxton six years, reported that he had 24 acres out of his plot cleared, fenced, and under cultivation. On six acres more the trees were felled. He had paid four installments on his farm, owned a yoke of oxen, a wagon, and a mare and two colts. His 14-year-old boy was at school, and was reading Virgil. In the home, besides bed and bedding, chairs, and tables, there was a rocking chair and a large, new safe. Water was brought to the visitor in a clean tumbler set on a plate. A neighbouring cabin had carpet on the floor and some crude prints on the walls. All the cabins had large brick fireplaces. Reverend Mr. King's own house, built of logs with high steep roof, dormer windows, and a porch the whole length, was somewhat larger than the others.[6]

What these people actually accomplished at Buxton amid conditions so different from what they had known in the past is altogether remarkable. Some had known little of farm work before coming to the colony, while all of them must have found the Canadian climate something of a hardship, even in the summer. Outside of the farm work, they showed ability as mechanics and tradesmen. One who visited them in the 1850s said:[7]

> The best country tavern in Kent is kept by Mr. West, at Buxton. Mr. T. Stringer is one of the most enterprising tradesmen in the county, and he is a Buxtonian, a coloured man. I broke my carriage near there. The woodwork, as well as the iron, was broken. I never had better repairing done to either the woodwork or the ironwork of my carriage, I never had better shoeing than was done to my horses, in Buxton, in February 1852, by a black man, a native of Kentucky — in a word, the work that was done after the pattern of Charles Peyton Lucas. They are blessed with able mechanics, good farmers, enterprising men, and women worthy of them and they are training the rising generation to principles such as will give them the best places in the esteem and the service of their countrymen at some day not far distant.

A few years sufficed to remove most of the prejudice that had shown itself in the opposition of the Larwill faction at Chatham at the inception of the colony. When Reverend Samuel Ringgold Ward visited the colony in the early 1850s, he found that instead of lowering the land values of adjoining properties, as some had predicted would result from establishing a Negro colony in Kent County, the Buxton Settlement had actually raised the values of adjoining farms. The Buxton settlers were spoken of by the white people as good farmers, good customers, and good neighbours. There were white children attending the Buxton school, and white people in the Sunday church services.

Perhaps no finer testimony to the success of the whole undertaking has been recorded than that of Dr. Samuel G. Howe, who came to Canada for the Freedmen's Inquiry Commission. He wrote:

> Buxton is certainly a very interesting place. Sixteen years ago it was a wilderness. Now, good highways are laid out in all directions through the forest, and by their side, standing back 33 feet from the road, are about 200 cottages, all built in the same pattern, all looking neat and comfortable; around each one is a cleared place of several acres which is well cultivated. The fences are in good order, the barns seem well fitted, and cattle and horses, and pigs and poultry abound. There are signs of industry and thrift and comfort everywhere; signs of intemperance, of idleness, of want nowhere. There is no tavern and no groggery; but there is a chapel and a schoolhouse. Most interesting of all are the inhabitants. Twenty years ago most of them were slaves, who owned nothing, not even their children. Now they own themselves; they own their houses and farms; and they have their wives and children about them. They are enfranchised citizens of a government, which protects their rights…. The present condition of all these colonists as compared to their former one is remarkable…. This settlement is a perfect success. Here are men who were bred in slavery, who came here and purchased land at the government price, cleared it, bought their own

implements, built their own houses after a model and have supported themselves in all material circumstances and now support their schools, in part.… I consider that this settlement has done as well as a white settlement would have done under the same circumstance.[8]

The Buxton Settlement had its part in the John Brown affair. A letter written by John Brown Jr., from Sandusky, Ohio, on August 27, 1859, and addressed to "Friend Henrie," (John H. Kagi, one of his lieutenants), speaks of men in Hamilton, Chatham, Buxton, etc., suitable for the enterprise. "At Dr. W's house (presumably in Hamilton) we formed an association," he says, "the officers consisting of chairman, treasurer and corresponding secretary, the business of which is to hunt up good workmen and raise the means among themselves to send them forward.… No minutes of the organization nor any of its proceeding are or will be preserved in writing. I formed similar association in Chat — and also at B-x-t-n."

John Brown Jr. also speaks of going to Buxton, where he found "the man, the leading spirit in that affair."

"On Thursday night last," said he, "I went with him on foot 12 miles; much of the way through mere paths and sought out in the bush some of the choicest. Had a meeting after ten o'clock at night in his house. His wife is a heroine and he will be on hand as soon as his family can be provided for."[9]

Such is the earlier history of the experiment in Canada of taking bondsmen and placing before them the opportunity not only to make a living in freedom, but also to rise on the social scale. How well these people took advantage of their opportunity is shown not only by the material progress they made, but by the fact that they gained for themselves the respect of their white neighbours, a respect that continues today for their many descendants who still comprise the Buxton community in Kent County, Ontario.

7

Agriculture Among the Negro Refugees in Upper Canada

Journal of Negro History, *vol. 21, no. 3 (July 1936), 304–12*

The bulk of the Negroes who came into the Province of Upper Canada (now Ontario) in the period before the Civil War had a background in agriculture; and it was quite natural, therefore, that in their new environment they would tend to turn to the land as a source of livelihood. In this tendency, they were encouraged by the government of the province and by their own leaders. Though the Negro immigration was neither sufficiently large nor sufficiently permanent to affect in any marked way the agriculture of the province, it did demonstrate rather forcibly that the Negro, when given opportunity and freedom, was not inferior to some other races in his ability to improve his condition. When, in the last year of the Civil War, Dr. Samuel G. Howe visited Canada as a representative of the Freedmen's Inquiry Commission to investigate the economic and social conditions of the Negroes resident there, he was much impressed by this fact, and commented upon it at some length in his report.

Negroes were to be found in Upper Canada from the very beginnings of the province. There were even some Negroes held in slavery during the first quarter century, although in the second session of the Legislative Assembly a bill had been introduced and unanimously passed that prohibited the bringing in of any more slaves, and made provision for the gradual extinction of such slavery as then existed. Upper Canada occupies the honourable position of having been the first British colony to abolish slavery. At a very early date, therefore, a tradition of freedom was created, which revealed itself conspicuously when, at a later date, the province became a refuge for runaway slaves and for those whose freedom was endangered by the Fugitive Slave Law.

Agriculture Among the Negro Refugees in Upper Canada

Dr. Howe, in the course of his inquiry into the condition of the refugees in Upper Canada, gave attention to the Negroes in the towns and cities rather than those in the country districts. At that particular time (1864), there was a considerable Negro population in the towns in the western part of the province, and indications of race prejudice were occasionally in evidence, particularly with respect to the presence of Negro children in the common schools. Social questions of this kind bulk large in the Howe report, possibly because they were conditions with which the investigator was himself familiar; nevertheless, he makes quite definite observations on the Negro farmers whom he encountered. He concluded that, in general, the Negro farmers were probably better off than were those of the race who were living in the towns. He found them generally owning the land they occupied, having in many cases paid off mortgages and having a clear title. From the standpoint of cleanliness and comfort, he found the Negro farmhouses differing in no respect from those of neighbouring white settlers, and he found much evidence of distinct progress shown in permanent dwellings and barns, enclosed fields, and livestock.

Besides visiting and interviewing individual farmers, Dr. Howe inspected the Buxton Settlement, in Kent County, which had been founded in 1848 by Reverend William King, a Scottish Presbyterian clergyman. Of Buxton colony, Dr. Howe wrote:

> Buxton is certainly a very interesting place. Sixteen years ago it was a wilderness. Now, good highways are laid out in all directions through the forest; and by their side, standing back 33 feet from the road, are about 200 cottages, all built on the same pattern, all looking neat and comfortable. Around each one is a cleared space, of several acres, which is well cultivated. The fences are in good order; the barns are well filled; and cattle, and horses, and pigs, and poultry, abound. There are signs of industry, and thrift, and comfort, everywhere; signs of intemperance, of idleness, of want, nowhere. There is no tavern, and no groggery; but there is a

chapel and schoolhouse. Most interesting of all are the inhabitants. Twenty years ago, most of them were slaves, who owned nothing, not even their children. Now they own themselves; they own their houses and farms; and they have their wives and children about them. They are enfranchised citizens of a government which protects their rights.[1]

The Buxton Settlement, or Elgin Association as it was legally known, had received a charter from the Parliament of Canada in 1850 empowering it to acquire and hold lands in Kent County, and to sell these lands to the coloured settlers. The success that attended the venture was largely due to Reverend Mr. King. Born in Scotland, he had lived for a time in Louisiana, and by marriage and the subsequent death of his wife found himself the owner of 15 slaves. Being averse to selling them, he determined to take them to Canada and to establish there a colony to which others of their race might also come. He received the support of the synod of the Presbyterian Church of Canada, this body assisting in bringing the plan to the attention of the government and in securing the legislation relating to the land grant of 9,000 acres.

By 1852 there were 75 coloured families at Buxton, a total population of about 400, with 350 acres of land cleared and more than 200 acres under cultivation. A year later, the fourth annual report showed 130 families, numbering 520 persons, having 500 acres of land cleared, 135 acres partially cleared, and 415 acres under cultivation.

The colony then possessed 128 cattle, 15 horses, 30 sheep, and 250 hogs.

The annual report for 1854 recorded yet further advances. Cleared land totalled 726 acres, with 174 acres partially cleared and 577 acres under cultivation. A year later, there were 827 acres of cleared and fenced land, with 216 acres chopped and ready to go under the plough in 1856. Livestock in 1855 consisted of 190 cattle and oxen, 40 horses, 38 sheep, and 600 hogs. In this year, a sawmill and a gristmill were put into operation. It was estimated that at this time there was standing timber on the colony lands worth more than $125,000.

The New York *Tribune* sent a reporter to Buxton in 1857, when the colony was seven years old. He estimated the population at about 800. More than 1,000 acres of land had then been cleared, while on 200 acres more the trees had been felled, and the land would go under cultivation in the following year. The acreage under cultivation in 1857 was reported to be as follows: wheat, 200 acres; oats, 70 acres; potatoes, 80 acres; other crops, 120 acres. The livestock consisted of 200 cattle, 80 oxen, 300 hogs, 52 horses, and a small number of sheep.

At the close of the Civil War, there was a desire on the part of some of the Buxton colonists to return to their former homes in the South, though in this they received no encouragement from Washington when their plans became known. By 1873, the directors of the Elgin Association, feeling that their work had been accomplished, wound up its affairs. Every man who had entered the colony had had it firmly impressed upon him that independence and ownership of property was to be his goal, and a large number had achieved that condition. Buxton remains to this day the most distinctly Negro community in all Canada.[2]

Wilberforce, a settlement about twenty miles north of the present city of London, Ontario, was an earlier attempt at colonization. About the year 1829, enforcement of the Black Laws of Ohio drove out a considerable number of Negroes from of the City of Cincinnati. Of those who came to Canada, a part settled at Wilberforce. Benjamin Lundy, the early abolitionist, visited the place in 1832, during the course of his journey through the province from the Niagara to the Detroit River. In his account of the settlement, he wrote:

> They have purchased nearly 2,000 acres in the whole, 200 of which are cleared and about 60 sown with wheat. The settlers have cut a wide road through seven miles and a quarter of very thickly and heavily timbered land for the Canada Company — the price for which was placed to their credit in the purchase of their several lots. It should be remarked that in clearing they leave no trees deadened and standing, as it is customary with many in new settlements; but cut all off, though the labour

is great. They have about 100 head of cattle and swine, and a few horses. Oxen are mostly used with them for hauling, ploughing, etc. They have a good substantial sawmill erected on a branch of the Au Sable, within the precincts of their settlement, and, of course, they will have no difficulty in procuring lumber for building.[3]

Wilberforce was not as successful as Buxton, partly because of faulty management of its financial affairs and partly through the racial hostility of incoming Irish settlers toward the presence of a body of Negroes. The most complete account of the experiment is found in the narrative of Austin Steward,[4] a member of the colony.

There are numerous references to this settlement in the Canadian travel literature of the 1830s and 1840s. Patrick Shirreff, who passed through in 1834, said of it:

On the boundary of the Huron tract, next to the London district, we passed a Negro settlement. The houses of the coloured people seemed of particular construction, having the chimney stack on the outside of the log-house, and which stack is composed of thin sawn timber, placed horizontally, and mixed with clay. Their chief crop was Indian corn, well cultivated. Before my departure from Britain I had heard of this settlement instanced as a complete failure, and used as an argument against the emancipation of slaves, then a general topic of conversation. The houses, barns, fences and general appearance are certainly mean enough, but I considered it in most respects equal and in some superior to settlements of whites in the Huron tract of the same standing of three years.[5]

When the Fugitive Slave Act became effective in the fall of 1850, thousands of Negroes who had been living in the northern states realized that their situation was dangerous, and a large number moved over into Canada. The movement was particularly marked along the Detroit

River, and towns like Windsor, Amherstburg, and Chatham found their coloured populations suddenly increased. With winter coming on, the situation called for immediate action to meet the calls for relief. By the spring of 1851, it was clearly shown that organization was necessary, and at a meeting held in the city hall of Detroit on May 21, 1851, the Refugee Home Society was founded. The aims of the society were to purchase land in Canada and to settle the Negro refugees on small plots that they would be permitted to purchase on very liberal terms.

In the working out of their plans, the society found an able helper in a Windsor Negro, Henry Bibb, who, at the beginning of 1850, had founded a little weekly paper, the *Voice of the Fugitive,* to set forth the needs and to champion the cause of his people.[6] Bibb had probably as much part as anyone in the founding of the Refugee Home Society, which he had advocated in the columns of his paper for weeks before the Detroit meeting. No official records of the society appear to have survived, but here and there one may come upon notices of its activities. The second annual report of the Anti-Slavery Society of Canada (1853) stated that at that time the Refugee Home Society had purchased 1,328 acres of land, of which 600 acres had been taken up by settlers. As the plots were to be 25 acres to a family, this would mean 24 families. When Benjamin Drew visited Canada a year later, he found that the society had nearly 2,000 acres of land, of which half had been taken up. It was to this colony that Mrs. Laura S. Haviland came as a teacher. In her autobiography, she says that the colonists raised corn, potatoes, and other vegetables, as well as some wheat. Reverend William M. Mitchell, who was a missionary among his own people, makes the following reference to the colony in his book, *The Underground Railroad*:

> About ten miles from Windsor there is a settlement of 5,000 acres which extends over a part of Essex County. It is called the Fugitives' Home. Several years ago a very enterprising and intelligent fugitive slave ... bought land from the government, divided it into 20 acre plots and sold it to other fugitives, giving them five to ten years for payments. Emigrants settled here in such large numbers

that it is called the Fugitives' Home. The larger portion of the land is still uncultivated, a great deal is highly cultivated and many are doing well.

Bibb, in his paper, continually emphasized the importance of placing the Negroes on the land and keeping them engaged in agriculture rather than permitting them to drift into the casual and seasonal labour in the towns. He, himself, in the spring of 1851, went about the western end of the province addressing gatherings of his people on agriculture. The Detroit market offered some special opportunity to those who were near the river to dispose of their farm produce. In the *Voice of the Fugitive* for June 2, 1851, Bibb says: "We saw a coloured friend of ours today cross on the ferryboat with about 200 dozen of eggs, six or eight turkeys, with chickens and butter also, and they are continually going over with loads of a like character."

The Hisson family of Glen Allan in the Queen's Bush, Peel Township, standing outside their home, circa 1920. Identified (left to right): Annabelle (born January 1912), Father Edward John Hisson (1881–1949), Elsie, Mother Mabel M. (Lawson) Hisson (1890–1924); at back is Grandmother Lawson holding baby Ada (born 1918), unknown girl beside. Photographer unknown. *Courtesy of the Wellington County Museum and Archives, ph 5786.*

In the mild climate of the Detroit River region, early vegetables could be grown in abundance, and Bibb speaks of seeing sweet potatoes brought to market by the Negro farmers. Tobacco was also grown in quantity.

Apart from the organized colonies, such as Buxton and the Refugee Home Settlement, there were other groups of Negro farmers settled in communities throughout the province without any official organization. Reverend Hiram Wilson, who was a missionary to Negroes at St. Catharines, in the Niagara district, wrote in Bibb's paper on December 3, 1851, describing a visit that he had made to a Negro settlement near Cayuga in Haldimand County. At a distance of a mile from the Grand River, he found about a score of families, and two miles distant a smaller group, making in all about 24 families. They had individual farms of from 50 to 150 acres, aggregating about 2,000 acres. Comfortable log cabins were set down in clearings of 20 to 30 acres. The land had been bought from the government at $3.50 an acre, deeds to be given when full payment was made. The land was described as generally level or slightly undulating, the soil being a dark loam, and the timber being of considerable value. Mr. Wilson described the Negro farmers as contented and cheerful. The adults were almost all of them ex-slaves, though one free Negro was said to have purchased his wife and children, paying $1,000 for them.

Henry Bibb sent a communication to a convention of coloured people held in Cincinnati in 1852 in which he stated that wild lands were to be had in the vicinity of Windsor and within five miles of the Detroit River at from $3 to $5 and acre.[7]

This district, he said, produced from 25 to 40 bushels of wheat an acre, and any crops that did well on Ohio soil flourished equally in this part of Upper Canada. He added:

> There is no difficulty in selling any kind of produce that the farmers can produce, and that without travelling over a distance of ten miles with it. Corn is worth 50¢ per bushel, wheat 65¢, oats 31¢, potatoes 50¢, butter 15¢, lard 10¢, pork $4.50, beef $3.50, eggs 20¢ per dozen, and chickens $1.50 per dozen the year round. The farmer

who cannot live in Canada West, with rich and fertile soil beneath his feet, with a mild climate and an anti-slavery government over his head, possessing commercial advantages inferior to none in North America, must be a little too lazy to work and would die a pauper should he be placed in a country flowing with milk and honey.

Of the Negro farmers in Canada before 1865, it may be said that they succeeded about as well as the average immigrant from other countries who came without capital. Their slavery background often affected them adversely in the earlier period of their residence in Canada, and some suffered from the more severe climate. They came to Canada, for the most part, during a state of emergency, and many thought of their stay in Canada as merely a phase that would end with a change of domestic policy in the United States. After the Civil War there was considerable migration from Canada back to the United States, but the numerous Black faces still to be encountered in southwestern Ontario bear evidence to the fact that many remained in the land that had given them protection.

8

Fugitive Slave Provides Focal Point for Change in Canadian Law

London Free Press *(August 23, 1958), 24*

Kent County and the Town of Chatham had a considerable coloured population in 1841, and newcomers from plantations in the South arrived so frequently that there was probably little attention paid to Nelson Hackett, a fugitive from the State of Arkansas, when he first appeared in Chatham about the end of August of that year.

He was perhaps more noticeable than most newly arrived fugitives, for he rode an excellent horse, had a comfortable saddle, carried a fine beaver overcoat, and sported a gold watch.

Runaway slaves did not usually show such evidence of personal property. He freely admitted that he was a runaway, and was accepted as such by those of his own race and by those white citizens as came in contact with him.

But there came a surprise within a short period after his arrival in Chatham.

His former owner, one Alfred Wallace, a merchant of Fayetteville, Arkansas, had followed him to Chatham and promptly swore out an affidavit charging Hackett with the theft of the horse, saddle, overcoat, and watch, and demanding their immediate return, at the same time demanding that the fugitive be arrested.

Since Hackett admitted to the stealing, the local magistrate at once remanded the man to jail pending the winter assizes.

He little knew that this man's case was one that would become of intense interest to the Parliament of Great Britain, and that it would likewise become one of the highlights of the anti-slavery controversy, and be written about long years afterwards by historians of the period.

Alfred Wallace, the former owner of the man, was not solely interested in recovering his horse and other belongings. He wanted the man himself, who was of much greater monetary value, probably $1,500 as slave values rated at that time.

Accordingly, he made a side trip to Detroit, consulted lawyers there, and prepared for action in the Canadian courts. Among others, he enlisted the aid of the governor of Michigan, who, on the basis of thefts admitted by Hackett, requested the surrender of the fugitive as a criminal.

This posed a problem for the attorney general of Canada, who promptly asked two questions: Had Hackett been indicted by a court of law, and if so, where?

Had Arkansas, the state of original jurisdiction, requested his surrender? The answer in both cases was in the negative. Due to these legal technicalities, the demand for Hackett's surrender was refused by the Canadian authorities.

Thereupon, Wallace returned to his home state and entered criminal charges against the man held in the jail at Chatham. A county grand jury promptly indicted the fugitive in Canada on a charge of grand larceny, and Governor Yell followed by requesting that the Canadian authorities deliver Hackett for trial before an Arkansas court. This application came before the Executive Council in December 1841, and since there seemed to be evidence warranting extradition, the council gave its approval to such a course.

Hackett was surrendered and returned to Arkansas. There, without trial of any kind, he was promptly restored to his master. That was chapter one of the Hackett affair.

Abolitionists in the United States and in England at once saw that a dangerous precedent had been set. Indictment for theft had been made a device to recover runaway slaves, and thereby the security of all refugees in Canada was jeopardized.

Protests went to Congress, and the American Anti-Slavery Society at once called the attention of British abolitionists to the Arkansas extradition incident. The matter was at once placed before Lord Aberdeen, Britain's foreign minister. The incident was soon in public debate on both sides of the Atlantic. The surrender of Hackett was denounced as "immoral and unconstitutional." It was not the liberty of one man that was at stake, but rather of thousands. Thomas Clarkson, in England, warned that the slaveholders would pester the government of Canada with thousands of applications.

The controversy took a new turn after publication of the terms of the new Webster-Ashburton Treaty, since Article X provided for mutual surrender of fugitive criminals. Assurance was given by Lord Aberdeen in England and by Sir Charles Metcalfe, the governor general in Canada, that the slave's right to residence in Canada would be preserved. The agitation against the "infamous Article X" created widespread interest in England, and echoes of it were as widely heard in the northern states.

The assurances of political leaders that the menace of the noxious article would be met resulted in the passing by Parliament of the treaty without change, but colonial governors were ordered to transmit all extradition records to England, while detailed instructions about extradition were transmitted to all provincial administrations.

By May 1844, even Thomas Clarkson was ready to admit that the menace of Article X had been removed, and that the security of the former slaves living in Canada had been restored.

The slaveholders made efforts during the next few years to safeguard their property, and in 1850 secured the passing by Congress of the notorious Fugitive Slave Act.

While it was expected that there would be renewed efforts at securing the return of fugitives through indictments for crime, stiffened British policy had its effect, and there were no further applications of this kind until the famous John Anderson case in 1861. By that time the states were at war, and the question was left to the issue of arms.

9

The Work of the American Missionary Association Among Negro Refugees in Canada West, 1848-64

Ontario Historical Society, Papers and Records *vol. 21 (1924),* *198-205*

Between 1848 and 1864, the American Missionary Association[1] was the most active agency carrying on any sort of religious work among the Negro refugees in Upper Canada (Ontario). The reports of the association during those years contain many references to the Canadian work, and throw a good deal of light upon the social conditions of these people, who had sought homes under the British flag. The American Missionary Association was, from its foundation, openly opposed to slavery, and much of its work was with the Black race in the United States. When attention was drawn to the fact that thousands of Negroes were living in Canada, it was natural that the association should extend its operations, even into another country, to take care of these people.

The Canadian work was unattractive, unpromising, apparently irresponsive, and even almost hostile at times, but the representatives of the association kept steadily at work, and in the end laid the foundations upon which the present church life of the Canadian Negro is largely built. The annual report for 1854 states some of the difficulties that had to be faced. In part, it says:

> In a former report the executive committee stated that the Canada Mission was one of the most unpromising fields of labour under their care and a longer experience has not tended to change that opinion. The victims of oppression who have but recently escaped from the house of bondage, having seen the minister of religion in alliance

with the oppressors, prostituting his office to the support of wrong, have had cultivated within them feelings of suspicion not easily overcome. These feelings have been fostered and taken advantage of by a few evil disposed and designing men who have been willing to keep the people in ignorance to subserve their own purposes.[2]

Similar statements with regard to the difficulties of the Canadian field appear in other reports. "The field is emphatically a hard one and requires much faith and patience from those who work there," says the report of 1857,[3] while that for 1861, in drawing attention to the deplorable conditions in which many Negroes reached Canada, said that some, goaded to madness, were almost ready to curse the whole white race.[4]

The tendency of the Negro communities to split up into many small religious groups was one difficulty that taxed the patience of the association's representatives.[5] Out of this tendency to form new religious societies grew the begging evil, which was vigorously condemned by the better class of the Negroes themselves. How to teach self-reliance to a people who had but little of this quality was a problem. Some of the Negroes believed that the establishment of Negro colonies would improve matters. Henry Bibb[6] came to the front around 1850 with a proposal to purchase 30,000 acres of land from the government, this to be sold to Negro settlers on terms that would enable them to become independent by their own industry. His was not the only proposal of this kind, the Elgin Association Settlement[7] in what is now Kent County, Ontario, being quite successful. The work in Canada was not altogether disappointing by any means. "The fugitives in Canada are not what their enemies represent them to be," said the annual report issued in 1860.[8] "Very many of them are moral, enterprising, industrious and thriving, showing that the liberty they have assumed is rightly used.… Good schools and a faithful ministry ought to be liberally sustained among the fugitives in Canada."

Prior to 1848, the American Missionary Association had made contributions to the work of missionaries among the Negroes in Canada, designating such work in its reports as the Canadian Mission. In that year, however, the association undertook to support three missionaries then working in Canada: Reverend Isaac Rice at Fort Malden (now called Amherstburg and situated on the Detroit River), and Mr. and Mrs. J.S. Brooks, at Mount Hope.[9] Support was also to be given to Reverend Hiram Wilson, who had been dividing his time between Amherstburg and the Dawn Settlement, near Lake St. Clair. This arrangement being unsatisfactory to the association, he now gave up the work at Dawn. Amherstburg was the really strategic point for missionary work, as more fugitives crossed into Canada at this point than anywhere else on the frontier.[10] Those who planned to go farther inland usually remained for a few days, at least, knowing that, having crossed the boundary line, not even the Fugitive Slave Law could touch them. Isaac Rice had had a school in operation since about 1838, and there was much religious activity of one kind and another among the Negroes in the village. Levi Coffin, the abolitionist, visited Amherstburg in 1844 and speaks well of the work that was being done by Isaac Rice:

> While at this place, we made our headquarters at Isaac J. Rice's missionary buildings where he had a large school for coloured children. He had laboured here, among the coloured people, mostly fugitives, for six years. He was a devoted, self-denying worker, had received very little pecuniary help, and had suffered my privations. He was well situated in Ohio as pastor of a Presbyterian church, and had fine prospects before him, but believed that the Lord called him to this field of missionary labour among the fugitive slaves who came here by hundreds and by thousands, poor, destitute and ignorant, suffering from all the evil influences of slavery. We entered into deep sympathy with him in his labours, realizing the great need there was here for just such an institution as he had established. He had sheltered at this missionary home many hundreds of fugitives till other homes for them could be found. This was the great landing point, the principal terminus of the Underground Railroad of the west.[11]

It was a heavy task that Isaac Rice faced at Amherstburg. Some idea of his difficulties may be gathered from a letter that he wrote to the *Western Citizen* of Chicago in 1849.[12] In this letter, he says that for three months past he has been unable to do any mission work. He had no money to pay the freight charges on boxes of supplies sent for relief work. All the money he had received had been spent on the school and mission house. Clothing was needed badly by the destitute fugitives arriving daily. Over 50 had come in that summer, and these and others had to be looked after. He asked that $300 be supplied to him to keep his work going. In *The Liberator* of August 23, 1850, there is a letter from Milly Morse, Foxboro, in which she appeals for help for Rice and his work: "He has suffered much in silence and given himself up for the good of the slave," says this letter. "He has lived principally on bread and beans and without the means to purchase these." The letter goes on to say that Rice has divided his own goods with the fugitives, until he is actually suffering for want of proper clothing, that he has sold his watch and even his beds to get food, that he clothed 300 fugitives in one year, including a mother who arrived with her four children, and that, of the 20,000 Negroes in Canada, 3,000 are near him in the southwestern part of the province. His mission buildings were reported completed at this time and, with stoves, had cost $250. The first floor of the building was used for the school, in which there were 90 pupils, while the upper floor was used for receiving fugitives and looking after their immediate needs.

Amherstburg continued through all the period of its activity in Canada as the chief station of the American Missionary Association. It was a strategic point, since more refugees entered by that gateway than by any other, as has already been pointed out, and the response to the efforts of the missionaries seems to have been more marked here than elsewhere. The little village on the Detroit River must have been the scene of many dramatic incidents during those years, when the runaway slaves were crossing into Canada. Some of these incidents have been recorded. Reverend William M. Mitchell tells of a Negro named Hedgman who had been sold south from Kentucky, but who escaped and made his way to Canada. While in slavery, he had been separated from his wife and had lost all trace of her. Twelve years after he had escaped, the wife also managed to make her escape and crossed into Canada at Fort Malden, or Amherstburg. Friendless and lonely, she wandered about the streets of the village seeking shelter, and was attracted by the singing in a Negro chapel. Opening the door, she entered and the first person she saw was her husband, from whom she had been so long separated, and of whose whereabouts she had no knowledge.[13]

It is very noticeable that education took a prominent place in the philanthropic work conducted for the benefit of the refugees at the various places where they were settled in any number. Hard as was the struggle for existence in the new land, where everything was so unlike what they had been accustomed to, the Negroes seemed keen to take advantage of any educational opportunity that was afforded them, and where they did not have any schools of their own they sought admittance to the regular schools provided by the municipalities. The Canadian law gave the Negro every right of the white man, but practically there was often a distinction of colour in education. Separate schools for the Negroes were established, among other places, at Chatham, Amherstburg, and Windsor. There was a feeling among the white people in some places that there should be no choice as between public and separate schools. On the other hand, there was a feeling amongst the Negroes that they should maintain their right of entrance to the public schools.[14] When Benjamin Drew visited Amherstburg in 1854, he found the Negro separate school a small, low building, having neither blackboard nor chairs. Low, rough benches were placed against the walls with desks before them. The whole interior was comfortless and repulsive. The teacher was a Negro woman, apparently doing the best she could under the discouragement of poor surroundings and frequent absences of her pupils.[15] The situation was improved after this date, however, when the Colonial Church and School Society of England opened up a school. When Dr. Samuel G. Howe visited Amherstburg in the early 1860s he found 90 coloured children enrolled, with an average attendance of 60.[16] An educational movement among the Negroes themselves had its origin at Fort Malden in 1854 when the first "True Band" was formed. Similar societies afterwards existed in the other settlements. The True Bands were open to both sexes, and a small monthly fee was charged. The aims of the bands were to improve the schools, to increase school attendance, abate race prejudice, arbitrate disputes between members of the race, to assist the destitute, suppress begging, and in all other ways possible work for the betterment of the refugees in Canada.[17]

The American Missionary Association doubtless realized that there would be great difficulties to be faced in the Canadian field, and some of these difficulties reflect themselves in the annual reports. The annual report for 1849 is typical of later reports in its record of obstacles to be overcome. Isaac Rice left the association in this year to become an evangelist among the coloured Baptists. Goods that were collected in both the United States and Canada for the benefit of sufferers failed to reach their destinations. The work at the Dawn Settlement dwindled, the managers being embarrassed by debt. Incompetent trustees had projected a college, when common schools were the real need.[18]

At Mount Hope, the work in charge of Mr. and Mrs. Brooks[19] was disturbed by the migration of their flock to a point near Georgian Bay, where they had been attracted by government grants of land. There was a need generally for competent teachers.

The Travis family settled in the Queen's Bush, Normanby Township, before moving on to Buxton. *Courtesy of Buxton Historic Site and Museum.*

On the other hand, there were some encouraging signs. About one third of the adults had professed religion. The settlement at London, which was visited this year by Reverend J.P. Bardwell, was found to be making headway, though the Negro community was divided among three rival sects, each with its own chapel or meeting house. At London there was a free school, a temperance society with 100 members, and most of the coloured people were in comfortable circumstances, several being freeholders, and some in business. At Dawn, Hiram Wilson and his wife carried on two schools, Mrs. Wilson having 25 women and girls in her charge. One of these was a grandmother who learned to read and write in three months. About two miles from Dawn was another school conducted by a Miss Huntington, working under the Baptist board.

In this year, 1849, the expenditure on the Canadian work amounted to $650. The departure of Reverend Isaac Rice does not seem to have been regarded as a very serious loss. Of his piety there could be no question, but he is described as eccentric and as having little influence with the larger portion of the coloured people. The name of Reverend E.E. Kirkland appears in this report as being stationed about ten miles from Amherstburg, and there is also a reference to Henry Bibb as a collector for the Colporteurs* and Slaves Bible Fund.

The annual report for 1850[20] records the work done at Amherstburg, St. Catharines, and Mount Hope. Reverend Hiram Wilson removed to St. Catharines in this year, leaving Dawn for good. In the course of his movements, during the latter part of the year, he saw a good deal of the results of the Fugitive Slave Law.[21] His estimate was that 3,000 fugitives had entered Canada recently, and the immigration was still continuing. "That law," he says, "has done a direful work not only in spreading terror among the coloured people of the nominally free states but in breaking up families and driving them in a desolate and forlorn condition to these northern shores to encounter the rigor of a cold climate and an unusually severe winter." He cites the arrival of a refugee from Utica, New York, whose right foot was so badly frozen that the bone protruded.

---

* Editors' Note: A colporteur or colporter was a person who carried Bibles and gave them out to those in need. He was not a clergyman but an assistant missionary.

Reverend David Hotchkiss was at Amherstburg this year, and found some opposition from coloured preachers who were continually trying to establish new societies, with the usual accompaniment of appointing an agent and starting begging tours. Miss Susan Teall continued at Mount Hope, but reported that the work there was diminishing owing to the continued removal of the people.

The next year saw some additional workers in the field. At New Canaan, Reverend Kirkland, with his wife and Miss Theodosia Lyon, worked with the fugitives, while the name of Mary A. Shadd[22] appears as the representative of the association at Windsor. At Mount Hope, Miss Susan Teall was joined by Miss Mary Teall, presumably a relative. Reverend Mr. Kirkland reports that in the townships of his district there are between 3,000 and 4,000 fugitives. There are four or five schools, in which two of the teachers are coloured, but even at that from one half to three quarters of the children do not attend school.

"Our settlement is rapidly enlarging," he reports. "The Fugitive Slave Law appears to be a dead letter in its operation, judging from the number who get safely to Canada."[23]

Reverend Hiram Wilson, writing from St. Catharines,[24] reports that he has organized a refugee slaves' friend society, the membership of which includes some of the most representative citizens of the place. His report includes this interesting incident: In July (1851) 12 former slaves, of both sexes, were brought to St. Catharines by a North Carolina slaveholder and given into Wilson's care. Their master had died a year before, and in his will had given them their freedom, leaving also some considerable property to be used for their benefit. Mr. Wilson also reports the arrival of over a dozen fugitives just before he sent in his report.

Difficulties encountered in carrying on the work in Canada are again pointed out in this report, issued in 1852: "The missionary in Canada finds many whom he labours to bless who regard his efforts with great disfavour. There is a class of preachers and self-constituted collecting agents who, to retain their own influence, are labouring, some of them avowedly, to drive every white missionary from the colony. The influence of this class of men has been very extensive."

This British Methodist Episcopal church stood on the 4th Line of Peel Township (Queen's Bush) and was the heart and soul of the surrounding community. Reverend Samuel Brown was a charismatic preacher who held camp meetings for more than 5,000 people in the bush on his adjacent farm during the 1850s. Photo circa 1945. Photographer unknown. *Courtesy of the Wellington County Museum and Archives, ph 5965.*

The report issued in 1853 also draws attention to the opposition to white missionaries, which was added to by the misrepresentation of some of the coloured preachers. The Mount Hope station was closed in 1852, as the Negroes had moved away from that district. The Kirklands continued to labour at New Canaan, assisted by Miss Lyon and Miss Mary C. Beals, a newcomer. Hiram Wilson was at St. Catharines, the Tealls at Mount Hope until it closed, and Mary Shadd was also reported as working again at Windsor.

From this time on, there seems to have been comparatively little growth in the Canadian mission work. In 1853, only one school was in operation, the teachers in which were Miss Beals, Miss Lyon, and Miss Abigail B. Martin. The need for strong men is stated in the 1854 report, but they do not seem to have been found. The name of Reverend David Hotchkiss appears most prominently in the reports from this date. He made his headquarters at Windsor for the next two or three years and then removed to Rochester, not far distant. He appears to have been closely allied with Henry Bibb's project of the Refugee's Home Society. His field was a hard one, for Windsor had its full complement of small sects. The report issued in 1856 states that he has been preaching to small congregations at four places, and that his wife has been teaching school. The next year's report gives details of serious trouble that developed. The house that he used for a church was burned following threats, and when he opened up services in another house this was also burned. In the report for 1858, it is stated that Reverend Mr. Hotchkiss is now at Rochester, where he has organized his church, and his wife's school has nearly 40 scholars. "There are numbers who cannot come to school for want of suitable clothing," says this report. "They are nearly naked."

The report issued in 1859 reports that Reverend Hotchkiss is located at Rochester, but is also looking after missions at Little River, Pike's Creek, and Puce River, all in the southwestern part of the province. There has been a marked revival of religion, and at Puce River there are 25 members, with religious services well-attended. This year, Mrs. Hotchkiss had to give up her school work due to failing health. The name of Reverend L.C. Chambers (coloured) appears for the first time, with headquarters at Dresden.

In 1859, Reverend Hotchkiss and Reverend Chambers were the association's two mission workers in the Canadian field. Chambers was removed to Ingersoll, during the year, where there was a church of 45, and he also preached in London on alternate Sundays to a congregation with a membership of 65.[25] Mrs. Hotchkiss died November 27, 1859, aged 57, after nine years' work in Canada. The work under Mr. Hotchkiss seems to have grown. He required total abstinence from his members, and was able to report 16 members at Little River, 22 at Puce River, and six at Pike's Creek.

The secretary of the foreign department of the American Missionary Association visited Canada in the early part of 1860, and his observations on the Canadian work were printed in March, April, and May numbers of the *American Missionary*. The 1861 report estimated the Negro population of Upper Canada at about 40,000 "by the most reliable estimates."[26] There was much that was deplorable in the condition of the fugitives. "They reach Canada almost literally naked, hungry, destitute and in want of all things." Emphasis is laid upon the need for more missioners and more schools, "for in many parts of Canada they are shut out from public schools."

The opening of the Civil War disturbed the American Missionary Association's work seriously. Records of the Canadian field become more scanty until, in the *American Missionary* for July 1864, there appears this significant statement: "The mission among the refugees in Canada has been suspended. Its last missionary, Reverend L.C. Chambers is now sustained by the people among whom he labours. Some aid has been given and may be continued to sustain teachers there."

There was, of course, less need for the activities of the association in Canada once the movement of fugitive slaves to Canada ceased, and this change came early in the war years. After the war, many of the Negroes who had located in Canada returned to the United States, and those who remained found it less difficult to make a living. Their descendants still exist in large numbers in several counties of western Ontario, particularly Essex and Kent, an outflow of the great Negro population of the republic to the south.

10

Slaves' Church

London Free Press *(June 24, 1954), 4*

A curious chapter in the history of London schools is described in an article appearing in the current issue of *Ontario History*, the journal of The Ontario Historical Society. Professor John T. Cooper, of McGill University, a former Londoner and graduate of Western, has, through careful research, pieced together the story of the mission to fugitive slaves that was established in this city by the Colonial Church and School Society of England. There is a reference to this mission in the first city directory of London, published in 1857, where the Reverend Dr. Isaac Hellmuth's name is given as "superintendent of the Society in British North America and Missionary to the fugitive slaves in London."

This office, and responsibility in so far as it is related to London, may have been of a rather nominal character, as Reverend Hellmuth, who was later bishop of Huron, was carrying other heavy responsibilities at this time. The active missionary at London in the three years 1854–56 was Reverend Marmaduke Dillon, and Mr. Cooper deals with him more particularly in his article.*

The 1850s, as is well-known, brought many fugitives from southern plantations into western Ontario, and the influx of coloured folk became a torrent after the passing of the Fugitive Slave Act in 1850. Thereafter, most northern states were not safe for people with black skin. They were liable to be taken up, even though legally free, and charged with being runaways. In the courts that dealt with such cases, the cards were stacked

---

* Editors' Note: This is John T. Cooper, "Mission to the Fugitive Slaves in London," *Ontario History* vol. 54 (1954), 133–39. Although Landon repeatedly referred to "Reverend Martin Dillon," the missionary's name was Marmaduke Dillon, which has been corrected throughout this volume.

against them in a notorious manner, and there were tragic incidents in the years after 1850 when innocent people found themselves seized as runaways and shipped off to the South.

There were even attempts to get at the coloured people in Canada, but these were fruitless, though there were some incidents that might have had serious endings.

Marmaduke Dillon, the man who came to London, had formerly been in the Leeward Islands, which were British possessions. At an earlier date, he had been an officer in the 39th Regiment, but had sold his commission and studied for holy orders. In 1851, when he applied for work in a "colder" climate, he was 38 years of age and in poor health.

Reverend Marmaduke Dillon came to Canada in the summer of 1854. Journeying toward London, he received a licence from the Reverend John Strachan, of Toronto, whose immense diocese at that time included the London area. Before entering upon his work, however, Dillon visited other sections of the western area where Negroes were numerous, and was confirmed in his preference for London as a scene of his work. He found hearty support, first of all from the rector of St. Paul's in London, the Reverend Benjamin Cronyn, and then from a group of Anglican laymen, among whom we find such well-known names as Brough, Flood, Goodhue, Hayward, Wilson, Lawrason, Becher, and Labatt.

On November 1854, operations began when a school was opened in the military barracks, since no school building was available. Eleven children showed up the first day, but by the end of the week there were 50. There were both white and coloured children enrolled, the white children being from the soldiers' families. Two student teachers, Sarah and Mary Ann Titre, natives of Dominica, were assistants in the school, and Dillon was able to claim that this was "the first instance, either in the United States or in this country, in which coloured persons have been introduced as teachers of mixed classes," and he afterward added: "It succeeded."

Throughout 1855 the Free Coloured Mission flourished. The teaching staff was increased by the appointment of a catechist, from Newfoundland, named Hurst, and a female teacher, Miss Jemima Williams, whom Dillon described as "of middle age," though when she died five years later she had but reached the advanced age of 29. We learn

Teacher Jemima Williams surrounded by students of the Colonial Church and School Society school at the military barracks in London (Canada West), circa 1859. *Courtesy of Lande Canadiana Collection, Rare Books and Special Collections Division, McGill University Library.*

that the school's basic offerings to its pupils were: "Scripture reading, junior reading, spelling and alphabet, writing on paper, writing on slates, geography and arithmetic." But, by midsummer of 1855, the studies also included grammar, geography, mental arithmetic, natural history, natural philosophy, and plain needlework.

A letter written by Miss Williams in 1855 tells us that Mr. Hurst had taught the children to sing nicely, and of herself she says, "My principal object in imparting instruction is to give a clear and concise view of their state of nature, and the means which God has provided for their Salvation.... I also give them some instruction in writing, and in 'counting up' as they call arithmetic."

The school reached its peak in 1855. In that year, the coloured people of London and the western area celebrated Emancipation Day in London with a public demonstration and a religious service, which Mr. Dillon conducted in St. Paul's Church. Between 600 and 700 marched with banners flying and headed by a band from the barracks. Mr. Dillon preached from the text, "A new commandment give I unto you, that ye love one another." In the afternoon there was a luncheon, which was attended by the mayor of the city and many of the best citizens.

But from that time on there came sadder days. The two Titre sisters, teachers in the school, fell ill, both becoming tubercular. In the early months of 1856, Dillon also began to fail in health. There were financial worries, which, coming upon a man not himself of robust type, brought about a nervous breakdown. He became involved in a feud with the catechist Hurst, so that finally the Bishop of Toronto had to intervene. Dillon eventually resigned and returned to England. Later, however, he returned to Canada, entered the Diocese of Huron, and served at Port Stanley and Port Dover. He died at that latter place in the winter of 1884.

There is another aspect of the missionary work on behalf of the Negro fugitives that remains to be written. This is the record of the work carried on by the African American Missionary Association in the counties of Essex and Kent, particularly.

This work began as early as 1848 and continued almost to the end of the American Civil War, after which the association devoted its chief efforts to the people in the southern states recently emancipated from slavery and so badly in need of guidance and help. Education took a prominent place in all of the work of this American organization, which had its effect on the Canadian counties where its representatives carried on their work.

11

"We are Free," Answer of Slave to "Old Massa"

London Free Press *(August 23, 1924), 18*

More than 65 years ago a St. Thomas schoolboy stood by on Talbot Street while two Southern slave owners tried, by every kind of argument, to induce a couple of coloured men, formerly their property, to go back with them to Kentucky. The debate between the white men and the Black men was long, but in the end the former slaves refused to have anything to do with their former masters, and one of them gave the most conclusive of all reasons for his stand when he said: "Massa, in this country we are free."

A few days ago the boy, now himself in his seventies, met one of the two Black men who figured in that episode of the late 1850s. Dr. James H. Coyne, of St. Thomas, distinguished writer and historian, went to Mount Salem and visited Lloyd Graves, ex-slave, whom he had not seen since about the time of the incident, which he witnessed as a small boy.

Dr. Coyne recalled to Lloyd Graves that he had been there when the old master tried to induce him to return to slavery. The ex-slave at once narrated, in clear and concise fashion, the events connected with that visit of his former owner, and as well the events that attended his escape from slavery and his journeying to Canada and freedom via the Underground Railroad.

Lloyd Graves, from all data that can be secured, is now past the century mark. He came to Canada in the 1850s, probably about 1854, and was then 30 years of age. The visit from his old master was probably about 1858 or 1859. He has been a resident of Elgin County ever since he reached this country, and today he is at work every day in the acre and a half of garden that he owns in the Village of Mount Salem.

His wife is more than 80 years of age. She says that as a very little girl she knew Lloyd Graves as a grown man. She is convinced that he is 100 years old, and there seems little reason to doubt it, even in the absence of any documentary evidence. What is remarkable, however, is the energy, alertness, and freedom from infirmities of this man, whose life is a connecting link with an era long since passed into history. Only his hearing is impaired, and even this not to an extent that prevents a visitor from conversing with him.

Of men and women who actually knew the sting of slavery, there must be comparatively few, indeed, in this country today. The great migration of refugees to Canada was in the 1850s, and the beginning of the Civil War in 1861 stopped this stream. After the war, many Black people who were in Canada returned to the South, thus materially reducing the coloured population in later years. Here, however, is a man born in slavery, one of those who escaped and made his way to Canada, and he is still able to recall many incidents, both of his slave life and the perilous journey from Kentucky to Canada about 1854.

His story is that he was the property of a man named Graves, living not far from Florence, Kentucky. When he was but a young man, the Mexican War came, and he recalls that the young white men went off to the war. That would have been in 1846. Occasionally, he heard of a place called Canada, where men were free, but he had no idea where Canada was or how to get there. It is a rather interesting fact that the Negroes in Kentucky knew of Canada after their masters returned from campaigning in the War of 1812, in which the Kentuckians played so large a part.

The desire for freedom was awakened in Lloyd Graves, as in many other slaves, by learning that he was to be "sold South." That was the fate which all dreaded, for "down South" were the harsher conditions of slavery that surrounded cotton plantations and sugar production. The old man still grows excited as he speaks of the terror that came into his soul when he chanced to hear a remark that indicated his possible fate.

Negroes who made their way to Canada were a superior class for two reasons: One was that only those of energy and initiative would undertake the risks and perils that were involved. In the second place, only those of good stamina were likely to overcome the perils and hardships of the journey. It was a straight case of the survival of the fittest.

There was, however, machinery to aid those who sought the land of freedom. The Underground Railroad, that mysterious band of people, many of them Quakers, who risked their own freedom for the cause of the oppressed, stood ready to aid those who fled from the slave states. Once the fugitive had crossed the Ohio River (really the River Jordan of his spiritual songs) this machinery would begin to operate and aid the refugee in his journey north.

Lloyd Graves knew little of this underground system, but when escape became his main thought, he soon learned more. He came into touch with people who knew the system because they were themselves the victims of slavery. On a nearby plantation, the slaves had been liberated by an enlightened owner, all except one, a woman, who was retained by the sister of the owner for a term of years. During her service, this slave married another slave and had a child, a boy. The father escaped to Canada, the mother eventually became free in accordance with the terms of the will, but the boy, following the condition of his mother, was held as a slave, and efforts on the part of the parents to buy him had repeatedly failed. These were the people with whom Lloyd Graves came into contact, and they promised him that if he would kidnap the child they would see him through to Canada.

It was a perilous plan in every way. The boy was guarded by an elderly Negress, and the room in which he slept had the window fastened by a nail. It was necessary to take a confederate into confidence, one George Barton, who, by the way, was the second of the coloured men whose conversation Dr. Coyne listened to on that day in the 1850s. George had access to the cabin where the boy was kept, and he removed the nail. Lloyd Graves opened the window, took the boy by the throat, and made a dash for the woods. So tightly did he have the child by the throat to prevent an outcry that he nearly caused the boy to suffocate then and there, but was able to restore him once he had gotten out of sight of the cabin.

Their master's best horses were used by Graves and Barton to make their way to the Ohio River. It was a Saturday night when they made their escape, and at dawn on Sunday morning they were peering across, through the mist, at the other shore, the promised land. Their friends were on hand to help them, and they were taken boldly across on the ferry. Pursuers were close behind them, but too late to stop their progress. Landing in Cincinnati, they were taken to an abolitionist home and concealed in the attic. Pursuers quickly arrived and took out a warrant to search the place. They searched in the lower floors, but overlooked the attic. The fugitives were ordered to change their clothes for others from a great stock that was contained in this garret. Then began a typical journey by the "underground." Concealed in a wagon, Graves and Barton were taken the first stage of the journey north, then hidden again in an abolitionist home. Sometimes it was necessary to remain hidden for days when the pursuit became more keen than usual. At other times, good progress would be made for a day or two. Yet every moment was an adventure, for there were plenty of pro-slavery people, ready to detain Black men going north in the hope of securing a reward.

Later stages of the journey were made by railroad, ending at Cleveland, where the fugitives were put on board a steamer, due to sail that night, and warned not to leave it under any circumstances. During the hours that intervened there came on board various persons who looked at them critically and apparently discussed their possible origins, but no attempt was made to arrest them. At night the boat sailed and landed the Kentucky slaves in the Village of Port Stanley. Captain Barr, who was in command of the boat, appears to have been closely in touch with the "underground" workers and sympathetic toward their efforts. Lloyd Graves says that when they landed at Port Stanley the captain took him aside and gave him some advice, which he has always treasured. He told him that this was a free country, but that a man must work. If he didn't work, people would have no use for him, but if he was honest and ready to work he would find plenty of people ready to help him.

And this very common sense advice was taken to heart by the Black man, who today says that he never in all his life had to go looking for work, there was always work for him to go at, and in his last days he has the satisfaction of owning his own home and owing no man.

Fifty-seven years ago, on August 20, 1867, Graves was married to Amanda Irons, of St. Thomas, born in Canada of parents who were slaves. This week the people of the vicinity, in good neighbourly fashion, took occasion to honour this aged couple, the bridegroom past the century mark and the bride of our confederation year, now in her eighties. The district has a very high regard for these people, who are among its oldest residents and whose whole lives have been marked by industry, honesty, and courtesy. Lloyd Graves will tell you that he paid for his plot of land in two years, and there is scarcely a foot of it that is not in cultivation. From the little frame cottage to the gate, the walk is bordered by old-fashioned flowers that extend off to the side, as well. There are some fruit trees, but the greater part of the home plot is now given over to corn, potatoes, cabbage, and other vegetables, among which the old master of the place hoes and weeds long hours each day.

Lloyd Graves says from the first he wanted to work on a farm. His earliest employer was Henry Lindon of St. Thomas, but eventually he carried out his idea and located out in the country. There is no other coloured family, save one, in this part of the county, though there are some in St. Thomas.

In conversation with Dr. Coyne the other day, the old man gave some humorous details regarding the visit to St. Thomas of the white slave owners whose efforts to take him back were fruitless. There was in St. Thomas at that time a coloured barber named Stewart, who came to George Barton, comrade of Graves in his flight, and suggested to him a scheme for getting some money out of "old massa." Stewart proposed that he should write on behalf of George, stating that the fugitives were sick and in need, and would return if money was sent to pay doctor's bills and their passage back. Stewart asked that, for his trouble, he get half of what money came. Eventually the money arrived, but back in Kentucky there was soon received another letter from St. Thomas saying that doctor's bills were exceptionally high and that little was left after they were paid. Would master not send more money in order that they might leave this wretched country? Master was deceived into sending a second remittance, but further appeals were unheeded, and eventually the owner turned up at St. Thomas himself.

Graves says that he received a message at the place where he was working that a stranger wanted to see him. He thought it was some farmer in the district who wanted to hire him and hastened to the hotel. He says when his old master suddenly faced him, he could not utter a sound, he was so taken back The master offered him a glass of brandy, and this brought back his courage and he stiffened his mind to resist all arguments that might be advanced as to why he should return. The owner told him of the distress of his relatives at his flight, and how much he was missed about the house and plantation. He offered him a horse and bridle when he came back, but all to no purpose. The Black man knew that in Canada he was free and no arguments could alter his decision to stay where he was. In the end the slave owners had to desert without their property.

The story that Lloyd Graves tells of his earlier life is but an episode in the great struggle that culminated in the downfall of the slavery system in the United States. In the breaking down of that system, this country had a certain indirect influence in as much as Canada provided a refuge for all who could make their way to its borders. Thousands of slaves did make their way to Canada, a black stream that quickened during the 1840s and became large in the early 1850s. On the eve of the Civil War, there were probably 30,000 Black people in Canada. There are not nearly that many today, but as a minor section of our Canadian population they have a highly romantic history, some of which has been written, but most of which has passed into oblivion.

12

Fugitive Slaves in London Before 1860

Transactions of London & Middlesex Historical Society, *vol. 10* (1919), 25–38

To gain any comprehensive idea of the condition that surrounded the refugees from slavery in Canada in the period before the Civil War, it would be necessary to make a careful examination of a number of the communities that afforded homes and livelihoods to the runaways and their families. Marked differences would be noted in the condition of the refugees in the various communities. There would also be differences in the attitude of the white population towards these strangers in their midst. Occasionally there was prejudice shown, some intolerance that jarred on the generally broadminded view of Canadians. This did not pass unobserved by the Negroes themselves nor by their friends, yet none could be more grateful than these people for even the crumbs of liberty and opportunity from the Canadian table. Despite the small population at the time of the very considerable immigration of Negroes in the 1840s and 1850s, there was never anything in this country that could be properly described as a Negro problem, and in general the relations of whites and Blacks were marked by a friendliness against which any occasional ill will showed in quite marked contrast.

A study of the condition of the refugees in London before the Civil War may be regarded as typical of the conditions that prevailed in cities like Hamilton and Toronto, but hardly as typical of Windsor, Chatham, or even St. Catharines, which were towns having large coloured populations. Conditions in London would, of course, differ much from those found in organized refugee settlements such as the Elgin Association at Buxton, Kent County, or the Refugee Home Settlement in Essex County, near Windsor. The testimony of observers, both white and Black, of the period of the 1850s, is that probably in no other place were the Blacks treated with such friendliness as in Toronto. Similar testimony is borne to an ill will more manifest at Chatham than elsewhere. Not that there was ill treatment at Chatham, far from it, but there was more prejudice there, due in part to the attitude of a member for Parliament for Essex County, who did not hesitate to declare himself the refugees' friend when an election impended, but blackguarded [disparaged] the race at other times, even on the floor of the Canadian Parliament. [This was Colonel John Prince.]

London's geographical situation had its part in making this city one of the Canadian refugee centres. The 1850s, in particular, were years when an inland city had much to commend it to a runaway slave. Kidnappings took place occasionally at Windsor, Niagara, and other border points, some of these of the boldest character and in utter defiance of Canadian law. Few of the slavers, however, would attempt to kidnap a slave in an inland town, though they would come here once in a while seeking to persuade the slave to return, or endeavouring to lure him to a border town where an attempt at kidnapping might stand a chance of success. The Black man who reached the Forest City could feel that he was a free man, and that no one could threaten his liberty.

Then, too, the city was easy to access from whatever point the runaway entered Upper Canada. From the Niagara River on the east, from the Detroit River on the west, and from Cleveland and Port Stanley on the south, arrivals in London are recorded, some of them escorted to their destination by border abolitionists or by "conductors" on the Underground Railroad who had guided them out of slavery and through the dangers of the supposedly free North. For those were days when the Fugitive Slave Law could take a runaway, even on the streets of Boston.

The refugees who reached Canada tended to drift to the towns and cities. They were more likely to meet friends there, perhaps relatives who had come that way before them. In addition, there were more immediate opportunities to make a living, a matter of importance seeing that the great majority of the fugitives reached Canada in absolute destitution. London offered fair opportunity to the newcomer. In the 1850s it was an active little city, surrounded, as now, by well-tilled farms, which created for it an extensive trade. While opportunities to rise high on the social scale were absent, the City of London would at least provide a living for any coloured man or woman willing to work. And, in general, it must be said, to the credit of the refugees, that they did work, and that a majority of them did rise, more or less, on the social scale by their exertions. The names of several pioneer coloured men come quickly to mind who showed themselves as good citizens, and earned the full respect of their white fellow citizens. Their children hold that same respect in London today.

It is difficult to arrive at any definite figure as to the number of coloured refugees in London before the outbreak of the Civil War. Figures that are derived from various sources are contradictory. The *History of Middlesex*, published here in 1889, says that in 1839 there were "over 200" coloured people in London. It adds that in 1853 there were 276 coloured people in London owning real estate valued at $13,504.

Drew's *North Side View of Slavery*, published at Boston in 1856, says that at that time there were 350 coloured people out of a total population of 12,000. James B. Brown's *Views of Canada and the Colonists* (Edinburgh, 1851) gives the coloured population of London District as 480, of whom 374 were males, a very great preponderance, but not unlikely at that time.

Dr. Samuel G. Howe's *Refugees from Slavery in Canada West* (Boston, 1863), quotes the mayor of London as saying that there are 75 coloured families in London, though the latest census had shown only 36 coloured people in the city. This statement was plainly incorrect, as the census of 1860–61 shows 171 coloured people in London.

William M. Mitchell's *Underground Railroad* (London, 1860), gives the coloured population as 500 out of a total of 12,000. This is probably exaggerated. The London school report of 1862, made at a time when the question of segregation of coloured children was arousing feeling, shows 55 coloured families, 153 children, 96 of school age, and 50 attending school (Quoted by Howe on page 105 of *Refugees from Slavery in Canada West*).

It seems safe to say that in the late 1850s there were about 300 coloured people in London, and that figure had probably not been exceeded at any earlier date.

There is good evidence that the refugees in London found it fairly easy to make their living. Some of them gathered considerable property, and one or two showed business ability. The *History of Middlesex* gives their holdings of real estate in 1853 as $13,504. Reverend William M. Mitchell, in his *Underground Railroad,* says that beggary and pauperism were unknown in London.

Dr. Howe, when he visited London in 1863 as a representative of the United States Freedmen's Inquiry Commission, was told by Reverend Dr. Proudfoot that he didn't know a beggar among the Negroes. The mayor of the city said that while there were none of wealth, there were many Negroes owning a single lot. Dr. Howe remarks on the thrift evident in their very tidy homes, in their gardens, and in the general good state of repair of their property. There is ample testimony that the refugees always earned their own way, and never depended on others.

Drew's *North-Side View of Slavery* gives considerable data regarding individual Negroes in London. A.B. Jones is quoted as saying that he arrived without a cent, got work at once, and has now placed his family beyond want. Moreover, he thinks, any coloured man with industry can do the same. Drew states in a footnote that Jones resided on Grey Street, in a brick dwelling as good or better than the average house in London, a place worth $4,000, and that he also owned other property in the city — a brick dwelling in the business section comprising two stores that rent for between $700 and $800 per annum, and several building lots in the immediate vicinity of the Great Western freight depot. "Mr. Jones," says Drew, "is of unmixed African blood." Mention is made of this same man by Samuel R. Ward in his *Autobiography of a Fugitive Negro* (London, 1855). He says that Jones has his shop, his residence, and most of his town property on one of the best streets in the centre of the town. Ward also makes mention of the fact that there were some coloured families in London whose condition was equal, if not superior, to many of the inhabitants of either colour.

Alfred T. Jones, a brother of A.B. Jones, was another prosperous refugee. He kept a drug store on Ridout Street, opposite the exchange [market]. He told Drew that he was closing out his affairs in London in order to go to England in connection with a suit involving his title to Dundas Street property valued at $45,000. The case had already gone through chancery in the provincial courts, and was now appealed.

Nelson Moss, described by Ward as the "best cordwainer [shoemaker] in Middlesex County," told Drew that there were a few wealthy coloured people, and a good many well off. Some who had arrived without the price of a night's lodging now had houses and lands of their own. John Holmes informed Drew that he owned 22 acres of land. He had recently sold a house and lot to the railroad at a profit. He regretted that he had not invested in London real estate at an earlier date. Had he done so, he would have been well-to-do. He blamed lack of education for the slow progress of some of the coloured people. John D. Moore showed a good spirit in his interview. "I can't complain," he said. "I am doing well here and am satisfied with Canada."

Christopher Hamilton said he had made a comfortable living. He thought the coloured people in London were saving, and did not waste their means. Alexander Hamilton told Drew that he arrived in Canada in 1834 penniless. Today he had three houses and several lots of land in London. Henry Moorehead had only been in London a short time, but was doing well.

Benjamin Miller said, "All make a living and some lay up money." He had property worth $1,800, and had raised a family of eight out of his eighteen children in London. There was no begging by the refugees, he said. He himself had served as pastor of the Methodist church on Thames Street for several years without pay. He had travelled extensively in Canada, and generally speaking he found the coloured people doing well, "uncommon well considering the way they came."

In some of the Ontario towns where the refugees settled in numbers, they tended to live by themselves in one district or street, with results that were generally regarded as unsatisfactory, as race segregation usually is. In the larger cities, however, there was a tendency to scatter about among the whites, this being particularly true in Toronto.

In London, the nearest approach to a Negro quarter was the little low-lying district west of the gas house towards the river, which, until a very few years ago, bore the name of "Nigger Hollow," though for long there had been few, if any, coloured people living there. At one time there was a coloured Methodist church near the corner of Horton and Thames streets. This has long since disappeared.* Grey Street was also the home of quite a number of refugees in the earlier days, as the district is for their descendants today. The vicinity of Wellington Street Bridge also found quite a number of coloured people. Their occupations were what might be expected in view of their social status and lack of education. They were mostly engaged in hotel work, whitewashing and plastering, cleaning, carting, and like occupations, though there were a number of skilled workmen among the London refugees, and a few in business.

Mr. William Mayo, who came to London about 1840, says that he and the other members of the family were brought from Hamilton to London by a Negro teamster who solicited the job. There were quite a number of Negroes in the city at that time, he says, perhaps more than there are today, in his opinion.

Taken as a whole, the evidence presented by impartial observers of the time is that the Negro refugees were steady and industrious, getting along well in Canada considering all their handicaps. Dr. J. Wilson Moore of Philadelphia, who visited this city before the war, was struck by the air of neatness and comfort displayed at the homes of the London fugitives.

The morality of the refugees in Canada affords a most interesting commentary on the effects of freedom. The constant violations of domestic relations under slavery was bound to react on the slaves' home lives, and to take away the incentive to constancy. Yet, upon arriving in Canada, one of the first things married slaves did was to have their plantation union reaffirmed by the form of marriage legal in this country. Dr. Howe observed that the refugees tended to settle in families, and to hallow marriage, and that sensuality lessened under freedom. Mrs. Laura Haviland, who was engaged in educational work with the Negroes in Essex County, has left some interesting evidence of this in her book, *A Woman's Life Work*. The religious instruction given to the fugitives by devoted workers in Canada had some part, no doubt, in Canada. Mrs. Haviland has left a record of her experiences, which is probably typical of what was being done in London and elsewhere. On Sundays, her schoolhouse near Windsor

---

* Editors' Note: Here Landon was mistaken. The church is still standing near the corner of Thames Street and Horton Street in London, Ontario.

This building that served as the African Methodist Episcopal Church in London, Ontario, between 1848 and 1869, is now a private residence. *Courtesy of Glen Curnoe.*

would be thronged, persons coming five and six miles to be present. The reading of the Bible was a great delight to the Negroes, though none of them could do little more than spell out the more simple portions a word at a time. Dr. Howe noted that in Canada the religion of the Negroes was "less nasal and more practical" than in slavery. Religious instincts were shown in charity to the sick and to newcomers, and in their attitude toward women. Dr. Howe was also pleased to note as a characteristic of the Negroes in Canada that there was no spirit of vengeance manifested against those who had so wronged them in the past, no desire to go back and take it out on the old master. Rather, there was a disposition to let the dead past bury its dead and to look to the present and the future. The general improvement of the refugees in Canada was very well summed up by Dr. Howe when he said: "The refugees in Canada earn a living and gather property; they build churches and send their children to schools; they improve in manners and morals, not because they are picked men but because they are free men."

It would appear, from the testimony of a number of observers of the conditions in London in the 1850s and early 1860s, that there was some prejudice shown against the Negroes. Dr. Samuel G. Howe, who visited London as representative of the United States Freedmen's Inquiry Commission, makes repeated mention in his report of this condition in London and cites cases where he believes the Negroes were unfairly treated. While in London, he interviewed several people with regard to this problem, and Dr. Proudfoot told him that the prejudice was growing. That was in 1863.

"But it is not a British feeling." Dr. Proudfoot explained. "It does not spring from our people but from your people coming over here. There are many Americans here and great deference is paid to their feelings. We have a great deal of northern feeling here. The sympathy for the North is much greater than you would imagine."

Dr. Alfred T. Jones (coloured) told Dr. Howe that there was a "mean prejudice" in London that was not found in the United States. John Shipton (coloured) also found prejudice greater in London than in the States and thought it would be a good deal worse but for the protection of the Canadian law.

Dr. Howe placed the blame for the prejudice on the schools, particularly on the headmaster of the union school, who was opposed to having white and Black together. This teacher he quotes as saying: "It does not work well with us to have coloured children in school with the whites. In our community there is more prejudice against the coloured people and the children receive it from their parents. The coloured children must feel it for the white children refuse to play with them in the playgrounds."

One of the other teachers in the school expressed the opinion that the coloured children would be better educated, and that conditions would be improved generally, if the Negroes were sent to separate schools. The coloured children would not then be subjected to so much annoyance. This teacher added that some white children of the lower order didn't mind sitting with Negroes, but that there were others more particular who didn't like it at all.

Dr. Howe comments, with a touch of bitterness, on the sad sight in the playground of this London school "where coloured children stood aside and looked wistfully at groups of whites playing games from which they were excluded. Such scenes," he adds, "do not occur in the playground at Hamilton because the teacher takes care, by showing personal interest in the coloured children, to elevate them in the eyes of their comrades. Moreover, it is not likely that the school committee of London would persist in efforts to expel coloured children from public schools and to degrade them in the public eye if one humane master should publicly protest against it as any citizen has a right to do."

When Dr. Howe visited London in 1863, there was a contest under way to segregate the coloured children, as had already been done in some other western Ontario municipalities. The coloured people had announced that they would fight this move, and they were led in their opposition by Dr. Alfred T. Jones, who himself had been a slave until he was 20 years old. He pointed out to Dr. Howe that his eight children had all been born in London, and that they were as much British subjects as any white child. Such a course as that proposed by the school board would, he contended, make them grow up to hate the country instead of loving it. He predicted that the close of the war then raging would see a general exodus of the refugees back to the United States.

A report of a sub-committee to the London school board in 1862 spoke of prejudice even amongst the children, of the close proximity of the Negroes being distasteful to the whites, and of the want of sympathy between white teachers and coloured children. By a vote of ten to three, a decision was reached to place all the coloured children in a separate school "when financially practicable." This condition was never reached.

Evidence of some prejudice at a date much earlier is given in Benjamin Drew's *North-Side View of Slavery*. Drew came to Canada about 1855 to see how the refugees were making out in the new land, and to see how far they had improved their condition in freedom. He makes a strong case against slavery by showing that freedom made men out of the former chattels. He mentions prejudice against the Negroes in the city schools, but praises the work of the Colonial Church and School Society. The bulk of the Negro children seemed to be in the care of this society.

Alfred T. Jones (coloured) is quoted by Drew, as he was quoted by Howe eight or nine years later. He speaks of a "second hand prejudice" among old country people, but thought there would be less of this were it not that practically all the refugees were poor and ignorant, and so did not properly represent their race. Frances Henderson told Drew that there was "much prejudice" against the Negro, and cited cases where Negroes had practically been turned away from hotels. John Holmes (coloured) said there was still some prejudice, but not as much as there used to be. He speaks of coloured people having been insulted when they came out of white churches. John D. Moore (coloured) mentioned prejudice amongst the lower class of whites, but praised the protection of the law and was philosophical about any feeling among the whites.

Reverend Samuel R. Ward, writing about the same period, says in his *Autobiography of the Fugitive Negro* that "there is not a town in Canada where the respectable coloured people enjoy more of the esteem of the best classes than London."

"Here, too," he adds, "the lower classes are, according to their custom, Negro haters."

It is not difficult to understand why in a city like London there should arise some of this ill feeling. To some extent, the Black men came into the unskilled labour market in competition with the lower classes of whites, and wherever this occurred, whether in the United States or Canada, there was some feeling aroused. A second influence was that of wealthy Southerners who sojourned in Canada and were popular in the society of the day. I have been told that during the Civil War a number of Southern men left their families in London, some of them living at the Tecumseh House. There would be no sympathy among these people for runaway slaves, and their attitude would be reflected among some of their Canadian friends. A third influence lay in the suspicion of all things Yankee. The fact that the Northern Yankees were fighting the Negro's battle would tend to arouse some ill feeling against the refugee, who was likely to be regarded as having stirred up more turmoil than he was worth. Reverend Dr. Proudfoot speaks of the prejudice as being due to Americans who had come to Canada. In 1863, there would have been both Southern refugee whites and Northern scalawags in London, neither of whom had much use for the coloured people.

This must be said for Canada that, though there was in some places

John H. Alexander and pupils of the King Street School, Amherstburg, circa 1890. Mr. Alexander was the principal until 1912 when this segregated school was closed. *Courtesy of the Archives of Ontario, Alvin D. McCurdy fonds, F 207-16-5-2-25.*

a prejudice against the Negro, he was always protected in his rights by Canadian law. Instances where any lawlessness was shown toward the Black men are exceedingly rare. There is a case recorded in Kent County where a number of white men attempted to stop a Negro from building his home on his own land. They tore down each night what he would built up in the day until he presented himself with a gun and gave them warning that he would protect his property. Then they left him at peace. I have found no instance of this or anything approaching it in London. The chief difficulty here had to do with the schools. Outside of that, there was practically no trouble of any kind.

Professor Wilbur H. Siebert, of Ohio State University, worked out some years ago the varied and tortuous routes by which the fugitives from the South came to safety in Canada. His map of the Underground Railroad would have been worth thousands of dollars to the slave owners of any Southern state before the war. Along the northern boundary of

New York and Pennsylvania, that is on the Lake Ontario and the Niagara frontier, there were ten points from which the fugitives crossed to Canada. These were Ogdensburg, Cape Vincent, Port Ontario, Oswego, some port near Rochester, Lewiston, Suspension Bridge, Black Rock, Buffalo, Dunkirk, and Erie. Of these, the four on the Niagara River were the most important and brought the greater number of runaways to freedom. Refugees coming in at any of these points tended to go to Toronto, St. Catharines, Hamilton, and, in a few cases, to Brantford.

The Ohio ports brought more to this district, particularly to London. On Lake Erie there were eight stations that were the termini of the long trips from the slave South. These were Ashtabula, Painesville, Cleveland, Sandusky, Toledo, Huron, Lorain, and Conneaut. Refugees leaving those ports landed in the majority of cases at Long Point, Port Burwell, Port Stanley, or Point Pelee, though a few would land on the Detroit River. The Detroit River was the most important of all places of entry into Canada. At Fort Malden (Amherstburg) as many as 30 fugitives a day entered Canada, while probably as many more came in at Windsor and Sandwich.

Dr. Alexander Milton Ross of Toronto, who made daring trips into the slave states in the 1850s, spreading news of Canada among the slaves, and in several cases helping them to escape, describes the experiences of a Negro man and woman who were finally landed in London, coming in via Port Stanley. Dr. Ross was mixed up in the John Brown raid at Harper's Ferry in 1859, but a few months after that tragedy, while the South was still excited, he decided to renew his operations and accordingly went to Harrodsburg, Kentucky, giving out that he was a Canadian looking for a farm. He amused himself by hunting in the woods in his leisure time, and the man with whom he was bargaining for a farm allowed a very intelligent mulatto to accompany him. The slave told Ross that he had been separated from his wife one month after they were married, the woman being sold to a hotelkeeper in Covington, and that he himself was likely to be sold down the river to Texas. He begged Ross to try and get them both to Canada. Ross explained to him that if he wanted liberty, he would have to be ready to sacrifice for it. He explained that if he reached Cincinnati, he would be sheltered and protected and gave him the names of people there who would be ready to aid. Ross further said that he would go to Covington and try to get the woman away, and that the two would be united in Cincinnati. On the following Saturday night, the Negro, Peter, made good his escape, being aided by the compass and other necessaries supplied to him by Ross. On the Friday Ross went to Covington and put up at the hotel where Polly, the woman, was owned. The hotelkeeper told Ross that he had paid $1,200 for her but was inclined to grumble because she wouldn't take up with his Negro man. He promised her a good lashing if she didn't give in, and told Ross that he knew how to manage such. He would send her down to New Orleans, where she would bring $2,000 because she was "likely." Ross managed to get a word with the woman secretly, and told her that her husband intended to run away, and that she was to make an effort to join him in Cincinnati. Ross promised to help her. He then went over the river to Cincinnati, but on Sunday night, at midnight, he crossed the river in a small boat, met the Negress at a point agreed upon, and in an hour had her in Ohio. Putting the woman in a cab, they drove to a point near a friend's home, then dismounted and entered the house by the rear door.

Ross told Polly that as soon as her husband arrived they would both be sent on to Cleveland, where he would meet them and help them on to Canada. He accordingly went on to Cleveland to make further arrangements, and in a few days received word that Peter had arrived safely, though with badly torn feet. A few days later, another letter reached Dr. Ross stating that freight car number 705 had been hired to convey a box containing one package of "hardware" and one of "dry goods" to Cleveland. The key to the car was enclosed. The train, of which this car was part, was due in Cleveland on a Tuesday evening. That morning, Dr. Ross drove into Cleveland from the home where he had been stopping just outside the city, and as he passed one of the chief hotels, who should be standing outside but the Harrodsburg farmer, the owner of Peter. Ross made his way unobserved by the slaver, and went to the harbour, where, after a long search, he found a schooner loading for Port Stanley and sailing the next day, if the weather were favourable. The captain agreed to stow away the two fugitives and to carry them to Canada. Toward night, Dr. Ross went to the freight depot and met the train bearing the precious shipment. He unlocked the door, went in, and closed the door after him. There was no sign of life, but he called in a low voice: "Peter." The reply came at once. "Yes, massa, shall I open the box?" There were the two poor creatures, in a dry-goods box just sufficiently large enough for them to sit up in. They were helped out, placed in a closed carriage, driven to the harbour, and hidden in the schooner. After midnight, sail was made, and Port Stanley reached the following evening.

"When our little vessel was safely moored alongside the pier," says Dr. Ross in his narrative, "I led my two companions on shore, and told them that they were now in a land where freedom was guaranteed to all. Two happier beings I never saw. We kneeled together on the soil of Canada and thanked the Almighty Father for His aid and protection. Next day I took them to London and obtained situations for both Peter and his wife."

It would be interesting to know who these people were whose first names were Peter and Polly.

The Negroes in London were quite ready to strike a blow at slavery, as the following incident will show. In 1850, a St. Louis man named W.R. Merwin was travelling through Canada accompanied by a slave boy ten or twelve years of age. At London, he was seen by some coloured men who were at the depot and they wired to friends in Chatham to meet the train there and look into the case. As soon as the train reached Chatham, a body of coloured men entered the car where Merwin was sitting and summarily emancipated the boy by taking him away and putting him in hiding. Merwin promptly laid a charge of abduction, claiming that the boy was taken from him against his own desires. The case came on in to court, and dragged along for some time but came to nothing because the boy had disappeared and because it was discovered that Merwin was not a Southern man at all, but a travelling agent who had kidnapped the boy in Paterson, New Jersey, and was evidently planning to take him South and sell him. There is an account of the incident in the *Globe* of October 8, 1858, and in the issue of December 10 of the same year there is a further reference, the Detroit *Advertiser* of November 27, being quoted as saying that the mother of the boy has arrived from Paterson to take her son back.

This story derives additional interest from the fact that it is told in similar detail in the sketch* of Elijah Leonard, which was published in

---

* Editors' Note: Elijah Leonard, *The Honourable Elijah Leonard: A Memoire* (London, ON: n.d.), 47–8.

this city [London] some years ago. Leonard says that he was at the Grand Trunk depot and saw the man pacing up and down the platform with the boy. He called attention of a Negro, Anderson Diddrick, to the case, who at once got busy. When the case came to trial in Chatham, Elijah Leonard was called as a witness, but the papers were miscarried and he did not attend. The case attracted considerable attention in some of the American papers, exaggerated reports being published telling of the rescue of the boy having been brought about by a mob numbering between 300 and 400, and armed with guns and knives. The Chatham *Planet* gave a prompt denial to this, stating that there was no riotous conduct, no violence, no threats, but that all was done peaceably but firmly.

The Anti-Slavery Society of Canada was founded at Toronto in 1851, and in pursuance of its work proceeded to establish branches in various cities, London being one of the earliest. In September 1852, Reverend Samuel Ringgold Ward, a coloured man, visited London and preached in the Methodist New Connexion Chapel (the present Salvation Army Citadel). Following his visit, the branch of the Anti-Slavery Society was formed, with the following officers: President: Reverend William McClure, pastor of the Methodist New Connexion Chapel; Secretary-Treasurer: Reverend Robert Boyd, the pastor of the Baptist Church (now Wrighton's hide warehouse); Directors: Reverend W.F. Clarke, pastor of the Congregational Church, then on King Street; Reverend John Scott, first pastor of St. Andrew's Church; Dr. Salter; John Fraser; Dr. Wanless; William Rowland; and A.B. Jones.

The *History of Middlesex* says (page 357) that the opening of a fugitive chapel followed the organization of the branch of the Anti-Slavery Society, and that other measures were taken, looking both to the comfort of the refugees and also to means for rescuing slaves in the South from their inhuman conditions. The same work speaks, (page 36), of a refugee chapel and alms house being established here by the Colonial Church and School Society, of which Reverend Isaac Hellmuth was in charge. The Colonial Church Society's school is mentioned in the *London Directory* for 1856–57. Reverend Mr. Dillon was head of the mission in London at that time. He is mentioned in Drew's *North-Side View of Slavery*, in his account of conditions among the refugees in London.

There are those still living in Canada who knew what it meant to get out of the South and make their way, against great odds in some cases, to the land of liberty. The following story was given to me within the last few weeks by Mrs. W.J. Hardin, who resides at 21 Wellington Road, and whose sister, Mrs. Harper, lives at 56 High Street. These aged women reached this city on March 25, 1855, and although neither was a slave, their exit from the South was attended with considerable danger and much discomfort.

Mrs. Hardin says that she is the daughter of a Negro mother and a father half-Indian and half-German. Her father was a freeman who, seeing her mother in slavery and taking a fancy to her, bought her freedom and made her his wife. A family of 15 children were born in Kentucky. About 1855, hints were brought to the mother's attention that a plot was afoot to enslave her and the children and sell them all south. She forthwith determined to move to some safer place, and arranged to leave on the next boat going from Bowling Green, Kentucky.

Mrs. Hardin was herself married by this time, but her husband was in California. When she saw her mother packing, she decided that she would leave, too, and so all started north, old Mother Butcher [Mrs. Hardin's mother], several of her daughters, and their children. At Evanston, Ohio, the boat was held up by ice, and they proceeded by train to Cincinnati. On the way, they met with a man named Lawrence, from this city, an uncle of the late Shack Martin [a barber in London for many years], and it was probably through him that London came to be their goal. At Cincinnati the party divided, some coming openly on the railroad to Toledo, while the others journeyed more secretly by the Underground Railroad to Detroit, where finally all were united. Abolitionist friends gave some help here, the party finally landed in London on a cold March day, knowing no one and practically penniless. But the hearts of the fugitives who had attained the goal were always open to their helpless fellows, and at the railroad depot in London they were taken in charge by William Hamilton, a coloured baker at the corner of York and Ridout streets, who took the whole party, eight in all, to his home.

"When we left Kentucky they were starting to sow the crops," says Mrs. Hardin, "but when we landed in London that day it was cold and bleak, with snow and frost everywhere."

After a few days spent at the Hamilton home, the party was lodged in Jones's Hotel, where they were charged $1 a day each for very poor accommodation. While sitting in the waiting room one day, Mrs. Hardin was approached by a stranger who asked her name, and on being told asked her husband's name. The stranger was Henry Howard, a coloured man who had done well and who knew her husband. He took the whole party to his home, kept them there for some weeks, then assisted them in securing a house and making a home.

They did not find the struggle at all easy. The first directory of the City of London records the name of Mrs. P. Butcher, at the corner of Cartwright and Great Market streets, whose occupation is given as sewing and washing. The family did whatever work came their way to make both ends meet. A few years later, while the Civil War was raging and when London was a home for many Southern families, Mrs. Hardin found her services much in demand as cook for Southerners far from their home and longing for the dishes so common in Dixie.

Mrs. Hardin says that two or three times a week she would fill a basket with real Southern dishes and take it to the rooms of some family at the Tecumseh House, who would then call in other Southern families for the meal. She also did sewing and washing for them, all of which assisted the family.

From 1855–60 there was a large influx of coloured folk, she says, but many of these returned to the United States when the war was over. She did not know most of them, as she was too busy trying to make a living to bother much with the newcomers from slavery. Though most of her family were Baptists, she was a Methodist and attended the coloured church, which in the 1850s was located at the corner of Horton and Thames streets.

In the *History of Middlesex* (1889) the statement is made on page 36 that "in May 1858 John Brown, with his abolition lieutenants, Kagi and Stevens, resided in Canada, passing their leisure hours at London or Hamilton and their working hours at Chatham, drafting the constitution of their proposed provisional government of the United States."

It was in April 1858 that Brown was in this part of the country on his first visit to Canada. Osborne P. Anderson describes his visit to Chatham as follows:

The first visit of John Brown to Chatham was in April 1858. Wherever he went around, though an entire stranger, he made a profound impression upon those who saw or became acquainted with him. Some supposed him a staid but modernized Quaker, others a solid business man from 'somewhere' and without question a philanthropist. His long white beard, thoughtful and reverend brow and physiognomy, his sturdy measured tread, as he circulated about with his hands under the pendant coat tails of plain brown tweed, with other garments to match, revived to those honored with his acquaintance and knowing of this history, the memory of a Puritan of the most exalted type (*A Voice from Harper's Ferry* [1861], 9).

Brown's visit to Canada was really a prelude to the disastrous raid on the government arsenal at Harper's Ferry, the design of which was to strike a blow at slavery by making all slave property unsafe. R.J. Hinton, in his book, *John Brown and His Men,* says on page 70 that "in the early part of April John Brown visited St. Catharines, Ingersoll, Hamilton, and Chatham in Canada West to prepare for the convention he wished to convene just before he entered on his active work. He was also reported at this time at Sandusky, Ohio, and Detroit, Mich."

I have found no direct evidence that Brown ever visited London, though it is not at all unlikely that he was here in 1858 conferring with the fugitives and with the friends of the fugitives in this city. If the story of Canada's relation to some of the striking episodes of the abolition movement and the Civil War could be known, we would doubtless have some marked surprises. How many, for instance, know that on August 7, 1864, there took place in this city [London] a conference between three commissioners of the Confederate States government and representatives of the powerful secret political organization in the northwestern states known as the Knights of the Golden Circle, the object of which was to separate the northwestern states from the Union and form a second rebelling Confederacy?

13

Records Illustrating the Condition of Refugees from Slavery in Upper Canada Before 1860[1]

Journal of Negro History, *vol. 13, no. 2 (April 1928), 199–206*

I

The fourth annual report of the American Anti-Slavery Society contains the statement of an agent of the society who was employed "to investigate the conditions and prospects of the coloured people in Upper Canada." The report says:

> He finds a population of about 10,000, almost entirely fugitives from American oppression. Having crossed the line with no other wealth than their own bodies and souls, many of them have made themselves quite comfortable, and some have become even wealthy. Several schools have sprung up among them by the efforts of the agent. Full and satisfactory evidence of their good behaviour and value as citizens has been given by the highest civil authorities and by men of standing of different sects and parties.

The following letters were received by the agent, in reply to his inquiries, from gentlemen in Toronto whose character is too well-known to need any description. First from the Honourable R.G. Dunlop, member of the provincial parliament:

House of Assembly, Toronto,
Jan. 27, 1837
Dear Sir:

Permit me to assure you that I feel much pleasure in replying to your communication of yesterday, and in recording my testimony, whether in my private capacity as a subject, or in my public as a magistrate and representative of the people, it gives me infinite satisfaction to say that after much observation and some experience I have arrived at this conclusion, viz., that there are not in His Majesty's dominions a more loyal, honest, industrious, temperate and independent class of citizens than the colored people of Upper Canada. Go on, therefore, my dear sir, in your work of charity, and let us pray fervently to the Most High, that He will look down with compassion on the degraded children of Africa, and lead them as He did the chosen people of old, from your modern Egypt of oppression.

I remain, dear sir,
Yours very sincerely,
R.G. Dunlop,
Captain of R.N., M.P. for the County of Huron.[2]

———————————————

———————————————

Toronto, Jan. 30, 1837
Sir:

In reply to your inquiries, I beg to offer as my opinion with much diffidence, 1st. That nearly all of them are opposed to every species of reform in the civil institutions of the colony – they are so extravagantly loyal to the Executive that to the utmost of their power they uphold all the abuses of government, and support those who profit by them. 2nd. As a people they are as well behaved as a majority of the whites and perhaps more temperate. 3rd. To your third question I would say, not "more numerous." 4th. Cases in which coloured people ask public charity are rare, as far as I can recollect. I am opposed to slavery, whether of whites or blacks, in every form. I wish to live long enough to see the people of this continent, of the humblest classes, educated and free, and held in respect, according to their conduct and attainments, without reference to country, color or worldly substance. But I regret that an unfounded fear of a union with the United States on the part of the coloured population should have induced them to oppose reform and free institutions in this colony, wherever they have had the power to do so. The apology I make for them in this matter is that they have not been educated as freemen.

I am, your respectful humble servant,
W.L. Mackenzie[3]

————————————————

————————————————

Sir:

In acknowledging the receipt of your letter of the 26th instant, containing certain inquiries relating to the people of color in this city, I have much pleasure in affording my testimony for the information of the Society of which you state yourself to be the agent, begging you will consider my observations as strictly applicable to the people of color within this city[4] and immediate neighborhood, to which alone my knowledge extends. In reply to your query No. 1, I believe them to be truly loyal subjects of the government. 2nd. As a people I have no reason to question their honesty or industry, and as far as my observation serves me, they appear to be both temperate and well-behaved. 3rd I am not aware that criminal cases are more numerous with them than with others in proportion to their numbers. But with respect to your 4th question I wish to be more explicit, that although I have been in the habit of daily contributing assistance to a vast number of destitute poor ever since my residence in this province, now seventeen years, I do not remember ever having been solicited for alms by more than one or two people of color during the whole course of that period.

I am, your respectful humble servant,
John H. Dunn,[5]
Receiver-General, Upper Canada

II

The two following letters are from correspondence between the Honourable Malcolm Cameron[6] and the coloured stockholders of the Elgin Association,[7] printed in the Montreal *Pilot* and copied in the *National Anti-Slavery Standard* of February 21, 1850.

To the Hon. Malcolm Cameron:

Sir, We the undersigned committee have been appointed by a number of colored stock holders of the Elgin Association to ask your views on a subject that chiefly concerns our civil rights. Your long residence in the western part of the province, where most of our people are settled, makes you well acquainted with our condition, and the many disadvantages under which we labour, in consequence of an unjust prejudice, which deprives our children, in a great measure, of the use of the common schools, and excludes us from participating in the rights and privileges guaranteed to us by law. This prejudice has lately assumed a hostile form, in an address published at Chatham in August last, the object of which is to prevent us from settling where we please, and if carried into effect, would eventually drive us from the province. As you represent the county where the Elgin Association has purchased land for colored settlers they wish to know if you are in favor of our settling there, or any other place that we may select in the province, and if you will aid us in obtaining all the rights and privileges we are entitled to by law. An answer at your earliest convenience will oblige the committee.

> Committee
>> Adolphus Judah
>> W.R. Abbott
>> David Hollin

(Mr. Cameron's reply:)

Gentlemen, In reply to your letter of this day I beg leave to say that the evil you complain of, relative to your position in common schools, was fully provided for in the new school bill which I had the honor to conduct through parliament last session and which comes into operation in January next.

I regretted very much the tone and sentiments of the resolutions and address to which you allude as having been passed at Chatham in August last, and I feel quite sure that they are not the sentiments of the great mass of the County of Kent. For my own part I have ever advocated the perfect equality of all mankind, and the right of all to every civil and religious privilege without regard to creed or color. And under the constitution we now enjoy all men are really "free and equal" and none can deny to the African anything granted to the Scotchmen the Irishmen or the Saxon; they have the right to purchase where they please, and settle in groups or singly as they like; and wherever they are, they will find me ready to defend and maintain the principles of civil and religious freedom to all, as the principle I hold most dear to myself and most sacred to my country.

I have the honor to be your obedient servant,
Malcolm Cameron

III

The following notes on the Negro settlements in the Detroit River district of Upper Canada appear in the *Voice of the Fugitive* of January 29, 1852:[8]

There is still a government school in operation at Sandwich with from 20 to 30 scholars. It is taught by Mr. Jackson, a man of colour; the school at Windsor is taught by Miss Mary Ann Shadd, a worthy coloured lady. She has between 18 and 20 scholars whom she is teaching in a private house.

The coloured people here have procured a lot on which to erect a school and meeting house, and have got an agent out collecting funds for that purpose and expect soon to erect the building.

Marble Village School. In 1856, an Englishman named Rowland Wingfield subdivided his land near the quarries in Anderdon Township, north of Amherstburg. Many lots were sold to African Canadians and their children attended this school, constructed on land donated by Wingfield. It was also called the Quarry School. *Courtesy of the Archives of Ontario 1002478.*

We visited during the past week, the colored settlement seven miles from Windsor; also the New Canaan settlement which is 11 miles east of Amherstburg. The former settlement has been sometimes called the Sandwich Industrial Society; a few years ago the African Methodist Episcopal Church sent out an agent, the Reverend T. Willis, who collected money enough to purchase 200 acres of wild land, which was bought and divided into ten acre plots, and sold out to coloured persons, on each of which they were to settle, with the exception of 10 or 20 acres which were reserved on which to build a school and meeting house. We found four or five families settled on the land, who seemed to be industriously engaged in clearing it off. We observed that they had erected the body of a log schoolhouse on the reserved lot; but there was no roof on it. There is a school in operation about one mile from the above, where there are several colored families settled who are the owners of farms containing from 30 to 100 acres of good land. The school is taught by Mrs. Prescott, a white lady.

In the New Canaan settlement they have a flourishing school, which is taught by Miss Lyon. Here they have a good schoolhouse and a very promising settlement around it of good, industrious coloured inhabitants, almost all of whom are the owners of the farms which they are clearing off and cultivating.

IV

The following letter from Hiram Wilson, dated St. Catharines, November. 12, 1851, appears in the *Voice of the Fugitive* of December 3, 1851:

My main object at present is to give your readers some account of a rural walk I have just taken to the Grand River and back, and of the colored settlement on that river, near Cayuga…. I started on Thursday last, having before me a clever walk (37 miles) to reach the settlement. The roads were very muddy and unpleasant most of the way. I had the pleasure, however, of passing through a very fine section of the country, which is particularly adapted to lumbering, grain growing and grazing. I passed many very extensive and beautiful farms, which were watered by the Chippewa River, and some fine buildings, though most of the houses were but indifferent in quality. The greatest evil I discovered by the way was the ruinous practice of drinking…. I found about one mile from Grand River an interesting settlement of 18 or 19 families, besides a small group of colored settlers, two miles distant on a public road, making in all about 24 families.

They all have farms, varying in quantity from 50 to 150 acres, the aggregate being 2,000 acres or more. I found on each lot a comfortable log cabin, and usually from 20 to 30 acres of cleared land, though some of the settlers have been there but three or four years. The land was purchased of the government at $31 an acre though some of the last purchasers will have to pay interest annually till the principal shall have been paid, when they can have their deeds. The land has on it much valuable timber, which is in great demand. It is generally level, or gradually undulating, and when cleared of trees and stumps reminds you somewhat of western prairies. The soil consists generally of a dark, rich loam, with a subsoil mostly of clay with here and there ridges overgrown with pine trees and shrubbery indicating the presence of sand near the surface.

I found the people generally cheerful, contented and happy, and the majority in quite comfortable circumstances. With rare exceptions the adults were formerly slaves in the south, though I came across one man who was free, but had earned as a blacksmith and paid one thousand dollars for the freedom of his wife and children.

Brother J.W. Logan[9] [*sic*] has arrived from Syracuse. Quite a number of others have lately come here from Syracuse and are likely to do well. I have lately visited the settlement at Norwich and prepared the way for a teacher, who is doubtless there by this time.

V

The following letter, apparently from an escaped slave to his former master, appears in the *Voice of the Fugitive* of January 29, 1852:

Sandwich, Jan. 12, 1852
J.A. Levy, Esq.

Respected Sir: When you purchased me, you promised that whenever I paid you the sum of $380, I should then be manumitted and set free. I should have staid with you, and paid the balance due you which is $50; I was truly unwilling to leave you until you were paid in full; but, respected sir, liberty is ever watchful, and I got an impression that you were about to sell me. This induced me to leave you, unwillingly I confess, but security to myself demanded the sacrifice. I am now free and in a free country. Still I wish to pay you the fifty dollars due, and if you will place my freedom papers, properly executed, in the hands of anyone in the city of New York, I will send a person with the balance due you to them, the same to be paid on delivery of the proper papers. You will please to address me, per mail, Post Office, Sandwich, Canada West.

With respectful regard, believe me, Sir, to be your sincere well-wisher,
J. Levy

VI

The following petition to the American Congress was adopted at a meeting of coloured people held in the town of St. Catharines, in Upper Canada, early in 1851. It was printed in the *Voice of the Fugitive* of February 26, 1851, with a note from Reverend Hiram Wilson, who had forwarded it:

Petition from American Exiles in Canada
To the Honorable, The Senate and House of Representatives of the United States in Congress assembled; the

petition of the undersigned, temporary residents in the Niagara District of Canada most humbly showeth:

That we, the petitioners, have been forced by an oppressive enactment of the Federal Government, called the Fugitive Slave Law, to leave our quiet homes in the nominally free states and seek protection under Her Britannic Majesty's just and powerful government, which knows no man by his complexion.

That although we are well satisfied with the government which now protects us, and can dwell in peace and quietude under the mild and benignant sway of Queen Victoria's sceptre, yet having been bred up in northern states, and never having forfeited the protection of a government which proudly proclaims its vast expanse of territory as an asylum for the oppressed of all nations; we respectfully ask that your Honorable Bodies may have the justice and magnanimity to repeal, with the least possible delay, the infamous Fugitive Slave Law, that we may return with safety if we choose, and have protection in our persons and property in our native land.

And your petitioners, as in duty bound, will ever pray, etc.

VII

The Genius of Universal Emancipation, November 18, 1826, quotes from the *Canadian Spectator*, published at Montreal, the following extract from a letter written by a gentleman residing at Sandwich on the Detroit River:

On the 12th August two hogsheads of Leaf Tobacco were shipped at Amherstburg, consigned to you, with a certificate from John Wilson, Esq., collector of that port, of their being the growth of this province. This tobacco belongs to an industrious, respectable Negro to whom I sold some land and who is one of a number of the same color whom I have advised to settle together and form a village; so far the undertaking is promising and the owner of the two hogsheads informs me that in a very short time he expected that at least 60 hogsheads of the same article would be raised in this small settlement.... I have sold nearly a 1000 acres [*sic*] of land in small parcels to a number of these poor fugitives.... It is their intention after they have paid for their lands to supply their wants in merchandise from Montreal.

14

Social Conditions Among the Negroes in Upper Canada Before 1865

Ontario Historical Society, Papers and Records, *vol. 22 (1925),* *144-61*

When the government of the United States emancipated the Negro slaves in the seceded states in 1863, there was instituted a Freedmen's Inquiry Commission to consider generally what should be done, both with slaves who had been freed by the operations of the war and those who should later become free. The members of this commission were Dr. Samuel G. Howe, Robert Dale Owen, and James McKaye.

Dr. Howe, soon after his appointment, visited Upper Canada, and later made a report to Secretary of War Stanton[1] that presents much information on the condition of the refugees who had entered the British province and were making their home there.

His findings were highly favourable to the fugitives, and one sentence of the report has been frequently quoted, where, after noting some of the advances made by these people in their new home, he adds: "The refugees earn a living, and gather property; they marry and respect women; they build churches and send their children to schools; they improve in manners and morals — not because they are picked men, but simply because they are free men."

Dr. Howe was deeply impressed with this idea, that it was freedom that improved the Negro. In Canada, he found the Black man facing severe hardships in many cases. The climate was harsh as compared with the South, sometimes there was difficulty in making a livelihood, and there was occasional prejudice. On the other hand, there was justice and opportunity and, above all, freedom. In the preface to his report, Dr. Howe says: "When everybody is asking what shall be done with

Dr. Samuel Gridley Howe was commissioned by President Lincoln to observe the lives of formerly enslaved African-American settlers in Canada. His 1863 report to the United States Freedmen's Inquiry Commission assisted in the planning for the education and employment of freed slaves after the Civil War. From Wilbur H. Siebert, *The Underground Railroad from Slavery to Freedom* (1898).

the Negroes — and many are afraid that they cannot take care of themselves if left alone — an account of the manner in which 20,000 of them are taking care of themselves in Canada may be interesting, even if it be imperfect, and contain superfluous speculations."

Dr. Howe's estimate of the number of Negro refugees in Canada was between 15,000 and 20,000.[2] This is but one of the many estimates, and it is rather difficult to arrive at any definite figure. The question is of some interest, however, as showing the effect of the refuge offered by Canada upon slaveholding in the South. For more than 30 years before the Civil War came, the slaveholders had protested against the British policy of protecting Negroes in Canada against their efforts to return them to slavery. The Canadian census figures are quite unreliable with regard to this class of people.

Reverend Samuel Ringgold Ward, himself a fugitive slave, says that the enumerators ignored the portion of their report designating colour.[3] Thus, we are left to draw some conclusion from the many and varying figures given by travellers, by the fugitives themselves, and by others who were interested. Richard J. Hinton, the biographer of John Brown, makes the highest estimate when he says that in 1858 there were at least 75,000 fugitives in Canada.[4] It is quite certain that this figure is far too high.

Reverend William M. Mitchell, a Negro missionary resident in Toronto, made an estimate of 60,000 in 1860,[5] and this estimate is supported by Reverend Dr. Willis, president of the Anti-Slavery Society of Canada, and by Reverend Hiram Wilson, a missionary among the fugitives.[6] Levi Coffin, when he visited Canada in 1844, was told that there were 40,000 Negroes in the country,[7] and this figure is also given by Reverend Samuel R. Ward in 1850.[8] The first annual report of the Anti-Slavery Society of Canada estimated the Negro population at 30,000, of whom about one fifth had arrived in the last two years. Josiah Henson, in 1852, put the figure at between 20,000–30,000,[9] "daily increasing," while James B. Brown, a British traveller, made an estimate of 30,000.[10] A resolution passed at a public meeting at Sandwich in 1852[11] speaks of 30,000 Negroes in Canada, and this figure is also given by John Scoble, writing in the *Anti-Slavery Reporter* in 1852.[12] The *National Anti-Slavery Standard* of September 5, 1850, quotes an address issued by fugitive slaves meeting at Cazenovia, the home of Gerrit Smith,* in which they say: "Including our children, we number in Canada at least 20,000. The total of our population in the free states far exceeds this." The *Voice of the Fugitive* of July 29, 1852, quotes from *The Liberator*: "It is stated that there are now in Canada about 30,000 of these poor refugees, 8,000 having been driven from the free states through the panic occasioned by the Fugitive Slave Law."

Henry Bibb, writing in the *Voice of the Fugitive*, of May 21, 1851, says: "From the best information we can get on the subject, there must be about 35,000 here now, more or less." He adds that before the passing of the Fugitive Slave Act there were about 30,000 Negroes in Canada, of whom at least 20,000 were refugees from slavery.

Reverend Samuel R. Ward, in making his estimate of 40,000, states that the majority were refugees from slavery. Apart from children born in Canada, he did not think that there were 3,000 freeborn Negroes in the country, though this class came in after 1850 in considerable numbers.

Figures of population for separate places show clearly that the majority of the Negroes were in the western part of the province. Windsor, Sandwich,

---

* Editors' Note: Gerrit Smith was an abolitionist, social reformer, and a three-time candidate (unsuccessful) for the American presidency.

Amherstburg, Chatham, Buxton, Dawn, and Colchester were all in the Detroit River district. Elsewhere, the Negroes were found in numbers in London, Ingersoll, Norwich, St. Catharines, Hamilton, Toronto, and in the Queen's Bush. The first annual report of the Anti-Slavery Society of Canada says that around 1852 there was a coloured population of 500 in Dawn (now Dresden), 1,200–1,500 in Colchester, 20 families at New Canaan, 300 families at Sandwich, 2,000 in the Queen's Bush, 800 at Hamilton, 800 at Toronto, 1,500 at St. Catharines and Niagara, 20 families at Wilberforce, north of London, and 50 actual settlers at Buxton.

Benjamin Drew[13] made the following [population] estimates in 1856: Toronto, about 1,000; St. Catharines, 800; Hamilton, 274; Galt, 40; London, 350; Chatham, 800 in the town and probably 1,200 more nearby; Buxton, 800; Dresden, 70; Windsor, 250.

Reverend William M. Mitchell gave the following figures in 1860: Toronto, 1,600; Hamilton, 600; St. Catharines, 200–250; London, 500; Chatham, 2,000; Windsor, 2,500; Sandwich, 2,000; Amherstburg, 800; Buxton, 800. He refers to Chatham as the headquarters of the race in Canada.

The 28th annual report of the American Anti-Slavery Society (New York 1861), refers to "the 1,000 refugees" in Toronto, and quotes an account from the Philadelphia *Friends' Review* of the visit of Joseph Morris, an Ohio Quaker, to Chatham, where he found 2,000 coloured people, one third of the whole population of the place. Their homes, he thought, compared favourably with those of the whites, and there were no cases of extreme destitution. He visited the Buxton colony, which presented an impression very agreeable and encouraging, and "he never saw any people more willing to rely on their own resources." Shrewsbury, on Lake Erie, was also visited, and here the coloured people "manifested a spirit of independence in respect to obtaining the means of living and educating their children. He thinks the unrestricted enjoyment of the privileges of citizenship largely promotes their improvement." All in all, this Ohio Quaker was much impressed by what he saw in Upper Canada.

The presence of the Negro refugees in Canada does not seem to have attracted any special attention until late in the 1840s. The Negro created no special problem, either for the government or for the local authorities. His status in Canada differed in no material respect from that of any other citizen. He had to work or starve, therefore he worked. If he transgressed the laws of the land, he was punished, though there does not seem to have been any unusual amount of crime among the Negroes. The Black man had the same civil rights as the white man; he exercised the franchise, and could participate in politics.

Under Canadian law, the Negroes were allowed to send their children to the common schools, or to have separate schools provided for them out of their share of the school funds. Separate schools were so established at a few places where prejudice had been manifested. There were also one or two private schools for Negro children, maintained by religious societies,[14] and in the distinctly Negro settlements, such as Buxton, Dawn, and the Refugee Home Settlement in Essex County, there were special schools. That at Buxton drew students from the northern states. The best work seems to have been done by the mission schools and those located in the colonies. An indication of the general interest taken in education is shown by the incorporation in 1859 of "The Association for the Education of the Coloured People of Canada," which succeeded and continued the work of "The Provincial Association for the Education and Elevation of the Coloured People of Canada," the object of which was to provide education for the coloured youth of the country.

Dr. Samuel G. Howe, when he visited Canada, noted that a surprisingly large number of the fugitives could read and write. In Chatham, he thought that the coloured children stood as well as the whites, while in the matter of attendance there was also little difference, except that the coloured children left school at an earlier age. The coloured children seemed to be dressed about as well as the white children in the mixed schools, but did not make as good an appearance in the separate schools. Howe thought the separate schools were ill-advised, and thought it a still greater mistake to ask for coloured teachers. The principal of the Chatham schools told him that the Negro children learned about as rapidly as the white children, but needed more attention.

Dr. Howe's criticism of the separate schools agreed with the views of some of the more intelligent of the refugees themselves. Henry Bibb was distinctly antagonistic toward any separation, and made frequent references to this matter in his paper. This was partly due to the occasional manifestations of prejudice against the Negroes in the matter of schools. Reverend William Troy, of Windsor, states that his children were turned out of the common school, along with other coloured children,[15] and Patrick Shirreff, a British traveller, refers to Negro children being kept out of a school near Chatham.[16]

Prejudice was almost sure to manifest itself occasionally in view of the nearby American influences. When the Elgin Association settlement, in Kent County, was beginning its work in 1849, there was considerable opposition manifested, and the Western District council in October of that year issued a resolution reading,[17] in part, as follows:

> This increased immigration of foreign Negroes into this part of the province is truly alarming. We cannot omit mentioning some facts for the corroboration of what we have stated. The Negroes who form at least one-third of the inhabitants of the township of Colchester attended the township meeting for the election of parish and township officers and insisted upon their right to vote, which was denied them by every individual white man at the meeting. The consequences of which was that the chairman of the meeting was prosecuted and thrown into heavy costs, which costs were paid by subscriptions from white inhabitants. As well as many others, in the same township of Colchester, the inhabitants have not been able to get schools in many school sections in consequence of the Negroes insisting on their right of sending their children to such schools. No white man will ever act with them in any public capacity, this fact is so glaring that no sheriff in this province would dare to summon coloured men to do jury duty. That such things have been done in other parts of the British Dominions we are well aware of, but we are convinced that the Canadians will never tolerate such conduct.

Reverend Samuel R. Ward, who was ever a doughty champion of the rights of his race, had a letter in reply to this resolution in which he denied that there was bad feeling between the two races in Colchester Township, and stated that the references to Negroes being kept off juries were untrue, as they had served in such a capacity in Toronto and elsewhere. The whole resolution was, in his opinion, an attempt to stir up racial hatred and influence Lord Elgin against the refugees. Referring to the outcome of the Colchester incident, he said: "Such is the even-handed justice and impartiality of British law, such the purity of the British courts. Thank God for this. There is a resort to which we may go when robbed and insulted."[18]

The attempt to block the granting of land to the Elgin Association was rebuked by the Montreal *Pilot*, which, reproducing correspondence that had passed between the Honourable Malcolm Cameron and the association's stockholders, said:

> We have on more than one occasion advocated the rights of our coloured fellow-citizens in this province and expressed our surprise and indignation at the attempt made to take them away. The opponents of free settlement may be reminded that we are not yet annexed and that it is far too soon to anticipate by an anti-British policy an event the probable occurrence of which is contemplated by the lovers of genuine freedom and independence with strong feeling of aversion. The prejudice against colour is a moral weakness, to say the least, of which an Englishman should be ashamed. It ought to have no place among us.[19]

Elsewhere,[20] Reverend Ward drew attention to cases of prejudice shown against Negroes, refusal to provide accommodation in taverns and on steamboats being the most glaring. J.T. Fisher of Toronto also complained of discrimination in the choosing of juries in Toronto.[21] *The Liberator* of January 3, 1851 has a reference to excitement in Canada West over the drawing of a colour line by the Sons of Temperance. There appears also to have been some trouble in 1852 at the annual militia training at St. Catharines, a Negro settlement being attacked.[22] On the other hand, Frederick Douglass could write to *The Liberator* stating that he had been received kindly at a hotel on the Canadian side, at Niagara, in marked contrast to treatment received in American cities. "Were it not cowardly, and perhaps selfish," he said, "I could wish to leave the United States and become a resident in Canada."[23]

There are numerous references by travellers and others to the condition of the Negroes in Canada at various times, and it is quite clear that the presence of Black people in this province was a matter of some interest to those who came examining the country. Reference has already been made to the visit to Upper Canada by Joseph Morris, an Ohio Quaker, who wrote his impressions for the Philadelphia *Friends' Review*. A correspondent of the New York *Tribune*, who also visited this province at about the same time (1860), says in his article: "Many of the coloured people are amassing wealth. All parties testify that the coloured man's condition is as good as that of any other emigrants."[24]

The Liberator of April 6, 1849 reprinted from the *True Wesleyan* the observations of one E. Smith under the heading: "Freed slaves, how they prosper."

The writer, on his visit to Canada, found the greater portion of the refugees engaged in farm work, not waiters, barbers, etc. They had been represented in the United States as lazy and improvident, but he saw evidence to the contrary. He wrote: "I saw quite a number who had pretty good farms and everything necessary for life and comfort around them. Some are worth hundreds and others thousands of dollars. The laws there make no distinction on account of colour. The coloured man can take rank and place with his white brother and the fugitives may become a part of the community and share their portion of its benefits."

About 1850, the board of the Baptist Missionary Convention of the State of New York sent two representatives, Messrs. Wheelock and Sheldon, to ascertain the condition of the coloured people, particularly those of the Baptist faith in Canada West. They found the white testimony quite favourable to the Negroes, who were described as generally moral and industrious. They urged in their report that the coloured Baptists in

Canada should be aided in maintaining schools and churches, but with regard to other forms of aid they wrote:

> We found in all the places we visited that respectable coloured people, in churches and out of churches, were united in their testimony that contributions of clothing and provisions, except for the aged and the sick, would prove a curse rather than a blessing. In the States there has been much said about the destitution and sufferings of the fugitives, and much has been done for their relief. This reported destitution and suffering, we find, has been greatly exaggerated. None need assistance of this kind but the aged and the sick.

The report adds that there has been much imposition practised on benevolent persons, collections having been taken up for the refugees, which never reached them. [25]

In *The Liberator* of July 30, 1852, appears a statement with regard to the refugees assigned by Reverend Dr. Willis, president of the Anti-Slavery Society of Canada,[26] and by Messrs. Henning and Hamilton, officers of

The Baptist Church in Toronto was founded by the much-loved Reverend Washington Christian and a group of fugitive slaves worshipping on the shores of Lake Ontario in 1826. The brick church at Queen and Victoria streets was constructed in 1841. By 1845, the mortgage had been paid off. Reverend Christian had spent two years in Jamaica on a preaching tour to raise the money, the white Baptist preachers of Toronto ministering to his congregation while he was away. From John Ross Robertson, *Landmarks of Toronto*, vol. 13, 1904.

the society. Their communication estimates the coloured population at the time of the passing of the Fugitive Slave Act at 20,000, but says that this was increased by from 4,000–5,000 within a few months after the passing of the act. Charges of mistreatment of the fugitives by Canadians are denied. "Every coloured man, as is well known, the moment he sets his feet on the Canadian soil, is forever free and not only free but he is on a level, in regard to every political and social advantage, with the white man. He can vote for members of Parliament and for magistrates and in every other popular election."

The communication states further that the Negro fugitives have their own churches, though they are not discriminated against in others, that they are not segregated in coaches or on steamers, and that they can have their own separate schools. "The coloured people in Canada have no grievance of any kind," is the conclusion of the communication.

The American and Foreign Anti-Slavery Society kept a friendly eye on the Canadian fugitives. The report for 1851 says:

> Several agents have, during the past year, proceeded to Canada to exert the best influence in their power over the fugitives that have flocked to the province in years past and especially those who have gone the past year. They are supplied with the means of instructing the coloured population, clothing some of the more destitute fugitives and aiding them in various ways to obtain employment, procure and cultivate land, and train up their children. Our friends in Canada are exerting a good influence in the same direction. It may not be improper for us to suggest that it is highly important that a plan, on a large scale, should be devised for the permanent employment of the people of colour in Canada under the direction of competent agents in agricultural and mechanical pursuits. [27]

The American Missionary Association also received regular reports from its workers in Canada. The annual report for 1855 says: "In general those who have gone there from the United States may provide for the wants of their families after a short residence there, especially if they meet a friendly hand and, more than all, good counsel on their arrival."[28]

Reverend William Troy, of Windsor, writing about 1860, stated his belief that nine tenths of the fugitives in Canada had received no aid for their physical wants from any source whatever. They showed a marked disposition to help each other, of which he gave several instances.[29]

An article by John Scoble, in the *Anti-Slavery Reporter*,[30] entitled "Refugee Slaves in Canada," estimates their number at 30,000 and increasing. He says: "By not a few of the French-Canadians, the Irish, and, though in not so great a degree the Scotch and English, they are regarded as an inferior caste and a degraded people, and, therefore, but little social intercourse exists between them. As a consequence of this unhappy state of things the coloured people are found mostly in isolated communities." Their needs, he thought, were chiefly a well-regulated body of schoolmasters, as superior a class of religious teachers, and easy means of procuring land. He doubts the wisdom of sending in much material aid, and says that the Negroes have themselves exposed gross cases of misappropriation of charity.

"It may be regarded as a fact," he writes, "that every industrious coloured person in West Canada may obtain employment in one form or another and be fairly remunerated for it, and that consequently aid is only wanted to meet temporary necessities, more particularly when the flight of the fugitive has been in the winter."

Benjamin Drew interviewed fugitive slaves living in Canada in 1855 and described the conditions under which they were living in his book, *The Refugee: A Northside View of Slavery* (1856). From Wilbur H. Siebert, *The Underground Railroad from Slavery to Freedom* (1898).

This writer stresses the need of better education facilities for both races. "In many districts of Canada West," he says, "the means of instruction are very scanty, and in some they do not exist at all." There is also need of a better-qualified ministry among the coloured people. "Many of the coloured preachers in Canada West are woefully ignorant," he writes, "thoroughly illiterate and much wanting in the reputation of good manners and a holy life.... It is sad to hear the things which are said and to witness those which are done by these people and which furnish subjects of jest and sport to the profane." He adds that this class of preacher tries to keep his people away from the whites.

In preparation for a state convention of coloured people, held at Cincinnati in January 1852, information was sought from Canada as to the success that was attending the fugitives there. Henry Bibb was asked to make a statement, which he published in his paper,[31] giving much interesting information concerning the refugees at this time. He was asked particularly with regard to the moral standards of his people, and his answer was that the morals of the fugitives in Canada were as high as among their people in the northern states, and compared favourably with the white population, though there was still need for improvement. "Mentally, we find our people far behind the intelligence of the age," he says in his statement.

> Just as in the States, we have scarcely any professional men among us, while we are well satisfied that they would be well supported in Canada West. We are sorry to be compelled to admit that along the frontier we have to contend with Yankee prejudice against colour, although unlike that which is so formidable in the United States. There it is bolstered up by law — here it has no foundation to stand upon and we can live it down. As to there being legal obstacles in the way of our advancement, we know of none. The laws that apply to the Black men apply with equal force to the white men also, and there is no distinction here among men based on the colour of the skin so far as the law is concerned, with but one exception, and that was asked for by the coloured people and the

Roman Catholics, and their prayer was granted. The request, however, was not made by the intelligent portion of the coloured population, but by a lot of ignoramuses who were made fools of and who knew not what they were doing. Such men are hardly fit to live or die. The prayer of the petitioners was that coloured persons might have separate schools for their children if they asked for them, and that the Catholics and Protestants might do the same — not that they shall have these distinctions but that they may have them if asked for. We are happy to inform you that there is no compulsion or necessity in Canada for coloured schools or coloured churches and that every man who respects himself will be respected.

It would be impossible for us to state adequately the pecuniary condition of the people of colour in Canada, but we should think they were worth not less than $200,000.… Wild lands may be bought within five miles of the Detroit River at from $3 to $5 acre, such as will produce from 25 to 40 bushels of wheat to the acre and on which anything will grow and do well that will do well in Ohio soil. There is no difficulty in selling any kind of produce here that the farmer can produce and that without traveling over a distance of 10 miles with it. Corn is worth 50¢ per bushel, wheat 65¢, oats 31¢, potatoes 50¢, butter 15¢, lard 10¢, pork $4.50, beef $3.50, eggs 20¢ per dozen and chickens $1.50 per dozen the year round. The farmer who cannot live in Canada West with rich fertile soil beneath his feet, with a mild climate and with an anti-slavery government over his head, possessing commercial advantages inferior to none in North America, must be a little too lazy to work and would die a pauper should he be placed in a country flowing with milk and honey.

A picture rather less favourable is presented in a letter from Isaac J. Rice, missionary at Amherstburg, appearing in *The Liberator* of

November 23, 1849. He is concerned over the helplessness of the people coming in. "Whole families reach us," he says, "needing clothing, provisions, a home for a few days until arrangements can be made for life, and all this amid strangers, the prejudiced. They are driven from schools in the States, they are no better here. If they go in schools by themselves, their portion of public money is allowed; but Canadians will not teach them, so that your teachers from the States must do it and aid them also about getting lands and various other ways. We have received at our house and clothed more than 50 from the South."

Conditions among the fugitives on the Detroit River at the end of 1850 and early in 1851 are described by A.L. Power of Farmington, Michigan, in a communication to Henry Bibb's newspaper and published in the February 12, 1851 issue. Mr. Power, with a Mr. Benham, crossed over to Windsor about the middle of January, bringing a team load of provisions, bedding, and wearing apparel collected at various points. They proceeded to "the barracks" near Windsor, where 16 or 18 families were sheltered.

"Most of them were in want of food and clothing; some were sick, and others could not get employment." They proceeded from Windsor to Sandwich.

> There we found some families in the most deplorable state of destitution that I ever saw. Some of them were sick, in miserable huts, without food or clothes sufficient to cover their shivering limbs; one family of eight or nine children, some of whom were almost in a state of nudity, without a bed in the house and the weather intensely cold. I was favourably impressed with the effort Mrs. Bibb has put forth in commencing a school for the education of the coloured children around here. We visited her school, some of the children read and spelled very well.... The room is badly constructed for a school, there being but one window and no desks or tables and poorly seated.

Negro refugees were found enrolled in the Canadian militia from an early date. There were coloured men on the Canadian side in the War of

1812, and during the troubles of 1837–38 they were much in evidence. Sir Francis Bond Head speaks of their promptness in answering the call to arms,[32] while Reverend Jermain W. Loguen says that he was in command of a Black company in 1838.[33] Reverend Josiah Henson, founder of the Dawn colony, was on active service during 1838, and did garrison duty at Amherstburg for several months. He was present when the schooner *Anne* affair took place in January 1838. "The coloured men," he says, "were willing to defend the government that had given them a home when they fled from slavery."[34]

A somewhat unusual comment on the loyalty of the Negroes in Canada, from no less a personage than William Lyon Mackenzie, is to be found in the fourth annual report of the American Anti-Slavery Society,[35] being a reply to an agent of the society who visited Canada at the beginning of 1837 and solicited from certain of the public men of the province their opinions of the Negroes as citizens. Mackenzie writes under the date of January 30, 1837:

> Sir, In reply to your inquiries I beg to offer as my opinion with much diffidence, 1st, That nearly all of them are opposed to every species of reform in the civil institutions of the colony — they are so extravagantly loyal to the Executive that to the utmost of their power they uphold all the abuses of government and support those who profit by them.
>
> 2nd; As a people they are as well behaved as a majority of the whites, and perhaps more temperate. 3rd; To your third question (regarding crime), I would say, not more numerous. 4th; Cases in which coloured people ask public charity are rare, as far as I can recollect. I am opposed to slavery whether of whites or Blacks, in every form. I wish to live long enough to see the people of this continent, of the humblest classes, educated and free, and held in respect, according to their conduct and attainments, without reference to country, colour, or worldly substance. But I regret that an unfounded

fear of a union with the United States on the part of the coloured population should have induced them to oppose reform and free institutions in this colony, whenever they have had the power to do so. The apology I make for them in this matter is that they have not been educated as freemen.

I am, your respectful, humble servant,
W.L. Mackenzie

In this report there also appear letters from Captain R.G. Dunlop, member of Parliament for the County of Huron, and from the Honourable John H. Dunn, receiver general for Upper Canada. Both speak well of the refugees. Captain Dunlop says that "There are not in His Majesty's dominions a more loyal, honest, industrious, temperate and independent class of citizens than the coloured people of Upper Canada," while Honourable Mr. Dunn speaks of them as "truly loyal subjects of the government ... both temperate and well behaved."

It was hardly to be expected that the refugees in Canada would be left entirely undisturbed by their former masters. There were several attempts to find some flaw in the Canadian laws that would enable fugitive slaves to be recovered by their masters. One of the earliest cases of this kind was that of a Negro named Moseby, who arrived at Niagara about 1836. His former owner traced him to Canada and applied for his surrender on the grounds that he had stolen a horse to make his good escape. The case came before the governor, Sir Francis Bond Head, who thought that the owner's application was in order. Moseby was arrested and lodged in the Niagara jail. There was widespread sympathy manifested for the unfortunate Negro, and petitions were sent to the governor on his behalf. Sir Francis Head replied that he must give the man up as a felon, though he would have armed the province to protect a slave. The Negroes in the Niagara district were particularly aroused, and declared that they would oppose by force any attempt to take Moseby out of Canada. The order finally came for the delivery of the prisoner to his owner, but when the Negro was brought out of the jail a mob attacked the officers and a fatal encounter resulted. In the resulting confusion Moseby escaped and was not pursued. William Kirby* is the authority for the statement that he [Moseby] resided until his death at St. Catharines and Niagara.[36]

Another case of similar nature also came before Sir Francis Bond Head, that of a slave named Jesse Happy,[37] who had run away from his master in Kentucky, also taking a horse to aid his escape. His return was demanded on a charge of horse stealing, but before giving a decision the governor referred the case to the colonial secretary in a memorandum dated at Toronto, October 8, 1837, and asking for instructions as to general policy. "I am by no means desirous," he wrote, "that this province should become an asylum for the guilty of any colour; at the same time the documents submitted with this dispatch will, I conceive, show that the subject of giving up fugitive slaves to the authorities of the adjoining Republican states is one respecting which it is highly desirable I should receive from Her Majesty's government specific instructions." Proceeding, the governor said:

> It may be argued that a slave escaping from bondage on his master's horse is a vicious struggle between two guilty parties, of which the slave owner is not only the aggressor, but the blackest criminal of the two. It is the case of the dealer in human flesh versus the stealer of horse flesh; and it may be argued that if the British government does not feel itself authorized to pass judgment on the plaintiff neither should it on the defendant. The clothes and even the manacles of the slave are undeniably the property of his master, and it may be argued that it is as much of a theft in the slave walking from slavery to liberty in his master's shoes as riding on his master's horse; and yet surely a slave

---

* Editors' Note: William Kirby (1817–1906) was the British-born editor of the *Niagara Mail* newspaper. It was published at Niagara-on-the-Lake, Kirby's tenure beginning in 1839. A prolific writer and poet, he produced a number of novels and historical works in his lifetime, and was president of Lundy's Lane Historical Society. His *Annuals of Niagara* (1896) is the most likely source for Landon's citation.

walking from slavery to liberty in his master's shoes as riding on his master's horse; and yet surely a slave breaking out of his master's house is not guilty of the same burglary which a thief would commit who should force the same locks and bolts in order to break in.

Sir Francis urged as a further objection to the rendition of fugitive slaves that, even if acquitted of crime by a state court, the fugitive would be no better off, for he would at once be seized and forced back into slavery. His conclusion was that "the slave states have no right, under the pretext of any human treaty to claim from the British government, which does not recognize slavery, beings who by slave law are not recognized as men, and who actually existed as brute beasts in moral darkness until on reaching British soil they heard, for the first time in their lives, the sacred words 'Let there be light and there was light.' From that moment, it is argued, they were created men, and if this be true, it is said that they cannot be held responsible for conduct prior to their existence."

The same question was brought before the British Colonial Office in 1840 in a communication from the coloured people of Upper Canada through Mr. Eduard de St. Remy.[38]*

A decision had been given by the British government in 1839 relative to the surrender of criminals and fugitives escaping from the Danish West Indies into the British possessions nearby, and the dispatch relating to this contained the following declaration: "Where the criminals, whether male or female, shall be satisfactorily proved to the British colonial authorities to have been guilty of murder or any other heinous crime

---

* Editors' Note: Eduard de St. Remy is a little-known figure in Canadian history. Born in England to Huguenot parents, his family had immigrated to Upper Canada from Jamaica by about 1832. His mother ran a private academy on the present grounds of Ryerson University at Toronto, and his brother, Edmond, became the French master at Upper Canada College between 1852 and 1860. De St. Remy was an associate of Upper Canada graduate Peter Gallego, the son of free African-American immigrant Philip Gallego of Virginia. Gallego and de St. Remy were officers of the largely African-Canadian British-American Anti-Slavery Society, founded at Toronto in the early 1830s, and both men corresponded with the New-York based *Colored American* on behalf of the organization.

which the laws of all nations visit with extreme punishment, the safety of society demands that such a criminal should be brought to justice, and it would become the duty of governors of colonies to afford every assistance for his apprehension and restitution to take his trial in the foreign colony in which his crime may have been committed."

The Canadian Negroes were suspicious that this seemingly fair instruction might have a bearing on their status as citizens of Upper Canada. What if charges were trumped up which would be accepted by the Canadian courts? They presented their point of view as follows:

> The coloured population of Canada distinctly disavow the desire of being screened from the punishment due to any offence cognizable by the regular tribunals, and which would give them the benefit of trial, although they might reasonably dread a surrender, even in such a case, from the consciousness that if acquitted they would again be involved in cruel, irremediable slavery; and they pray to be sheltered from the fabrications of masters who charge them with crimes of which they are themselves accusers, judges, juries and punishers.

Further supporting their claim, the petitioners pointed out the discriminations against Negroes in American courts of law and asked that there should be the most thorough sifting of evidence in any case where the surrender of a fugitive Negro was asked.

Two other fugitive cases may be noted briefly. In 1847, a Negro was arrested at Sandwich and charged with murder. An American philanthropist named Young interested himself in the matter, and it was shown that while the Negro had escaped from slavery the murder charge was a fabrication. He was consequently freed.[39] In 1856, a Negro named Archy Lanton was arrested in southwestern Ontario and charged with horse stealing. By the connivance of two magistrates, whose names are given as Wilkinson and Woodbridge, he was spirited away and probably taken back to slavery. The two magistrates were at once discharged from office. This appears to be the only case on record where Canadian law did not protect a fugitive.[40]

The most famous fugitive case in Canadian annals was that of the Missouri Negro, [John] Anderson, in 1860.[41] Anderson was arrested in Canada and charged with the murder of a Missouri planter, whom he had stabbed while attempting to make his escape from slavery. The alleged crime had happened seven years before, but the friends of the murdered slaver seem to have been steadily on the trail of the Negro. The trial attracted much attention in Canada, was dragged into the politics of the day, and even became the cause of a difference of opinion between the British and Canadian authorities over a question of jurisdiction of courts. Anderson was first brought to trial in Brantford, where ugly charges were made against the presiding magistrate. Following the trial in Brantford, an appeal was made for the release of the prisoner. This was refused, and the case came up before the Court of Queen's Bench, where the judges divided, Chief Justice Robinson and Justice Burns pronouncing against Anderson, with Justice McLean dissenting. At this stage, a writ of habeas corpus was issued by the Court of Queen's Bench in London, England. The right of a British court to interfere in this way was at once challenged by the Canadian government, but while the dispute was raging Anderson's case was brought before Chief Justice Draper in the Court of Common Pleas. Here, the prisoner was freed on the basis of certain technicalities. Anderson then disappears from view.

This attempt to secure the return of Anderson to his former state was brought under the extradition clause of the Webster-Ashburton Treaty of 1842, though it seems to be quite clear that the British government had not intended that this clause should ever be a means of rendering slaves back to their masters. At a public meeting held in Toronto on December 19, 1860, John Scoble, to whom reference has already been made, told of interviewing Lord Brougham and Lord Aberdeen when the bill was before Parliament, and when Scoble was secretary of the British Anti-Slavery Society. Lord Ashburton had told him that "the article in question was no more designed to touch the fugitive slave than to affect the case of deserters or parties charged with high treason." Lord Aberdeen also told Scoble that instructions would be sent to Canada that in the case of fugitive slaves, great care must be taken to see that the treaty did not work toward their ruin. When this was communicated to Lord Metcalfe, the governor of the day, he declared that he would never be a party to wronging a fugitive.[42]

The position of the British government on this question is further shown by the fact that, in moving the second reading of the bill to ratify the treaty, Lord Aberdeen stated that it was not intended to deliver up fugitives found in Canada. To escape from slavery was not, he felt, a crime; on the contrary, the condition of the slave attempting to escape was to be regarded with much sympathy. Lord Brougham agreed with this view, regarding it as a settled fact that a slave arriving in British territory would not, under any circumstances, be claimed or rendered liable to further service. Lord Ashburton's own view was set forth in a letter to Thomas Clarkson, president of the British Anti-Slavery Society, in which he stated that Negroes would be given up only for the crimes specifically mentioned in the treaty. The use of a boat or any means of escape was not robbery, and could not be so construed. Clarkson lost no time in communicating this view to the Canadian authorities, pointing out that Great Britain would watch with some anxiety the outcome of the treaty when brought into operation, and expressing the hope that Canadians would exercise all possible humanity toward the fugitives.[43]

Most of those who inquired into the condition of the refugees in Canada West noted a desire for economic independence. This is reflected in the steady succession of protests from their leaders against the sometimes unwise philanthropy on their behalf.

It is rather interesting to note these protests against gifts of food, clothing, etc., except for the sick and the aged. There are strong condemnations of "begging" by Reverend Samuel Ringgold Ward, Henry Bibb, and others. Bibb frequently draws attention to the "begging" propensities of Reverend Isaac J. Rice, the missionary at Amherstburg. At the beginning of 1852, Rice printed a little paper called the *Amherstburg Quarterly Mission Journal*, of which 5,000 copies were to be distributed and in which he appealed for clothes, bedding, provisions, etc., setting forth a grim picture of the needs.

"Nothing can be more false than such a misrepresentation of things," is the comment of Bibb. "How long are we to be represented as a nation of paupers, in nakedness and starvation? There is no respectable missionary who has not given his protest against the begging system, as derogatory to our character and a hindrance to our advancement, and the time has come when all such beggars should be considered and treated as impostors."[44]

At about the same time, a meeting was held at Ann Arbor, Michigan, where there were many refugees and many friends of refugees, protesting against agents coming from Canada unless they had the personal guarantee of the editor of the *Voice of the Fugitive*. It was stated that there were then five able-bodied men out begging for "the poor fugitives in Canada."

The desire for improvement expressed itself in various ways. At St. Catharines there was established a "Refugee Slaves' Friends Society" to bear testimony against slavery and to promote the education of the fugitives. Several influential men were associated with this society, including William H. Merritt, MPP, and Mayor Elias Adams. Temperance societies were formed in several of the settlements. At New Canaan almost every man, woman, and child was a member of the temperance society. The same was true to almost as great a degree at Windsor and Sandwich. At Amherstburg there was a "Young Men's Educating and Temperance Society" for some years.

During the 1850s, the industrial conditions of Canada West were favourable for the refugees, railway building providing work at good wages for many. Bibb's little paper (the *Voice of the Fugitive*) contains advertisements of railroad contractors and others looking for labourers. A typical advertisement (May 7, 1851) offers $10 a month and board. The issue of November 5, 1851 reports that over 2,500 Negroes are at work on the Canada Railway, the work being driven ahead rapidly in the expectation that trains would be running between Niagara Falls and Windsor within 15 months. The issue of Bibb's paper of April 22, 1852, carried an advertisement for 1,000 labourers to work on the Great Western Railway near Windsor. Many others turned their attention to agriculture and market gardening. The Detroit market, then as now, offered opportunities to Canadian producers of foodstuffs, and the refugees on the Canadian side of the river were quick to avail themselves of this.

"We saw a coloured friend of ours today cross on the ferry boat with about 200 dozen of eggs, six or eight turkeys, with chickens and butter also, and they are continually going over with loads of a like character." So writes Bibb in his paper in June 1852, supporting his earlier contention that "Canada is no place for barbers, bootblacks and table waiters.... We want farmers, mechanics and professional men." Elsewhere, he speaks of crops of tobacco and sweet potatoes satisfactorily raised and sold.[45]

The morality of the Negro refugees in Canada was commented upon by several observers of some note. The frequent violation of domestic relations in slavery conditions inevitably reacted upon the refugees' home lives, and took away one of the incentives to constancy. But, upon arriving in Canada, one of the first things many slaves did was to have their plantation union reaffirmed by the form of marriage legal in Canada.

Dr. Howe noticed that the refugees were settled in families, that marriage meant something to them, and that sensuality seemed less in freedom.* Mrs. Laura Haviland, who was engaged in missionary educational work among the refugees for some time, has much to say about the morals of the race in her book, *A Woman's Life Work*.[46] She found a keen desire for education among the refugees, and on Sundays the coloured people came in great numbers to her Sunday school. The reading of the Bible was apparently a real delight to these people, most of whom, if they could read at all, could only spell it laboriously out word by word. Dr. Howe notes that in Canada the religion of the Negroes was "less nasal and more practical" than among their race in the South. Their religious instincts were displayed in charity to the sick and to poverty-stricken newcomers. Their attitude toward women was courteous and honourable. Dr. Howe was pleased to find no spirit of vengeance against the old masters. Rather, there was a desire to forget the past now that they had begun life anew.

Occasionally, there were echoes in Canada of the colonization projects that were for so many years held up in the United States as a

---

* Editors' Note: Samuel Gridley Howe was referring to the upright and moral lives led by former slaves in Canada. In the United States, enslaved African-American women were subjected to unwanted sexual advances by their owners and other whites from whom they had no means of protecting themselves. This led to the unfair implication that it was the enslaved women who were immoral, rather than their owners, a charge that Howe denied from his own observations in Canada.

solution for the future of the Black race. In 1858 there was a convention held in Chatham, attended by delegates from the northern states, at which emigration to Africa was discussed, and a decision was reached to send Martin R. Delany to spy out the land. There was little inducement, however, for the refugees in Canada to leave their new-found freedom. They were themselves colonizationists by their own free will and could see their numbers increasing every year. Had the Civil War held off for another five years, the continued immigration of the Black race might have become more of a problem for the country, since even in the 1850s there were some who thought that more Negroes were coming in than could be properly looked after. With the opening of the war, however, the migration visibly slackened, and when the war was over quite a number of refugees left Canada, many returning to the South, where their relatives had remained. Thus, only a portion of those to whom Canada had offered freedom and security remained, and it is their descendants chiefly who are now found in the cities and towns of Ontario. In recent years, the number of coloured people in the province has not increased noticeably, although there has been an infusion of the race from the West Indies that differs slightly from the older stock, whose coming to Canada forms so romantic a page in our history.

15

Canadian Negroes and the Rebellion of 1837

Journal of Negro History, *vol. 7, no. 4 (October 1922), 377–79*

There are a number of interesting references in the literature of the times to the part played by Negro refugees in defending the frontier of Canada during the troubles of 1837–38. The outbreaks of rebellion in both Upper and Lower Canada in 1837 were followed by a series of petty attacks along the border in which American sympathizers participated.

Sandwich, on the Detroit River, was one of the objectives of the attacking parties, and there were also threats on the Niagara River frontier. One of the parties of "rebels" had taken possession of Navy Island, in the Niagara River, and a small ship, the *Caroline*, was used for conveying supplies. A Canadian party under the command of Commander Andrew Drew crossed the river, seized the ship and, after setting it on fire, allowed it to drift over the falls. This gave rise to an international issue and was the occasion of much bluster on both sides of the border that happily ended as bluster. All along the border on the American side there were "Hunter's Lodges"[1] organized during 1838, and this movement, joined with the widespread political disaffection, made the times unhappy for the Canadian provinces.

Sir Francis Bond Head, who was governor of Upper Canada when the troubles of 1837–38 began, and whose conduct did not tend materially to quelling the unrest, wrote his "apologia" a couple of years later. In it, he speaks of the loyalty of the coloured people, almost all of whom were refugees from slavery. He says:

> When our coloured population were informed that American citizens, sympathizing with their sufferings, had taken violent possession of Navy Island, for the double

object of liberating them from the domination of British rule, and of imparting to them the blessings of republican institutions, based upon the principle that all men are born equal, did our coloured brethren hail their approach? No, on the contrary, they hastened as volunteers in wagonloads to the Niagara frontier to beg from me permission that, in the intended attack upon Navy Island, they might be permitted to form the forlorn hope — in short they supplicated that they might be allowed to be foremost to defend the glorious institutions of Great Britain.[2]

Reverend Jermain W. Loguen, in the narrative of his life, says that he was urgently solicited by the Canadian government to accept the captaincy of a company of Black troops who had been enrolled during the troubles. As the affair was about all over due to the joint efforts of the Canadian and American governments, he did not accept the offer, but he makes this interesting comment:

The coloured population of Canada at that time was small compared to what it is now; nevertheless, it was sufficiently large to attract the attention of the government. They were almost to a man, fugitives from the States. They could not, therefore, be passive when the success of the invaders would break the only arm interposed for their security, and destroy the only asylum for African freedom in North America. The promptness with which several companies of Blacks were organized and equipped, and the desperate valor they displayed in this brief conflict, are an earnest of what may be expected from the

Josiah Henson of the Dawn Settlement as he appeared as an older man. In the 1837 Rebellion, he fought as a gunner on the side of the Crown. From his autobiography, *Uncle Tom's Story: An Autobiography of the Rev. Josiah Henson (Harriet Beecher Stowe's Uncle Tom) from 1789 to 1876*, edited by John Lobb, 1876.

swelling thousands of coloured fugitives collecting there, in the event of a war between the two countries.[3]

Josiah Henson, founder of the Dawn Settlement in Upper Canada and famous as the reputed original of Mrs. Harriet Beecher Stowe's Uncle Tom, says in his narrative that he was captain of the Second Company of Essex Coloured Volunteers, and that he and his men assisted in the defence of Fort Malden (Amherstburg) from Christmas 1837 to May 1838. He says further that he assisted in the capture of the schooner *Anne*, an affair that took place on January 9, 1838.[4]

John MacMullen, in his *History of Canada*, writes that among the troops on the border during 1838 "were two hundred Indians from Delaware, and a body of coloured men, settlers in the western part of the province, the poor hunted fugitives from American slavery, who had at length found liberty and security under the British flag."[5]

A rather interesting aftermath of the rebellion is contained in an item appearing in the *Amherstburg Courier* of March 10, 1849, reporting on a meeting of Negroes in Sandwich Township to protest against the Rebellion Losses Bill.[6] Colonel Prince was thanked for his opposition to the measure.[7]

Eighty years after the rebellion, the Negro men of Canada were again called upon to fight, this time in another land and in a conflict that was destined to affect every race in every land. The service that was rendered in the Canadian army by the coloured companies of pioneers will some day receive due recognition at the hands of an historian. In the meantime, it is not forgotten by the people of Canada.

16

Canadian Negroes and the John Brown Raid

Journal of Negro History, *vol. 6, no 2 (April 1921) 174–82*

Canada and Canadians were intimately connected with the most dramatic incident in the slavery struggle prior to the opening of the Civil War, the attack of John Brown and his men on the federal arsenal at Harper's Ferry, Virginia, on the night of Sunday, October 16, 1859. The blow that Brown struck at slavery in this attack had been planned on broad lines in Canada more than a year before, at a convention held in Chatham, Ontario, from May 8–10, 1858. In calling this convention in Canada, Brown doubtless had two objects in view: to escape observation and to interest Canadian Negroes in his plans for freeing their enslaved race on a scale never before dreamed of, and in a manner altogether new. It was Brown's idea to gather a band of determined and resourceful men, to plant them somewhere in the Appalachian Mountains near slave territory, and from their mountain fastness to run off the slaves, ever extending their area of operations and eventually settling the Negroes in the territory that they had long tilled for others. He believed that operations of this kind would soon demoralize slavery in the South, and he counted on getting enough help from Canada to give the initial impetus.

What went on at Chatham in May 1858 is fairly definitely known. Brown came to Chatham on April 30 and sent out invitations to what he termed "a quiet convention ... of true friends of freedom," requesting attendance on May 10. The sessions were held on May 8 and May 10, Saturday and Monday, and were attended by 12 white men and 33 Negroes. William C. Monroe, a coloured preacher, acted as chairman. Brown himself made the opening and principal speech of the convention, outlining plans for carrying on a guerilla warfare against the whites that would free the slaves, who might afterwards be settled in the more mountainous districts.

Fanatical white abolitionist John Brown spent the winter before his raid on the military arsenal at Harper's Ferry, Virginia, in Chatham, Ontario. From *The Underground Railroad from Slavery to Freedom* by Wilbur H. Siebert, 1898.

He expected that many of the free Negroes in the northern states would flock to his standard, that slaves in the South would do the same, and that some of the free Negroes in Canada would also accompany him.

The main business before the convention was the adoption of a constitution for the government of Brown's Black followers in the carrying out of his weird plan of forcible emancipation. Copies of the constitution were printed after the close of the Chatham gathering and later furnished as evidence against Brown and his companions when their plans came to ground and they were tried in the courts of Virginia. Brown himself was elected commander-in-chief, John H. Kagi was named secretary of war, George B. Gill, secretary of the treasury, Owen Brown, one of Brown's sons, treasurer, Richard Realf, secretary of state, and Alfred M. Ellsworth and Osborne Anderson, coloured, were named members of the congress.

It was more than a year before Brown could proceed with the execution of his plan. Delays of various kinds had upset his original plans, but early in June 1859, he went to Harper's Ferry with three companions and rented a farm near that town. Others joined them at intervals until at the time of their raid he had 18 followers, four of whom were Negroes. The story of the attack and its failure need not be told here. It is sufficient to say that when the fighting ended on Tuesday morning, October 18, John Brown himself was wounded and a prisoner; ten of his party, including two of his sons, were dead, and the others were fugitives from justice. Brown was given a preliminary examination on October 25, and on the following day was brought to trial at Charlestown. Public sentiment in Virginia undoubtedly called for a speedy trial, but there was evidence of panicky feeling in the speed with which John Brown was rushed to punishment. On Monday, October 31, the jury, after 45 minutes' deliberation, returned a verdict of guilty of treason, conspiracy with slaves to rebel, and murder in the first degree. On November 2, the sentence was pronounced, that Brown should be hanged on December 2. As the trap dropped under him that day, Colonel Preston, who commanded the military escort, pronounced the words: "So perish all such enemies of Virginia. All such enemies of the Union. All such foes of the human race." That was the unanimous sentiment of Virginia. But in the North, Longfellow wrote in his journal: "This will be a great date in our history; the date of a new revolution, quite as much needed as the old one."[1] And Henry David Thoreau declared: "Some 1,800 years ago Christ was crucified; this morning, perchance Captain Brown was hung. These are the two ends of a chain that is not without its links."[2]

John Brown's raid on Harper's Ferry made a profound impression in Canada. Although the Chatham convention had been secret, there were some Canadians who knew that Brown was mediating a bold stroke, and could see at once the connection between Chatham and Harper's Ferry. The raid was reported in detail in the Canadian press, and widely commented upon editorially. In a leading article extending over more than one column of its issue of November 4, 1859, the *Globe* of Toronto pointed out that the execution of Brown would but serve to make him remembered as "a brave man who periled property, family, life itself, for an alien race." His death, continued the editor, would make the raid valueless as political capital for the South, which might expect other Browns to arise. References in this article to the Chatham convention indicate that George Brown, editor of the *Globe*, knew what had been going on in Canada in May 1858. Three weeks later, the *Globe*, with fine discernment, declared that if the tension between the North and the South continued, civil war would be inevitable and "no force that the south can raise can hold the slaves if the north wills that they be free."[3] On the day of Brown's execution the *Globe* said: "His death will aid in awakening the North to that earnest spirit which can alone bring the South to understand its true position," and added that it was a "rare sight to witness the ascent of this fine spirit out of the money-hunting, cotton-worshipping American world."[4] Once again, with insight into American affairs, it predicted that "if a Republican president is elected next year, nothing short of a dissolution of the union will satisfy them (the cotton states)."

The special interest taken by the *Globe* in American affairs and its sane comment on the developments in the slavery struggle were due to George Brown's understanding of the situation, resulting from his residence for a time under the stars and stripes before coming to Canada. The feeling of the public in Toronto over the execution of John Brown was shown by the large memorial service held in St. Lawrence Hall on December 11, 1859, at which the chief speaker was Reverend Thomas M. Kinnaird, who himself had attended the Chatham convention.[5] In his address, Mr. Kinnaird referred to a talk he had had with Brown, in which the latter said that he intended to do something definite for the liberation of the slaves or perish in the attempt. The collection that was taken up at this meeting was forwarded to Mrs. Brown. At Montreal, a great mass meeting was held in St. Bonaventure Hall, attended by over one thoussnd people, at which resolutions of sympathy were passed. Among those on the platform at this meeting were L.H. Holton, afterwards a member of the Brown-Dorian and Macdonald-Dorian administrations,* and John Dougall, founder of the Montreal *Witness*. At Chatham and other places in the western part of the province similar meeting were held.

The slaveholding states were by no means blind to the amount of support and encouragement that was coming from Canada for the

---

* Editors' Note: Here Landon refers to the joint government of the Canadas by Quebec politician Antoine-Aimé Dorian and Canada West's George Brown. They governed for only two days in August 1858, after Prime Minister John A. Macdonald and George Étienne Cartier's ministry lost on a vote of non-confidence. Then, when Dorian and Brown's government fell, Macdonald and Cartier formed a new administration; this is known as the "Double Shuffle" in Canadian politics. In 1863–64, Dorian, with John Sandfield Macdonald again formed a joint government between Canada East (French Canada) and Canada West (what is now Ontario), the so-called Macdonald-Dorian administration.

abolitionists.[6] They were quite aware that Canada itself had an active abolitionist group. They probably had heard of the Chatham convention; they knew of it, at least, as soon as the raid was over. In his message to the legislature of Virginia immediately after the Harper's Ferry incident, Governor Wise made direct reference to the anti-slavery activity in Canada. "This was no result of ordinary crimes," he declared. " ... It was an extra-ordinary and actual invasion, by a sectional organization, especially upon slaveholders and upon their property in Negro slaves.... A provisional government was attempted in a British province, by our own countrymen, united to us in the faith of confederacy, combined with Canadians, to invade the slave-holding states ... for the purpose of stirring up universal insurrection of slaves throughout the whole south."[7]

Speaking further of what he conceived to be the spirit of the North he said: "It has organized in Canada and traversed and corresponded thence to New Orleans and from Boston to Iowa. It has established spies everywhere, and has secret agents in the heart of every slave state, and has secret associations and 'underground railroads' in every free state."[8]

Speaking on December 22, 1859, to a gathering of medical students who had left Philadelphia, Governor Wise is quoted as saying: "With God's help we will drive all the disunionists together back into Canada. Let the compact of fanaticism and intolerance be confined to British soil."[9] The New York *Herald* quoted Governor Wise as calling upon the president to notify the British government that Canada should no longer be allowed, by affording an asylum to fugitive slaves, to foster disunion and dissension in the United States. Wise even seems to have had the idea that the president might be bullied into provoking trouble with Great Britain over this question. "The war shall be carried into Canada," he said in one of his outbursts.[10]

Sympathy for the South was shown in the comment of a part of the Tory press in Canada, the *Leader* [of Toronto], declaring that Brown's attack on Harper's Ferry was an "insane raid" and predicting that the South would sacrifice the union before submitting to such spoliation.[11] The viewpoint of the *Leader* and its readers may be further illustrated by its declaration that the election campaign of 1860 was dominated by a "small section of ultra-abolitionists who make anti-slavery the beginning,

Osborne Perry Anderson was the only Canadian Black to join in the raid on Harper's Ferry in October 1859. He subsequently published his memoirs of John Brown's raid as *A Voice from Harper's Ferry*, 1861. *Courtesy of the University of Western Ontario Archives, Annie Straith Jamieson Collection.*

middle and end of their creed." As for Lincoln, he was characterized as "a mediocre man and a fourth-rate lawyer,"[12] but then some of the prominent American newspapers made quite as mistaken an estimate of Lincoln at that time.

The collapse of John Brown's great adventure at Harper's Ferry furnished complete proof to the South of Canada's relation to that event. The seizure of his papers and all that they told, the evidence at the trial at Charlestown, and the evidence secured by the senatorial committee that investigated the affair all confirmed the suspicion that in the British provinces to the north there was extensive plotting against the slavery system. The senatorial committee declared in its findings that the proceedings at Chatham had had as their object "to subvert the government of one or more of the States, and, of course, to that extent the government of the United States."[13] Questions were asked of the witnesses before the investigating committee, which showed that in the minds of the members of that committee there was a distinctly Canadian end to the Harper's Ferry tragedy.[14] Their suspicions may have been further confirmed by the fact that Brown's New England confederates, Sanborn, Stearns, and Howe, all fled to Canada immediately after the raid.

In the actual events at Harper's Ferry, the assistance given by Canada was small. Of the men who marched out with Brown on that fateful October night, only one could in any way be described as a Canadian.

This was Osborne Perry Anderson, a Negro born free in Pennsylvania. He was working as a printer in Chatham at the time of the convention and threw in his lot with Brown. He was one of those who escaped at Harper's Ferry. He later wrote an account of the affair, served during the latter part of the Civil War in the Northern army, and died at Washington in 1871. He is described by Hinton as "well educated, a man of natural dignity, modest, simple in character and manners."[15]

There naturally arises the question — why was the aid given to John Brown by the Canadian Negroes so meagre? That Brown had counted on considerable help in his enterprise from the men who joined with him in drafting the "provisional constitution" is certain. John Edwin Cook, one of Brown's close associates, declared in his confession, made after Harper's Ferry, that "men and money had both been promised from Chatham and other parts of Canada."[16] Yet, apart from Anderson, a Negro, only one other Canadian of either colour seems to have had any share in the raid. Dr. Alexander Milton Ross went to Richmond, Virginia, before the blow was struck, as he had promised Brown he would do, and was there when word came of its unhappy ending. Brown evidently counted on Ross being able to keep him in touch with developments at the capital of Virginia.

Chatham had been chosen as the place of meeting with special reference to the effect it might have on the large Negro population resident in the immediate vicinity. There were more Negroes within 50 miles of Chatham than in any other section of Canadian territory, and among them were men of intelligence, education, and daring, some of them experienced in slave raiding. Brown was justified in expecting help from them. There is also evidence that among the Negroes themselves there existed a secret organization, known under various names, having as its object to assist fugitives and resist their masters. Help from this organization was also expected.[17] Hinton says that Brown "never expected any more aid from them than that which would give a good impetus."[18] John Brown himself is quoted by Realf, one of his associates, as saying that he expected aid from the Negroes generally, both in Canada and in the United Sates,[19] but it must be remembered that his plans called for quality rather than quantity of assistance. A few daring men, planted in the mountains of Virginia, would have accomplished his initial purpose better than a thousand.

The real reason why the Canadian Negroes failed to respond in the summer of 1860, when Brown's men were gathering near the boundary line of slavery, seems to be that too great a delay followed after the Chatham convention. The convention was held on May 8 and May 10, 1858, but Brown did not attack Harper's Ferry until the night of October 16, 1859, nearly a year and a half later. The zeal for action that manifested itself in May 1858 had cooled off by October 1859, the magnetic influence of Brown himself had been withdrawn, and the Negroes had entered into new engagements. Frank B. Sanborn says he understood from Brown that he hoped to strike about the middle of May 1858, that is about a week after the convention or as soon as his forces could gather at the required point.[20] The delay was caused by the partial exposure of Brown's plans to Senator Henry Wilson by Hugh Forbes, who had been close to Brown. Panic seized Brown's chief white supporters in New England, the men who financed his various operations, and they decided that the plans must be changed. Brown was much discouraged by their decision, but being dependent upon them for support in his work he submitted and went west to Kansas. Among his exploits there was the running off of more than a dozen slaves, whom he landed safely at Windsor, Canada.

There was some effort made in the early summer of 1859 to enlist the support of the Canadian Negroes,[21] the mission being led by John Brown Jr., who was assisted by Reverend Jermain W. Loguen, a well-known Negro preacher and anti-slavery worker. Together they visited Hamilton, St. Catharines, Chatham, London, Buxton, and Windsor, helping also to organize branches of the League of Liberty among the Negroes. The letters of John Brown Jr. show that there was little enthusiasm for the cause, which, indeed, could only have been presented in an indefinite way. There was more interest at Chatham than elsewhere, as might be expected, but even there it was not sufficiently substantial to bring the men that were needed. Against this rather dismal picture, should be placed some evidence that there were a few Canadians on the way south when the end came.[22]

17

Abolitionist Interest in Upper Canada, 1830–65

Ontario History, *vol. 44 (1952), 165–72*

In the period between 1830 and 1860, during which the slavery issue in the United States was resolved, three groups of the American people had a particular interest in Upper Canada, in each case arising out of their personal relation to the slavery system.

The first of these groups was made up of the Negro slaves, who, since the close of the War of 1812, had been running off from the plantations and, with the help of Quakers and other friendly persons, making their way to freedom in Canada.

The second group was made up of the slaveholders, suffering heavy losses by the disappearance of their property, together with those, chiefly but not entirely in the South, who for business reasons were favourable toward the system.

The third group comprised the opponents of slavery who saw in the freedom of Canada an opportunity for refugees to live as respectable human beings, and also an influence of considerable importance in the moral crusade in which they were engaged.

Much has been written about the first group, their means of escape from slavery, their journeyings to Upper Canada, the aid they received through the Underground Railroad system, and their subsequent experiences in their new home. Scholars have also examined the slaveholders' losses and the efforts made, even in Upper Canada itself, to recover this human property. Less has been written, however, about the interest in Upper Canada shown by abolitionists and other opponents of slavery, and it is with the third mentioned aspect of the slavery question that this paper will deal.

Slaves began to run off to Canada at an early date. Soldiers who had served in the campaigns of the War of 1812 brought back word that no slavery existed in the British province to the north, and it was not long before this was being whispered widely among the slaves. Soon it was reported from the South that slaves were disappearing, while in Upper Canada it was recorded that they were arriving. Captain Charles Stuart, himself an ardent abolitionist, who later engaged actively in the struggle in both England and the United States, has recorded that as early as the five years 1817–22, while he was living in Amherstburg, about 150 refugees came to that place. Captain Stuart proceeded to settle them on small plots of land, and stated that he found them "quite equal to any class of labourers in the country."[1]

From decade to decade, the number of fugitives arriving in the province increased. There were more in the 1830s than in the 1820s, more in the 1840s than in the 1830s, and when the 1850s arrived it was a veritable black stream crossed the international boundary at certain points. This increased migration was a sequel to the new Fugitive Slave Act of 1850, replacing older and somewhat ineffective legislation that had been passed in 1793. The South demanded drastic machinery to recover its runaway slaves, but it paid a high price, for probably nothing else in this decade did more to turn Northern opinion against slavery. Opposition to the act took various forms: state legislation forbidding the use of local jails to house captured runaways, riots when arrested slaves were brought into court, bold rescues, and other forms of defiance. The Fugitive Slave Act of 1850 may properly be regarded as one of the influences that led to the conflict between northern and southern states.

It was estimated early in 1850 that there were about 20,000 Negroes in Upper Canada, most of them in the southwestern section and in the Niagara area, but some also in towns and cities elsewhere. During the year after the passing of the Fugitive Slave Act, probably 5,000 more came in, many of these being from the northern states, since the new act gravely imperilled their safety. This migration continued throughout the whole decade, ceasing only when the Civil War was at its height.

The migration after 1850 had immediate consequences for Upper Canada. The arrival of hundreds of fugitives, many with nothing but the clothes they wore, created serious social problems. It was to meet these

The passage by the United States Congress of the Fugitive Slave Law of 1850 spurred a greatly intensified immigration to Canada. More than 10,000 fugitive slaves and free African Americans crossed the border in the decade before the Civil War. From *The Underground Railroad* by William Still (Philadelphia: Porter & Coates, 1872).

problems, and at the same time to educate the Canadian people on the general question of slavery, that the Anti-Slavery Society of Canada came into existence. Nine days before President [Millard] Fillmore signed the bill passed by Congress, a public meeting was held in the Mechanics' Institute at Toronto "to consider the propriety of taking steps for a public demonstration on behalf of the slaves now flying from bondage to Canada." A second gathering took place on February 26, 1851, in the city hall, with the mayor of the city in the chair. Out of this gathering came the new society with Reverend Michael Willis, principal of Knox Presbyterian College as president; Reverend William McClure, a Methodist minister of the New Connexion branch, as secretary, and Captain Charles Stuart, now living in retirement near Georgian Bay, as corresponding secretary. George Brown, editor of the *Globe,* and Oliver Mowat, destined later to become premier of Ontario, were original members of the executive. Brown's association with the society was of particular value because of the support that his newspaper could provide.

The organization of this distinctively Canadian anti-slavery body is closely linked up with the interest in the Negro in Canada, which for many years had been displayed by the anti-slavery groups in the United States. These people, aware of the fact that the government of Canada received the fugitives and accorded them civil rights, in their turn gave extensive and amazingly efficient help to the Black people, particularly through the machinery of the Underground Railroad. But they went even beyond this by maintaining an interest in the fugitives after they reached Canada, often providing further generous aid. From time to time individuals came into the province, examined conditions, and published their findings in the anti-slavery journals or in book form. It was excellent propaganda for the general anti-slavery cause in the United States.

The first of such visitors whom I have record was Benjamin Lundy, a Quaker born in New Jersey who, as early as 1815, was founder of an anti-slavery society at St. Clairsville, Ohio, established an anti-slavery newspaper, *The Genius of Universal Emancipation,* at Mount Pleasant, Ohio in 1821, and continued its publication at various places, though with occasional interruptions, until 1839. He was for 35 years one of the most unwearied advocates of the freedom of the slave.

Lundy visited Upper Canada in 1832, chiefly with the idea in mind of examining conditions in the Wilberforce Negro settlement in Middlesex County, north of present-day London. Ohio Quakers had secured land from the Canada Company for a group of Negroes driven out of Cincinnati by the enforcement of rigorous Black Laws. If the reports he had received proved correct, Lundy believed that Wilberforce might become an important refuge and place of settlement for coloured people, and would be an alternative to Liberia, in Africa, which had been established a decade earlier by the American Colonization Society as a home for emancipated slaves.

Lundy spent several days at Wilberforce, and his impressions of the place were set down in a series of articles in his newspaper, *The Genius of Universal Emancipation,* in the issues of March, April and May 1832.[2] He had high hopes for the future of Wilberforce, but they were not realized for, after a few years, the colony dwindled and it is today but a memory. Yet, strangely, more has been written about Wilberforce and men associated with it than has been written about any other Negro colony in Upper Canada.[3]

An interesting visitor to Upper Canada in 1844 and again in 1854 was Levi Coffin, who, because of his long and intimate connection with the Underground Railroad, was popularly known as its "president." A prominent businessman in Cincinnati, he had aided hundreds of fugitives on their way to Canada, so that when he visited the province he encountered scores of men and women whom he had met and aided in the past. His home and his warehouses in Cincinnati were well-known as stations on the underground, and were equipped with secret chambers and tunnels to the outside, together with other means of providing for the safety of his charges.

Coffin crossed into Canada at Detroit in September 1844, and proceeded to visit all the Negro communities in Essex County, then went on to Chatham and London and north to Wilberforce. This colony, he tells us, was the only place he visited at which he did not meet people who had slept under his roof or fed at his table on their way to freedom. The explanation of this would be that the original arrivals at Wilberforce were from Cincinnati itself and, while probably aided by Coffin, they did not require the shelter that he gave to others passing through the city. In all he spent about two months in Upper Canada, travelling about on horseback, as there were then no railroads.[4] He gives 40,000 as an estimate of the number of fugitives in Upper Canada at this date. He was again in the province in 1854 and, as before, met many whom he had aided in their movement to Canada. He tells of attending an Emancipation Day celebration a few miles south of Windsor that drew coloured people from a wide area, and was marked by great enthusiasm. On this later visit, Coffin was accompanied by his wife and daughter and by Mrs. Laura S. Haviland, a Michigan woman who worked for several years among the refugees and whose narrative provides us with many interesting details of their lives and experiences.[5]

Negroes who had themselves come up from slavery and knew the system firsthand were used effectively, in both the United States and Canada, in educating the public on the evils of the system. Three such men who were used by the Anti-Slavery Society of Canada during the 1850s were Samuel Ringgold Ward, Jermain Wesley Loguen, and the famous Frederick Douglass. All three were effective speakers, and Douglass had an international reputation as a platform orator.

Ward was born of slave parents on a Maryland plantation in 1817, and gained freedom when his parents ran away to New Jersey and later to New York. He showed ability as a speaker early on, and in 1839 became an agent of the American Anti-Slavery Society. In 1844, he campaigned nationally for the Liberty Party on behalf of James G. Birney, its candidate for the presidency. In 1851, he was implicated in the rescue at Syracuse of the fugitive William Henry ("Jerry"),[6] a runaway from Missouri, and fled to Canada for safety. Here, he almost at once became associated with the new anti-slavery society and was engaged as its agent, lecturing, organizing branches, and aiding newly arrived refugees. In April 1853 he was sent to England, where he created a sensation as an orator and in ten months collected £1,200 for the society's work. He was sometimes referred to in the United States as "the Black Daniel Webster."

Jermain Wesley Loguen, born about 1813 in Tennessee, the natural son of a white resident and a slave mother who had been kidnapped in Ohio, made his escape from slavery by the Underground Railroad about 1835. Making his way through Kentucky, southern Indiana, and Michigan he crossed at Detroit into Canada and went on to Hamilton. He later removed to New York State, where he was first a teacher and then an elder in the African Methodist Episcopal Zion Church, holding pastorates between 1843 and 1850. He was living in Troy, New York, when the Fugitive Slave Act was passed and, finding his safety imperilled, he went to Syracuse, where his home became a station on the Underground Railroad. Here and elsewhere he is said to have assisted 1,500 fugitives on their way to freedom in Canada. In 1851, he, like Samuel R. Ward, was a participant in the "Jerry" rescue at Syracuse and found it wise to take refuge in Canada for a time.

He was still facing an indictment when he returned to Syracuse in 1852, but popular sentiment was such that he was never brought to trial. Later, in the 1850s, he again visited Canada, this time with John Brown Jr. on behalf of the Liberty League, and possibly also to further John Brown's plans. He was made a bishop of his church in 1868, and was re-elected in 1872, but died in the same year.

Frederick Douglass was the outstanding Black abolitionist. Born a slave on a Maryland plantation, he was first introduced to the abolition movement when he attended a Massachusetts anti-slavery convention in 1841. After speaking there, he was employed by several societies and was soon one of the best-known orators in the United States. In 1847 he began publication of a newspaper, the *North Star*. This led to a break with William Lloyd Garrison, of *The Liberator*, who had hitherto been his chief sponsor. The name *North Star* was changed in 1850 to *Frederick Douglass' Paper*. It is an important source in anti-slavery history. Douglass was active in Negro conventions, in the Underground Railroad, and in other efforts to improve the condition of his race. A historian of the Negro in America says of him: "He was endowed with the physical attributes of an orator; a magnificent tall body, a head crowned with a mass of hair, deep-set flashing eyes, a firm chin and a rich melodious voice. Few anti-slavery leaders did so much to carry the case of the slave to the people of the United States and Europe in the generation before the Civil War."[7]

Douglass came to Toronto at the time of the organization of the Anti-Slavery Society of Canada in 1851, and we find him recorded among those present at a conference held in George Brown's office at the *Globe* on March 31, 1851. Subsequently, he was a speaker at meetings held by the society, as was also Samuel R. Ward, already mentioned. Other speakers who gave aid to the society were George Thompson, MP, the noted English abolitionist, John Scoble, secretary of the British and Foreign Anti-Slavery Society, and Reverend Samuel J. May. May was a Massachusetts Unitarian clergyman and an ardent reformer. He interested himself in such a variety of humanitarian and betterment efforts that Bronson Alcott once described him as "the Lord's chore boy." He was for a time secretary and general agent of the Massachusetts Anti-Slavery Society, and an agent also of the Underground Railroad, his home being a station on the route.

Many more names might be mentioned of anti-slavery workers who gave aid to Canada. Elihu Burritt, often referred to as "the learned blacksmith," lectured in both Toronto and Hamilton in the spring of 1857. On March 7, 1857, in St. Lawrence Hall, Toronto, he explained a proposition for the peaceful extinction of slavery in the United States by a united effort of both sections of the republic.[8] Benjamin Drew was another friend of the refugees who visited this province in the early 1850s,

Newly opened on King Street in Toronto, the St. Lawrence Hall hosted the inaugural meeting of the Canadian Anti-Slavery Society on February 26, 1851. This photo is dated 1867. *Courtesy of the Archives of Ontario, Octavius Thompson fonds, F 4356-0-0-0-43.*

travelling to 14 communities where Negroes were numerous, interviewing and securing narratives from no less than 129 individuals. His book, *A North-Side View of Slavery. The Refugee: or the Narratives of Fugitive Slaves in Canada Related by Themselves* (Boston, 1856), is a storehouse of material on the experiences and lives of these people and it was, at the time, a most effective reply to the apologists for slavery and their setting forth of the south-side view of slavery.

The anti-slavery journals, particularly Garrison's *Liberator*, gave much attention to the refugees in Upper Canada. After the passing of the Fugitive Slave Act, *The Liberator* gave almost weekly reports on the migration to Canada, much of it culled from a small Negro newspaper published at Windsor by Henry Bibb and bearing the name the *Voice of the Fugitive*.[9]

Attention has thus far been given chiefly to individuals who aided the anti-slavery cause in Canada. Mention must be made of the part played by one organization. The American Missionary Society, organized at Albany, New York, in 1846, and openly opposed to slavery in its policies, began making grants for work in Canada in its first year. The work thus supported was known as "The Canada Mission." In 1848, the society definitely undertook the support of three missionaries then working in the counties of Essex and Kent: Isaac J. Rice at Amherstburg, John S. Brooks at Mount Hope, and Hiram Wilson, who was dividing his time between Amherstburg and the Dawn Settlement. Amherstburg was the really strategic point, as most of the fugitives were landed there, and it was around Amherstburg that work was chiefly supported. Levi Coffin tells us that he made his headquarters with Isaac J. Rice when he visited Amherstburg in 1844, and he speaks of the heavy task that this missionary had to face. Education was always a feature in the society's work, and was supported generously. For 18 years its workers were active in the Canadian field, but the opening of the Civil War disturbed operations and, finally, in July 1864, the society's publication, the *American Missionary*, had this significant announcement: "The mission among the refugees in Canada has been suspended. Its last missionary, Reverend L.C. Chambers, is now sustained by the people among whom he labours. Some aid has been given and may be continued to sustain teachers there."

In 1858 Canada was visited by the most aggressive of all the abolitionists, John Brown. He was a veteran in the anti-slavery cause, and in the middle of the 1850s had been a spectacular figure in the conflict over slavery in the Territory of Kansas. He had begun to contemplate a blow at slavery that would startle the North out of its seeming indifference, and it was to organize this aggressive effort that he called his now famous "convention" at Chatham. For three days in May 1858, a mixed group of Black and white supporters considered plans laid before them for what was utter defiance of the government of the United States and indifference to their personal safety. Much has been written about this Chatham convention, which need not be repeated here, but it is interesting to note that one of the three buildings in which

Brown and his associates held their meetings is still in existence, as is also the home where he stayed while in Chatham.

The presence of a Judas in the group, who revealed its activities to Washington, delayed the blow until October 1859. It came at Harper's Ferry in Virginia, was a complete failure as an enterprise, and Brown and several of his followers were captured. Brown was placed on trial, condemned to death, and hanged on December 3, 1859. Less than 18 months later, war came between the North and South, a conflict that he had undoubtedly hastened. But his death on the gallows proved a rallying influence for the North. It was significant that the first Northern regiment to march to the front, the 12th Massachusetts, whistled and sang a new song as they marched through Boston streets — "John Brown's Body."

One more example of American interest in this country's relation to the slavery question must be mentioned. This was of an official character. During the war, large numbers of Negroes came into the custody and care of the Northern armies. This, along with a concern for the future, led to the appointment by Secretary of War Stanton in 1863 of a Freedmen's Inquiry Commission, consisting of Samuel Gridley Howe, Robert Dale Owen, and James McKaye. Howe came to Canada to investigate the condition of the refugees in this province and submitted his report in December 1863.[10] Howe was himself an ardent reformer and an abolitionist, and perhaps in some respects took too favourable a view of conditions; but his report, official in character, gives a good picture of the Negro population in this province at the end of the refugee period, for already emancipation had been proclaimed. I shall quote only the concluding paragraph of his report to President Lincoln and Secretary Stanton:

> Finally, the lesson taught by this and other emigrations is that the Negro does best when let alone, and that we must beware of all attempts to prolong his servitude, even under pretext of taking care of him. The white man has tried taking care of the Negro, by slavery, by apprenticeship, by colonization, and has failed

disastrously in all; now let the Negro try to take care of himself. For, as all the blood and tears of our people in this revolutionary struggle will be held as cheap, if they re-establish our Union in universal freedom so all the suffering and misery which his people may suffer in their efforts for self-guidance and support will be held cheap, if they bring about emancipation from the whites.[11]

Had this admonition made by Howe been heeded in the period after the Civil War, what a different situation might have been found in the reconstructed southern states.

18

Captain Charles Stuart, Abolitionist[1]

Profiles of a Province: Studies in the History of Ontario *(Toronto: Ontario Historical Society, 1967), 205–14.*

Few people in Canada or in the United States have ever heard the name of Captain Charles Stuart, though he spent years in each of these two countries. Nor is his name known in England, where, as in the other two countries and in the West Indies as well, he was an active participant in the anti-slavery movements of the first half of the nineteenth century. His name is not to be found in any recent history of the United States, nor in any account of the British emancipation movement, and the *Dictionary of American Biography* gives only a few lines to his career.

Yet here is a man who, after retirement from army service with the British East India Company, was active as a lecturer and pamphleteer during the anti-slavery crusade in England, gave like service to the movement in the United States, and in his later days was an officer in the Anti-Slavery Society of Canada when it was organized in 1851.

Moreover, he is the man whose influence brought Theodore Dwight Weld into the American struggle. The name of Weld is no longer absent from American histories, but today stands high on the roll of those who brought about the freedom of the slaves in the United States. In the revision of the American anti-slavery movement that has been going on during the last two decades the contribution of Weld as organizer and propagandist assumes steadily greater importance.

Those who knew Charles Stuart during his lifetime paid tribute to his deeply religious character. "One of the most devoted Christians I have ever known and an unwearied advocate of the oppressed African," was the judgment of James Cropper, the English philanthropist. "A true man of God, a perfect being" was Theodore Weld's judgment of his friend. There are other similar tributes.

For most of his life a bachelor, he ever went about doing good, and despite the austerity of his life and his many eccentricities he was always beloved. "He was the children's friend," said a contemporary, "for with the tenderness of a woman he had the spirit of a child."

During two periods of his life he resided in Canada. Between 1817 and 1822 he lived at Amherstburg, on the Detroit River. There, he first became acquainted with American slavery through his contact with the numerous fugitives who came to that terminus of the Underground Railroad. From the early 1850s until his death in 1865 he lived at Lora Bay, a little inlet on Georgian Bay, not far from the Village of Thornbury, and in the Thornbury Union Cemetery his grave can be seen today. He was in his 84th year when the end came.

Stuart's reasons for leaving the service of the East India Company are explained in a brief sketch of the man that is among the Weld papers in the William L. Clements Library at the University of Michigan. Stuart was born in Jamaica in 1783, son of a British army officer who had fought in the American Revolution. His parents were Scottish Presbyterians of an extreme Calvinistic type, and his mother, in particular, deeply influenced the boy's character. He was educated in Ireland, and at the age of 18 received a commission in the service of the East India Company. At retirement in 1815 he was "a captain in the 1st Battalion, 27th Regiment, and native infantry." So he described himself when taking the oath of allegiance after coming to Canada.

During his service in India, he was seriously wounded while assisting in the quelling of an insurrection and carried a bullet in his body to the end of his days. At a later date, a new colonel came to the regiment and invited his officers to dine with him on a Sunday, announcing that all of his official dinners would be held on Sundays. Stuart declined the invitation and told the colonel that he regarded his action as a profanation of the Sabbath. From this time, Stuart was regarded with an evil eye by his superior officer, and though he was respected by his fellow officers and his men, his influence was covertly destroyed. Feeling utterly baffled, he eventually resigned his commission and returned to England where, through the influence of friends, he was granted a pension of $800.

This explanation of his retirement differs from that given by Dr. John J. Bigsby, who met Stuart at Amherstburg around 1821, and is entirely different from the story that was current following Stuart's death in 1865. According to these versions, he was in disfavour because of some stand he had taken over the mutiny at Vellore in 1804. According to one story, he had protested against the cruelty in connection with the suppression of the outbreak and had been sent home. But as the mutiny at Vellore was in 1804, and Stuart did not retire until more than ten years later, there does not seem to be a connection between the two. Probably the version given in the Weld manuscript, and which appears to be in Weld's handwriting, is correct. No one knew Stuart better than Weld, or was more in his confidence.

There is no record of Stuart's activities between the time of his return to England and his departure for Canada. There is some indication that it was a period of intense religious conflict that became a crisis when he was at Montreal. "Many are the places," he wrote in his *Emigrant's Guide,* "which are endeared to me by melancholy or by pleasing recollections; but over Montreal, a memorial of struggle and of anxiety, of peace and hope, of truth and holiness, and love, of obedience and of conflict, of tears and joy, throws an influence more dear and sacred to my soul, than it ever before had experienced. In reviewing the days which I spent there in retirement ... as an unknown stranger, and desiring not to be known, a peculiar emotion is on my heart."

Stuart already had a sister in Upper Canada, and had been promised a land grant if he wished to settle in the province. He arrived early in 1817 bearing a letter from Henry Goulburn, undersecretary of state for war and the colonies, to Sir John Sherbrooke, governor of Canada, and also authorization for a grant of land. Governor Sherbrooke sent a copy of the letter to Francis Gore, lieutenant-governor of Upper Canada, recommending Stuart to his notice and protection.

"The object of this gentleman," he wrote, "is to become a settler in Upper Canada where he already has some friends. One of my correspondents acquaints me that Captain Stuart's precise reasons for quitting the Madras establishment are not known to him, but that he is

Charles Stuart shared his land grant of 1,000 acres at Amherstburg with fugitive slave families as they entered the province. Shown here are a cluster of people in front of a farmhouse in the area. The first commercial crop of tobacco in what is now Ontario was produced by Virginia fugitives on land given to them by Stuart. *Courtesy of the Archives of Ontario, McCurdy Collection, 5428.*

assured they are such as reflect no discredit upon him, either professionally or individually; that he was very desirous to have procured orders in the Church of England previous to his quitting England; but neither his own efforts or his friends could effect this object, it having of late been considered objectionable to ordain a soldier or a sailor."

Stuart's land grant was promptly approved, but for the time being he settled at Amherstburg, on the Detroit River. From there he wrote to Gore's successor, Sir Peregrine Maitland, expressing his desire to enter the church. Reverend John Strachan, the rector at York, had, he said, suggested that he seek official approval for a licence to read prayers and preach, and he himself, so he informed Maitland, looked forward to eventual ordination.

There was one impediment, however, that this pious bachelor put before Maitland. "My sentiment," he wrote, "is that intermarriage of Uncles and Nieces is perfectly consistent with God's Holy word and will;

and that restraints placed upon it in society, are the mere fabrications of that kind of reason which brings Divine wisdom to its own bar, and can believe a human inference more infallible than the Word of God."

Maitland, passing upon [ignoring] this theological question, saw no error in Stuart's views, but soon another question arose. Stuart wrote to say that while he would gladly have received ordination from other hands, he could not accept it from Bishop Jacob Mountain, "because I believe him to be an exceedingly antichristian overseer; a secular, not a spiritual character. The feelings and principles I would try to establish would be at decided variance with his principles and his life."

Stuart went to England in the autumn of 1819 and was absent from Canada for almost exactly a year. While abroad he published his first work, *The Emigrant's Guide to Upper Canada; or Sketches of the Present State of that Province, Collected from a Residence Therein During the Years 1817, 1818, 1819. Interspersed with Reflections.*

It was a curious production. Edward Allen Talbot, in his *Five Years Residence in the Canadas*, said that it might be much more appropriately entitled *The Pilgrim's Guide to the Celestial Regions*. While crediting the book with presenting some honest and valuable information respecting the country, Talbot's comment was that it contained "such a confused medley of polemical theology, whining cant and complimentary bombast, that it would require as much patience to travel through this duodecimo volume, as to make a pedestrian tour through the whole of the Upper Province."

Returning to Upper Canada in the autumn of 1820, Stuart reopened correspondence with Maitland, offering copious advice on a variety of subjects until the lieutenant-governor, wearied by the letters, said so in rather plain terms. But Stuart was not easily suppressed. Writing in January 1821, he said that he was both pleased and distressed by Maitland's words; pleased by his candid and gentle style, but regretful of the condemnation pointed at him.

"I have always been aware that you have no time for fruitless correspondence," he wrote, "and I distinctly perceive that my correspondence with you has been worse than useless." Then he added a few further suggestions for bettering the welfare of the province.

But Maitland was not the only one who was wearied by Stuart. At Amherstburg, where he had become a magistrate soon after his arrival in Upper Canada, he became involved in a heated dispute with one of the officers of the Fort Malden garrison over their respective jurisdictions in dealing with civil offences committed by members of the garrison. Colonel J.P. Hawkins wrote to the authorities at Toronto:

> Do pray endeavour to prevail on Sir Peregrine to cause instruction to be sent to this troublesome magistrate, not to interfere unnecessarily with matters that are purely military, as he really seems inclined to be troublesome.
>
> Believing him to be a good-hearted man, I have, hitherto kept on tolerable terms with him, though he has more than once before interfered improperly. In one instance he committed one of the men to gaol, and kept him there for many weeks before he could be tried, after all of which the man was acquitted on trial. You are doubtless aware of Captain Stuart's eccentricity of character, but perhaps not of his having a strong propensity to meddle in the affairs of other people; even, I believe, to the almost neglect of his own.

Stuart tendered his resignation as a local magistrate in October 1821, and peace descended on the Detroit River community.

There is no evidence that Stuart's desire to enter the church advanced further. His wish was to serve as a missionary to the Indians, in whose welfare he was deeply interested, as we see from his repeated communications to the lieutenant-governor. He admitted that he had little talent for acquiring languages. This would have militated against him as a missionary. After he returned from England, however, he found a new outlet for his religious and humanitarian zeal in the fugitives from Southern slavery who were about him at Amherstburg. He recorded that between 1817 and 1822 about 150 Negro fugitives came to the village. "I became more or less acquainted with them all," he wrote in the *West India Question*, "and found them quite equal to any class of labourers in the country ... one of them, a man named Adams, was one of the most interesting persons with whom I have ever met."

A more pleasing picture of Stuart than that by the officer at Fort Malden is given in the *Shoe and Canoe* by Dr. John Bigsby, who was attached to the British section of the commission occupied in the survey of the international boundary. Bigsby met Stuart at Amherstburg, and left this description of the man and his activities: "Although Captain Stewart [*sic*] resided at Amherstburg, and was still 35 years of age, he had passed many years in India, and had had some concern with the mutiny at Vellore; but his part in the affair must have been small; for his jealous masters dismissed him with full pay for life. He was handsome, frank and energetic. His iron frame was indifferent to luxuries or even comforts, any hut was a home, and any food was nourishment, provided he could be doing good to others; for he was, and is, a working Christian."

Bigsby found Stuart engaged in what he described as "waging successful war with the Negro slavery of the United States." He was providing homes for the fugitives from slavery by setting up a Negro colony on a small tract of land in the rear of the village. There, the refugees became his tenants. "The Negro village and the clearances were then just begun," wrote Bigsby. "As it was a very rainy season, the land seemed to be a swamp, and the huts very indifferent affairs, but were thought to be palaces by the freemen who inhabited them. Subsequently heavy crops were obtained from their farms. Captain Stuart had the goodness to walk over some of them with me; and I am glad that I had the discernment to cheer him on in his difficult undertaking."

Bigsby met Stuart again later in the year, near the mouth of the St. Clair River. While he was watching the flooded waters of the Black River, three men on horseback, with large-caped greatcoats, came to the opposite bank and shouted for the ferryman. As none was there, Bigsby took a large "pirogue" (a hollowed tree trunk) and, with a broad, heavy paddle, drove it to the opposite shore. In three trips, he took the party across. It was Stuart and two American clergymen on their way to establish a mission among the "Saguinaw" Indians, on the fertile banks of a river of that name emptying into Lake Huron.

Stuart's first period of residence in Canada terminated in 1822 when he went to Utica, New York, as principal of the Utica Academy, an institution that received its charter in 1814 and opened in 1818. It was an important move for Stuart. Henceforth, his life was to turn in new directions, and through his friendship with Theodore Dwight Weld he was to become one of the noteworthy figures in the anti-slavery cause. Stuart first met Weld at the home of Erastus Clark, a brother of Weld's mother. Clark, one of the founders and a trustee of Hamilton College, had undertaken to finance his nephew's education. When Clark died in 1825, Stuart at once offered to take on this financial obligation, making but one condition, namely, that young Theodore should report quarterly, in writing, on his spiritual progress, doubts, and difficulties. It was the beginning of an almost lifelong friendship.

During the later 1820s, when Reverend Charles G. Finney, the great revivalist, was stirring all of western New York with his preaching, Stuart and Weld came under his influence and were converted. Both joined Finney's "Holy Band" as assistant revivalists, touring the country, preaching, and exhorting. It was a prelude to their later labours in the cause of emancipation.

The curious relations between Stuart and Weld, which began at almost their first meeting, were closer and more intimate than would have been the case had they been father and son. They demonstrated their piety and their friendship in these early years by a daily sunrise "heart meeting," praying each for the other. In the letters that the older man wrote, there are expressions of fervent love. "Theodore," he wrote, "you are mine and I am yours. God made us one from the beginning.... I know that you love me in spite of my unmeetness* and unworthiness, and I love you the more for your love." Young Weld, in his turn, with deepest reverence, could say of Stuart: "While yet a boy I became acquainted with him, and from that time till now our intimacy has been almost that of an individual existence; and yet our creeds and speculative opinions, doctrinal views, and philosophical belief are as far apart as the poles. We are always disagreeing in opinion."

---

* Editors' Note: This comes from the New Testament, meaning unfitness or not deserving of such an honour.

This friendship, beginning in the 1820s, continued unshaken until the early 1860s. By that time Weld was going over to Unitarianism, and Stuart, believing that this would prevent their meeting in the next world, ceased to correspond with him, though in writing to others he still protested his deep love for the younger man. He had first probed Weld's views rather fully, putting to him a series of questions on doctrine. Finally, writing to Weld's brother and sister on September 9, 1861, he declared: "Although Theodore has entirely separated himself from me except indeed I would prefer him to Christ and I have ceased in consequence to correspond with him; yet have I never forgotten our former love and I ever mourn over his presently culpable apathy." During the remaining years of Stuart's life, there appears to have been no correspondence between the two men, whose friendship had hitherto been closer than that of brothers.

Stuart had entered the United States in 1822 but took no part in any anti-slavery effort at this time. Indeed, the decade was one of the most barren in the history of the struggle. The conflict from 1818–20 over the entrance of Missouri as a slave state had weakened the movement, and the anti-slavery societies that had flourished earlier, even in the South, tended to disappear at this time. Benjamin Lundy was almost the only man holding up the anti-slavery banner until the appearance of William Lloyd Garrison and *The Liberator* in 1831. Elsewhere, however, a great struggle was under way. In England, the agitation for emancipation of the slaves in the British colonies was making progress, and in 1829 Stuart decided that he would offer his help. He returned to England and enlisted as an agent and pamphleteer.

Discussion of the slavery issue had been under way in England for some time before Stuart's arrival, but there was widespread ignorance of the nature of the institution in the overseas island possessions. The Anti-Slavery Society consequently took it upon itself to educate public opinion, and sent out lecturers to proclaim the simple principle that "the system of colonial slavery is a crime in the sight of God, and ought to be immediately and forever abolished." The report of the agency committee of the society, presented in 1832, showed that six lecturers, of whom Stuart was one and George Thompson, the noted

English abolitionist, another, had been actively engaged, with Stuart having spoken in 26 towns. Soon, speakers were sent out in opposition by the Society of West India Planters and Merchants. In contrast to these defenders of slavery, who were liberally paid, Stuart met all of his expenses from his own pocket. He gave even wider service to the cause by writing several of the most effective pamphlets that appeared at the time. The best known was *The West India Question: Immediate Emancipation Safe and Practical* (London, 1832). This was reprinted again and again, both in England and in the United States, and in the republic became the approved statement of creed of the American Anti-Slavery Society.

Stuart entered into yet another phase of the great conflict, and aided the anti-slavery forces in the United States by completely discrediting the efforts of the American Colonization Society to secure approval and support in England for its work. This society was organized in the winter of 1816–17 with the purpose of transporting emancipated slaves to Africa. The little Republic of Liberia was the fruit of the society's activities, but it soon lost the confidence of both emancipationists and slaveholders. Elliot Cresson, its agent, wrote in 1831 in an unhappy note to Gerrit Smith, complaining of the violent attacks made upon the colonization society's principles and practices by "Captain Stuart, a disciple of Lundy and Garrison, who not satisfied with trying to print us down, has now added public denunciation." By 1832, the colonization society was in general bad odour in England, and all chance of support from that quarter was gone.

Official gratitude for Stuart's services was expressed in the 1832 report of the Anti-Slavery Society, which described him as "a persevering, uncompromising friend of the cause." He had plainly shown himself to be uncompromising, never hesitating to condemn those in high places who had any connection with slavery. In a long letter addressed to the Archbishop of Canterbury and published in the *Abolitionist* in 1833, he remonstrated over the fact that the great missionary organization of the Church of England, The Society for the Propagation of the Gospel, was itself a slaveholder and had been since 1710 through its ownership of the Codrington College Estates in Barbados.

Even the use of the driving whip had been admitted by the society as late as 1829 — six years after its abolition had been recommended by the British government. Stuart ridiculed the familiar excuse, repeated in the society's annual report, that the slaves were not ready for freedom, though they were being gradually brought to that state.

"I look in vain," Stuart wrote, "for a ground on which to support the untenable position that the right way in which to prepare a poor, ignorant man for liberty is to keep him a slave; especially when his preparation is conducted in a land of slavery and entrusted to distant stipendiaries."

In an appendix to *Remarks on the Colony of Liberia and the American Colonization Society*, one of the pamphlets that he published while in England, Stuart presented the Wilberforce Colony, near London in Upper Canada, as an alternative to Liberia. If the Negroes were to be encouraged to leave the United States it was preferable, he contended, that they go to Canada, where the coloured man was encouraged to do all he could to help himself. Included in the appendix was a testimonial from Sir John Colborne, lieutenant-governor of Upper Canada, to the character of Reverend Nathaniel Paul, agent of the Wilberforce Colony, who was then in England soliciting funds, particularly for the establishment of a college for young Negroes.

This idea of establishing a college in Upper Canada was a sequel to the refusal of the municipal council of New Haven, Connecticut, to permit the establishment of such an institution in that city. "When they persecute you in one city, flee to another," wrote Stuart. "The free coloured people have done so; they have abandoned New Haven to her white man's Christianity; and they have now fixed upon Wilberforce, in Upper Canada, as the place of their choice. There they are preparing to erect their college. There, amidst the Canadian forest wilds, they are preparing to place upon our brow a gem of the purest luster, which the United States have proudly dashed away. They need and implore our help."

During the whole period of his mission in England, Stuart corresponded with Weld, sending him copies of the pamphlets and other publications that were appearing and urging him to enter the struggle in the United States. John Quincy Adams once wrote to James Monroe saying that the influence of British emancipation "may prove an earthquake on this continent," and among the strongest influences on the Tappans* and other philanthropists at this time were the contemporary British debates on emancipation, material that was placed in their hands by Stuart and Weld.

Stuart returned to the United States in 1834 after five years of anti-slavery labour in England. For the next three years he gave his services to the crusade in the United States in close association and correspondence with Weld. He was one of the famous "Band of Seventy" sent out as lecturers in 1836 by the American Anti-Slavery Society, and experienced his share of the abuse and violence that these doughty warriors encountered. There are frequent references to his activities in the anti-slavery journals and newspapers of the time.

Prior to his departure for England in 1829, Stuart met Cordelia Weld, a sister of Theodore, and conceived a romantic affection that might have developed further had he remained in the country. But when he returned in 1834, while his admiration of Cordelia had not lessened, he realized that they were not destined for one another.

In August, 1834, Stuart wrote to Theodore: "She is not to be mine. There is altogether too great a discrepancy of temper and of mind between us. I see the fact now glaringly and wonder that I did not formerly perceive it." Cordelia's name does not appear further in the published correspondence.

When he left once again for England in August 1837, Stuart endeavoured to persuade Weld to go with him, but the latter was unwilling to leave the struggle in his own land. Stuart had intended to stay a year in England, but his plans were changed soon after his arrival in the homeland, and instead he sailed for the West Indies to observe firsthand what was happening under the new conditions created by emancipation. He was in Barbados in December, then went on to Jamaica and other islands and returned to England in 1839. While in Barbados, he learned of the insurrection in Upper Canada and wrote to Weld, asking him to ascertain

---

* Editors' Note: Brothers Arthur (1786–1865) and Lewis Tappan (1788–1863) were wealthy businessmen in New York who very generously supported abolitionist causes throughout the antebellum period, and were themselves founders of the American Anti-Slavery Society, along with William Lloyd Garrison and Theodore Dwight Weld, in 1833.

the situation of his relatives and provide them with aid if needed. He was back in England in time to attend the World Anti-Slavery Convention, called to consider the state of slavery in every land, especially in America, and to formulate a program for universal emancipation. Stuart received special recognition at this time, his friends in Parliament securing his promotion from the rank of retired captain to retired major, with an attendant increase in his pension. He was also made an honourary life member of the British and Foreign Anti-Slavery Society. He was continuously active, and his stay in England lengthened into years.

We get only fleeting glimpses of Stuart during this later period spent in England. He was active in British anti-slavery circles, concerned about the apprenticeship system in the West Indies, about conditions in the East Indies, and always deeply interested in what was going on in the United States. During 1846–47 he engaged actively in relief work in famine-stricken Ireland, and finally, in 1850, sailed directly to Canada.

"Duty seemed plainly to forbid my coming through the United States," he wrote on November 5, 1850, from Toronto to Weld, "and I lost the privilege of seeing you all, on my passage." In the same letter he wrote: "I myself am now residing with my eldest sister (Mary Rankin*) in this place. I expect, the Lord pleasing, to remain here until February, when it is my purpose to remove to the North and pursue the improvement of my property there; as well as to seek to serve, in love, the settlers around me."

In a letter to Weld from Lora [Bay], St. Vincent P.O., Canada West, dated April 22, 1852, he wrote: "I am settled here for the present direction — as above — and I have been lately married to a distant relation, whom I have known and loved as a pure and noble-minded woman, for upwards of 30 years.... Her father and two sisters, all lately from Ireland, are living with us and we form a little society."

Before leaving Toronto for his northern property, Stuart became the first corresponding secretary of the Anti-Slavery Society of Canada when it was organized in Toronto in February 1851. He was chosen for this office, we may surmise, because of his wide acquaintance with the

---

* Editors' note: Charles Stuart's sister Mary was married to Charles Rankin, the government surveyor for much of that region.

leading anti-slavery figures in both England and the United States, but his name does not appear on the list of officers after the first year. He made occasional visits to the United States. Thus, we find it recorded that both he and John Brown were at an abolitionist convention in Syracuse in 1855, and Frank B. Sanborn, another American abolitionist, has recorded that Stuart and Brown were at the home of Gerrit Smith on the night of February 22, 1858, when Brown unfolded his plan for a blow at slavery. In his *Recollections of Seventy Years*, Sanborn writes of going out for a walk with Smith while "Brown was left at home by the fire discussing points of theology with Charles Stewart [*sic*]." This was less than three months before Brown held his convention at Chatham, Canada West. Sanborn says that Brown arrived at the home of Gerrit Smith on the evening of February 18, and in an upper room unfolded his plans for a campaign somewhere in slave territory east of the Allegheny Mountains. He read to his friends the draft constitution drawn up by him in Frederick Douglass's home in Rochester for the government of the territory, large or small, that he might rescue by force from slavery.

Life at Lora Bay was peaceful. Writing to James G. Birney in March 1855, Stuart could say: "My present situation is replete with mercies.... The country where I am is a fine and growing one — much I suppose like that of Saginaw Bay, though not so far advanced yet, in improvements. We at present feel confined here, by duty; but we do not expect to remain here many years, should my life be so prolonged."

The Lora Bay property had originally been opened up by Charles Rankin, a relative, who had surveyed the wild lands west of Simcoe County for the government. The location was lot 37, concession 11, Collingwood Township, and Rankin was the township's first settler. Charles Stuart apparently took over the property before his return to Canada in 1850, and, on removing to the place after his marriage, built a commodious one-storey log house with a verandah the full width of the home. There were several large rooms, each with a stone fireplace, and smaller rooms in attached wings. The grounds were neatly planted with shrubs and flowers. At the rear was an addition in which Stuart had his sitting room and study. The ruins of the house were still visible many years later.

Charles Stuart ended his days at Lora Bay, Thornbury, Ontario. *Photo by Norm Frost.*

Traditions have come down of life at Lora Bay, and stories of the relations of Major Stuart with his neighbours, have been passed down. His servant went regularly to the nearest post office to pick up Stuart's mail, which continued to be extensive. Letters and papers were securely locked in a large leather military pouch. The story is still told of when the major himself came into the village and his servant opened the doors of the shops to announce his arrival. Stuart loved children and animals, and assisted in a local Sunday school. He found outlet for his reform instincts in the temperance cause, and occasionally spoke with old-time fire at community gatherings. He was stoutly opposed to the use of any product of slave labour, such as sugar or cotton, and substitutes had to be found by his family for these articles.

Stuart died at Lora Bay on May 26, 1865, just a few weeks after the close of the Civil War and the assassination of Abraham Lincoln. The 13th Amendment abolishing slavery had already been passed by Congress, at the time of Stuart's death and was before the states for ratification. He had lived to see the cause to which he had given his best years victorious, both in his own homeland and in his adopted country. He could say, as did one of old: "Now lettest thou thy servant depart in peace … for mine eyes have seen thy salvation." His confidential servant, Charles Grant, made the coffin out of pine boards hewn on the site of Stuart's home, and covered it with black cloth. He was buried on May 29, on a hill on his farm, the grave being surrounded by a fence. Later his body was removed to the Union Cemetery at Thornbury, Ontario, where the grave was marked by a plain stone bearing first the name of his sister-in-law, Isabella Watt, and, below, Stuart's name and the date of his death. At the base of the stone are the simple words: "The sweet remembrance of the just will flourish when they sleep in death."*

---

*Editors' Note: Annotated Bibliographical Note. For information on Stuart and Weld, see Gilbert H. Barnes. *The Antislavery Impulse, 1830–1844.* New York: D. Appleton-Century Co., 1933; Benjamin P. Thomas. *Theodore Weld, Crusader for Freedom.* New Brunswick, NJ: Rutgers University Press, 1950; Gilbert H. Barnes and Dwight L. Dumond, eds. *Letters of Theodore Dwight Weld, Angelina Grimké Weld and Sarah Grimké Weld, 1822–1844.* 2 vols. New York, London: D. Appleton-Century Co., Inc., 1934; Dwight L. Dumond, ed., *Letters of James Gillespie Birney, 1831–1857.* 2 vols. New York, London: D. Appleton-Century Co., Inc., 1938. The Weld-Grimké and Birney manuscripts are in the William L. Clements Library at the University of Michigan. [An excellent biography of Charles Stuart is: Anthony J. Barker, *Charles Stuart: Anglo-American Abolitionist* (Baton Rouge: Louisiana State University Press, 1986).]

19

The Anti-Slavery Society of Canada

Ontario History, *vol. 48, no. 3 (1956), 125–31*

The Anti-Slavery Society of Canada, organized in February 1851, gave expression to the feelings of many Canadians on the great issue of human bondage that was then agitating the people of the United States. At the same time, it provided the means by which practical aid might be given to the hundreds of Black people who in that period were seeking freedom and safety under the British flag.

The establishment of the society may properly be regarded as a direct outcome of the Fugitive Slave Act, which had been passed by Congress and received the signature of President Millard Fillmore on September 18, 1850. For this act, Fillmore received endless criticism and notoriety in the years following, as did all who had any connection with the bill, but today it is the considered opinion of historians that the president had almost no alternative. It was part of a carefully worked out series of compromises designed to settle a number of issues about which the slavery and anti-slavery sections of the United States felt most strongly, and which threatened, even in 1850, to break up the Union. Such a bill was authorized by the Constitution, the bill had been given the seal of Congress, and the ablest advisors of the president, Secretary of State [Daniel] Webster and Attorney-General Crittenden, had both declared the legislation constitutional.

The Fugitive Slave Act was a hateful measure in the eyes of anti-slavery people in the North. The slave who was taken up could not testify on his own behalf, and was refused a jury trial. Federal marshals and their deputies were required, under the penalty of heavy fines, to make unusual exertions to capture fugitives, and anyone aiding in the escape of a slave was liable to heavy fine or imprisonment, and to civil damages from the owner of the slave, as well. The alleged slave could virtually be turned over to anyone who claimed him, and the way was thus opened to great abuses in the enforcement of the measure. The American historian James Ford Rhodes has emphasized that the legislation demanded by the South was prompted "less by a desire to secure the return of fugitive slaves than as a taunt and reproach to that part of the North where anti-slavery sentiment ruled supremely."

The immediate result of the act was to start a migration of Black people to Canada and into the northern states bordering on Canada. It was accompanied by arrests, court hearings, and tragedies that had a profound influence on American public opinion. While the free Negro population in the northern states increased by nearly 30,000 in the decade after 1850, the gain was chiefly in three states: Ohio, Michigan, and Illinois, from which access to Canada was not difficult. Connecticut, on the other hand, had fewer people of colour in 1860 than in 1850, and there were half a dozen other states that barely held their own in this period. But it is estimated that between 15,000 and 20,000 Negroes entered Canada during the decade, increasing the coloured population to an estimated 40,000. The greater number of these settled in the southwestern part of Ontario, in Kent and Essex counties, though there were also many in Toronto, Hamilton, and in various communities in the Niagara district.

The arrival of so large a number of alien people in a province more sparsely settled than any of the northern states might have been expected to produce serious social problems, and indeed it did, but the records show that, in general, the Black people were received with kindness, and efforts were made to assist them in their chief needs. Canadians already knew something of the fugitive slaves because they had been entering the country ever since the close of the War of 1812, and the number of arrivals had increased decade by decade. Some of the churches had faced up to this home missionary challenge, schools had been established by missionary societies, and teachers supplied. There is even a record of a much earlier organization, the Upper Canada Anti-Slavery Society, organized in 1837.[1]

New, however, in 1850, with new and harsh legislation threatening the personal safety of every Black individual in the northern states, and with a considerable flight to Canada under way, a greater degree of organization became necessary to cope with the problems that were bound to arise.

American newspapers were quick to record what was taking place. Two weeks after President Fillmore had signed the bill, a Pittsburgh dispatch stated that: "all the waiters in the hotels have fled to Canada. Sunday, 30 fled; on Monday 40; on Tuesday 50; and on Wednesday 30 and up to that time the number that had left will not fall short of 300. They went in large numbers ... determined to die rather than be captured." Utica reported under date of October 2 that 17 fugitive slaves had passed through on a boat the day before bound for Canada.

There were dozens of such references in the next few weeks. The Negro population of Columbia, Pennsylvania, dropped from 983 to 487 after the passing of the bill. Out of one Baptist congregation in Buffalo more than 130 members fled across the border, a similar migration taking place among the members of a Methodist body. At Detroit one Baptist congregation lost 84 members. So it was during much of the decade. Fresh arrests or court hearings would stir anew the panic and send others northward. At Chicago in 1861, almost on the eve of the Civil War, more than 100 Negroes left on a single train following the arrest of a fugitive, taking nothing with them but the clothes on their backs.

Soon, too, from border points in Canada came reports of the arrival of the fugitives. Hiram Wilson, a missionary at St. Catharines, writing on December 13, 1850, said: "Probably not less than 3,000 have taken refuge in our country since the first of September. Only for the attitude of the North there would have been thousands more." He wrote that his church was thronged with fugitives, and that what was true of his district was also true of other parts of the province. Henry Bibb, of Windsor, editor of the *Voice of the Fugitive* and himself a coloured man, reported on December 3, 1851, that 17 had arrived that week. Thereafter, in almost every issue of his paper he recorded the number of arrivals and in many cases gave their names and the states from which they had come. In their trek to Canada, the fugitives were greatly assisted by the operators of the "Underground Railroad," which had never before been so active. Vigilance committees at border points, such as Cleveland and Detroit, made up of people with abolitionist views, also co-operated with the "underground" workers in providing facilities for the Negroes to get out of the country.

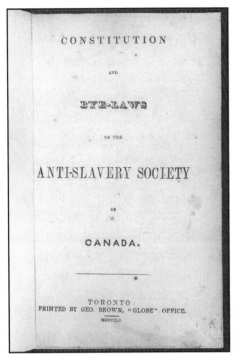

CONSTITUTION

AND

BYE-LAWS

OF THE

ANTI-SLAVERY SOCIETY

OF

CANADA.

TORONTO:
PRINTED BY GEO. BROWN, "GLOBE" OFFICE.
MDCCCLI.

The title page of the constitution and set of bylaws for the Anti-Slavery Society of Canada, published in 1851. *Courtesy of the Baldwin Room, TRL 326.6.A56.*

Sympathetic Canadians in the early part of 1851 realized that there was a definite Canadian responsibility in this crisis, and proceeded to meet this responsibility. We gain some information on the preliminary steps that were taken in the organization of the anti-slavery society from the memoirs of Reverend William McClure, a minister of the New Connexion Methodist Church, who was one of its early and active supporters.[2]

Mr. McClure notes in his diary that as early as October 9, 1850, exactly three weeks after the Fugitive Slave Bill had been signed and thus became law, a meeting was held at the Mechanics Institute in Toronto "on account of the coloured refugees." More definite is his reference to a meeting on February 22, 1851, "to arrange for the formation of an anti-slavery society." This was held at Reverend Dr. Geikie's church. Two days later, there was another meeting in the study of the Reverend Michael Willis, principal of Knox Presbyterian College. Finally, on February 26, came the public meeting held in the city hall, at which the Anti-Slavery Society of Canada came into being.

This meeting, large and enthusiastic, was reported to the extent of almost five columns in the [Toronto] *Globe* of March 1. The mayor of the city acted as chairman, and the opening prayer was made by Reverend Mr. Willis. The proceedings consisted chiefly of the moving and discussion of four main resolutions, which were all endorsed by the gathering and became the society's main platform. The first of these resolutions declared that "slavery is an outrage on the laws of humanity," and that "its

George Brown, publisher of the *Globe* and famously, Father of Confederation, was among the most ardent of Canadian abolitionists. The Brown family never wavered in its support of Black refugees in Canada and for the Union cause in the Civil War. *Courtesy of the Archives of Ontario, S 16268.*

continued practice demands the best exertions for its extinction." A second resolution, which was proposed by Reverend Dr. Willis, declared that the slave laws of the United States are "at variance with the best interests of man, as endowed by our great Creator with the privilege of life, liberty and the pursuit of happiness." A third resolution expressed sympathy with the aims and efforts of the abolitionists in the United States, while the fourth and concluding resolution proposed the formation of the Anti-Slavery Society of Canada. "The object," said the resolution "shall be to aid in the extinction of slavery all over the world by means exclusively lawful and peacable [*sic*], moral and religious, such as the diffusing of useful information and arguments, by tracts, newspapers, lectures and correspondence, and by manifesting sympathy with the houseless and homeless victims of slavery flying to our soil."

Reverend Dr. Willis was the choice for president when the assembly proceeded to its next business. It was a proper choice, and he so retained the confidence of the anti-slavery workers in Canada that he held the office until the society ceased to exist after the close of the Civil War. Reverend Mr. McClure, whose activity was rivalled only by that of the president, was named as secretary, with Andrew Hamilton as treasurer and Captain Charles Stuart corresponding secretary. An executive committee was also appointed, which included, among others, George Brown, editor of the *Globe*, and Oliver Mowat, later to become premier of the Province of Ontario.

The choice of Captain Charles Stuart as corresponding secretary of the new society was of special interest. He had recently settled on a farm near Thornbury, on Georgian Bay, after more than a quarter of a century of activity in anti-slavery societies in the United States, in England, and in the West Indies. He knew the leaders of the movements in other lands for freeing the slaves, and had long been powerful, both with his voice and his pen, on behalf of the slave. There was no man in Canada who had more practical experience in such work, and who was better fitted to relate to the Canadian effort in the struggle under way in the United States.

It was realized that a mere central organization would not be sufficient to meet the situation. Branches must be set up in the various towns throughout Ontario where Negroes had settled in any number. To this end, organizers and public speakers were sent out, among them being some men of the race for whose welfare the society had been established. Thus, we find extensive use being made of such men as Reverend Samuel Ringgold Ward and Reverend Jermain W. Loguen, both of whom had known firsthand what slavery meant to their race. Ward was appointed an agent of the society in 1851, and travelled widely over the province, awakening sympathy for the incoming fugitives and forming branches and women's auxiliaries. His autobiography, published in 1855, contains several chapters relating to the Negroes in Canada and to his own activities on their behalf. To further the work of the society, leaders in the anti-slavery movement elsewhere were brought to Canada to increase public interest. George Thompson, the eminent English abolitionist; Frederick Douglass, the Negro American orator; and the Reverend Samuel J. May of Syracuse were among those who gave aid of this nature. Mr. May preached in the George Street Unitarian Church while in Toronto.

The *Globe* was at all times a stout supporter of the aims and work of the society. George Brown's private generosity to the needy has been recorded by his biographer, but equally marked was the influence that he exerted through his newspaper. In this he was wholeheartedly supported by his brother, Gordon Brown, associated with him in the conduct of the *Globe*. Both men were outspoken in their hatred of anything that savoured of an alliance with or a concession to slavery. Canada, George Brown believed, should stand four-square against the whole system of human bondage. "We too are Americans," he declared on one occasion. "On us, as well as on them, lies the duty of preserving the honour of the continent. On us, as on them, rests the noble trust of shielding free institutions."

Newspapers, in Toronto and elsewhere, which differed in politics from the *Globe*, sometimes took a critical view of the efforts being made on behalf of the coloured people. The *Globe* rebuked the *Patriot* and *Examiner* for their lack of any positive position on the question of slavery while seemingly welcoming letters from correspondents who sneered at the efforts of the Canadian anti-slavery group. The *Argus*, published at Kingston, was quoted by *The Liberator* [Boston] of May 30, 1851, as saying: "That the inhabitants of Canada can sit still and look upon this struggle going on in the neighbouring republic is utterly impossible.... Every town and city along the line which boasts of a dozen Christians should have its branch anti-slavery society forming so many harbours of refuge where the weary and hunted fugitives may find protection from the human bloodhounds who pursue them."

The committee and auxiliaries of the parent society carried on work of considerable magnitude during the 1850s. The Ladies Auxiliary in Toronto reported that over 500 relief cases were dealt with during 1856–57. At that time, the society was distributing about £250 annually. The officers in 1856–57 were: president, Mrs. Arnold; treasurer, Mrs. Willis; corresponding secretary, Mrs. Henning; and recording secretary, Mrs. Brett. A men's committee that was active year after year, chiefly concerned itself with finding work for the newcomers, and sought particularly to place them on farms, work to which their backgrounds accustomed them.

Reverend William McClure, who had been active in the organization's work in Toronto in 1851, soon afterwards removed to London, and when a branch of the society was established in that city in 1852, he became its first president. Reverend R. Boyd was secretary-treasurer, and the directors included Reverend John Scott, a Presbyterian minister; Reverend W.F. Clarke, a Congregationalist; Dr. Salter and Dr. Wanless, physicians; and Messrs. John Fraser, William Rowland, and A.B. Jones. Soon after this branch was established, a fugitive chapel was set up, and measures were taken to improve the condition of the Negroes in the community.

The number of clergymen having a part in the movement is quite noticeable. Dr. Willis thought that every church synod and conference in Canada should give up one day of its sessions to prayer and humiliation over the presence of slavery so nearby. It was the duty of all churches, he held, to remonstrate on this question. At the 1857 meeting of the society, Reverend Dr. Dick protested that at times the church was the "bulwark of the system." There were churches in Canada, he said, that fraternized with those in the United States that patronized and openly supported slavery. He was equally outspoken on the attitude of the Sons of Temperance in deciding, against his protest, to shut out from Negroes its membership. There were other protests at this meeting concerning evidence of race prejudice that had been showing up in a few communities. Reverend Mr. Barrass, commenting on this, said that as the Negroes in Toronto set an example to the whites in morality, there was less reason for any such prejudice.

Thomas Henning, an active member of the society, emphasized that race prejudice was by no means general. Negroes were not excluded from schools, and the laws of the country were administered without respect to colour. He drew attention to the dismissal of a magistrate who had been suspected of conniving the return of a fugitive to slavery, and said that a member of Parliament who had sought to have a Negro immigrant stopped had been laughed at.

From the beginning, there were close fraternal relations between the Canadian organization and the anti-slavery societies of the United States. Dr. Willis was present at the 1851 meeting of the American and Foreign Anti-Slavery Society, and addressed that gathering. He was subsequently made a corresponding member. The reports of the Canadian society were sent to all of the abolitionist newspapers and journals, and were noted there. *The Liberator*, published by William Lloyd Garrison at Boston, showed a continued interest in the Canadian movement and regularly reported on its activities.

During the war years of the 1860s, the officers of the society followed the hostilities with deepest anxiety. There were periods when the success of Southern arms seemed to present the possibility of an independent slave republic with the institution fastened to it by constitutional machinery. Word of Lincoln's Emancipation Proclamation brought new confidence, and the annual meeting of the society on February 4, 1863, seems to have been one of the noteworthy events of its history. At this anniversary gathering, a resolution was unanimously carried that an address be presented to the government of the United States expressing the views of those assembled as to the important services rendered to the cause of freedom by President Lincoln and his administration.

As with so many other organizations of the past, all of the original records and correspondence of the society have disappeared through the years. For information concerning its establishment, its activities, and its workers we are now dependent on press reports and two or three of its annual printed reports, which alone have survived. Records of the branches throughout the province appear to have disappeared in the same way, and the very fact that there was such a society in Canada is probably known to few people.

20

The Negro Migration to Canada after the Passing of the Fugitive Slave Act

Journal of Negro History, *vol. 5, no.1 (January 1920), 22–36*

When President Millard Fillmore signed the Fugitive Slave Bill[1] on September 18, 1850, he started a Negro migration that continued up to the opening of the Civil War, resulting in thousands of people of colour crossing over into Canada, and causing many thousands more to move from one state to another seeking safety from their pursuers. While the free Negro population of the North increased by nearly 30,000 in the decade after 1850, the gain was chiefly in three states: Ohio, Michigan, and Illinois. Connecticut had fewer free people of colour in 1860 than in 1850, and there were half a dozen other states that barely held their own during the period. The three states showing gains were those bordering on Canada, where the runaway slave or the free man of colour in danger could flee when threatened.

It is estimated that from 15,000 to 20,000 Negroes entered Canada between 1850 and 1860, increasing the Negro population of the British provinces from about 40,000 to nearly 60,000. The greater part of the refugee population settled chiefly in what now comprises the counties of Essex and Kent, bordering on the Detroit River and Lake St. Clair. This large migration of an alien race into a country more sparsely settled than any of the northern states might have been expected to cause trouble, but records show that the Canadians received the refugees with kindness and gave them what help they could.[2] At the close of the Civil War, many of the Negroes in exile returned, thus relieving the situation in Canada.

The Fugitive Slave Bill had been signed but a month when William Lloyd Garrison pointed out in *The Liberator,* that a northward trek of free people of colour was already under way. "Alarmed at the operation

The masthead from the *Voice of the Fugitive*, 1851. From *The Underground Railroad: Next Stop, Toronto!* by Adrienne Shadd et al, 2002.

of the new Fugitive Slave Law, the fugitives from slavery are pressing northward. Many have been obliged to flee precipitately leaving behind them all the little they have acquired since they escaped from slavery."[3]

The American Anti-Slavery Society's report also notes the consternation into which the Negro population was thrown by the new legislation,[4] and from many other contemporary sources there may be obtained information showing the distressing results that followed immediately upon the signing of the bill. Reports of the large number of new arrivals were soon coming from Canada. Hiram Wilson, a missionary at St. Catharines, writing in *The Liberator* of December 13, 1850, says: "Probably not less than 3,000 have taken refuge in this country since the first of September. Only for the attitude of the north there would have been thousands more." He says that his church is thronged with fugitives, and that what is true of his own district is also true of other parts of southern Ontario.

Henry Bibb, in his paper, the *Voice of the Fugitive*,[5] published frequent reports of the number of fugitives arriving at Sandwich, on the Detroit River. In the issue of December 3, 1851, he reports 17 arrivals in a week. On April 22, 1852, he records 15 arrivals within the last few days, and notes that "the Underground Railroad is doing good business this spring." On May 20, 1852, he reports "quite an accession of refugees to our numbers during the last two weeks;" and on June 17 notes the visit of agents from Chester, Pennsylvania, preparatory to the movement of a large number of people of colour from that place to Canada. On the same date he says: "Numbers of free persons of colour are arriving in Canada from Pennsylvania and the District of Columbia, Ohio and Indiana. Sixteen passed by Windsor on the seventh and 20 on the eighth and the cry is 'Still they come.'" The immigration was increasing week by week, for on July 1 it was reported in the *Voice of the Fugitive* that "in a single day last week there were not less than 65 coloured emigrants landed at this place from the south.... As far as we can learn not less than 200 have arrived within our vicinity since last issue."

Almost every number of the paper during 1852 gives figures as to the arrivals of the refugees. On September 23, Bibb reported the arrival of three of his own brothers, while on November 4, 1852, there is recorded the arrival of 23 men, women, and children in 48 hours. Writing to *The Liberator* of November 12, 1852, Mary E. Bibb said that during the last ten days they had sheltered 23 arrivals in their own home. The American Missionary Association, which had workers among the fugitives in Canada, noted in its annual report for 1852 that there had been a large increase in the Negro population during the year,[6] while further testimony to the great activity along the border is given by the statement that the vigilance committee at Detroit assisted 1,200 refugees in one year, and that the Cleveland Vigilance Committee had a record of assisting more than a hundred a month to freedom.[7]

The northern newspapers of the period supply abundant information regarding the consternation into which the Negroes were thrown, and their movements to find places of safety. Two weeks after President Fillmore signed the Fugitive Slave Bill, a Pittsburgh dispatch to *The Liberator* stated that "nearly all the waiters in the hotels have fled to Canada. Sunday 30 fled; on Monday 40; on Tuesday 50; on Wednesday 30 and up to this time the number that has left will not fall short of 300. They went in large bodies, armed with pistols and bowie knives, determined to die rather than be captured."[8]

A Hartford dispatch of October 18, 1850, told of five Negroes leaving for Canada;[9] Utica reported under date of October 2 that 16 fugitive slaves passed through on a boat the day before, bound for Canada, all well armed and determined to fight to the last;[10] the Eastport *Sentinel* of March 12 noted that 12 fugitives had touched there on the steamer *Admiral* en route to St. John's; the New Bedford *Mercury* said: "We are pleased to announce that a very large number of fugitive slaves, aided by many of our most wealthy and respected citizens have left for Canada and parts unknown and that many more are on the point of departure."[11] The Concord, New Hampshire, *Statesman* reported: "Last Tuesday seven fugitives from slavery passed through this place ... and they probably reached Canada in safety on Wednesday last. Scarcely a day passes but more or less fugitives escape from the land of slavery to the freedom of Canada ... via this place over the track of the Northern Railroad."[12]

Many other examples of the effects of the Fugitive Slave Act might be noted. The Negro population of Columbia, Pennsylvania, dropped from 943 to 487 after the passing of the bill.[13] The members of the Negro community near Sandy Lake, in northwestern Pennsylvania, many of whom had farms partly paid for, sold out or gave away their property and went in a body to Canada.[14] In Boston, a fugitive slave congregation under Leonard A. Grimes had a church built when the blow fell. More than 40 members fled to Canada.[15] Out of one Baptist church in Buffalo, more than 130 members fled across the border, and a similar migration took place among the Negro Methodists of the same city, though they were more disposed to make a stand. At Rochester, all but two of the 114 members of the Negro Baptist church fled, headed by their pastor, while the Negro Baptist church at Detroit lost 84 members, some of whom abandoned their property in haste to get away.[16] A letter from William Still, agent of the Philadelphia Vigilance Committee, to Henry Bibb at Sandwich, says that there was much talk of emigration to Canada as the best course for the fugitives.[17] The *Corning Journal* illustrates the aid that was given to the fugitives by northern friends. Fifteen fugitives, men, women, and children, came in by train and stopped overnight. In the morning, a number of Corning people assisted them to Dunkirk and sent a committee to arrange for passage to Canada. The captain of the lake steamer on which they embarked very obligingly stopped at Fort Malden, on the Canadian side, for wood and water, and the runaways walked ashore to freedom. "The underground railroad is in fine working order," is the comment of the *Journal*. "Rarely does a collision occur, and once on the track passengers are sent through between sunrise and sunset."

That time did not dull the terrors of the Fugitive Slave Act is shown by the fact that every fresh arrest would cause panic in its neighbourhood. In Chicago in 1861, almost on the eve of the Civil War, more than 100 Negroes left on a single train following the arrest of a fugitive, taking nothing with them but the clothes on their backs and most leaving left good situations behind."[18]

The Underground Railroad system was never so successful in all of its history as it was after 1850. Despite the law, and the infamous activities of many of the slave-catchers, at least 3,000 fugitives got through to Canada within three months after the bill was signed. This was the estimate of both Henry Bibb and Hiram Wilson, and there were probably no men in Canada who were better acquainted with the situation than these two. In the *Voice of the Fugitive* of November 5, 1851, Bibb reported that: "the road is doing better business this fall than usual. The Fugitive Slave Law has given it more vitality, more activity, more passengers and more opposition which invariably accelerates business … We can run a lot of slaves through from almost any of the bordering slave states into Canada within 48 hours and we defy the slaveholders and their abettors to beat that if they can…. We have just received a fresh lot today and still there is room." The *Troy Argus* learned from "official sources" in 1859 that the Underground Railroad had been doing an unusually large business that year.[19]

The Detroit River at Detroit, Michigan, in 1850, was a favourite place for fugitives to cross into Canada. Image from *The Underground Railroad from Slavery to Freedom* by Wilbur H. Siebert, 1898.

Bibb's newspaper reports, December 2, 1852, that the underground is working well. "Slaveholders are frequently seen and heard, howling on their track up to the Detroit River's edge but dare not venture over lest the British lion should lay his paw upon their guilty heads." Bibb kept a watchful eye on slave-catchers coming to the Canadian border, and occasionally reported their presence in his paper. Underground activity was also noted in *The Liberator*. "The underground railroad and especially the express train, is doing a good business just now. We have good and competent conductors," was a statement in the issue of October 29, 1852.[20]

Not all those who fled to Canada left their property behind. The *Voice of the Fugitive* makes frequent reference to Negroes arriving with plenty of means to take care of themselves. "Men of capital with good property, some whom are worth thousands, are settling among us from the northern states," says the issue of October 22, 1851, while in the issue of July 1, 1852, it is noted that "22 from Indiana passed through to Amherstburg, with four fine covered wagons and eight horses. A few weeks ago six or eight such teams came from the same state into Canada. The Fugitive Slave Law is driving out brains and money." In a later issue it was stated that: "we know of several families of free people of colour who have moved here from the northern states this summer who have brought with them property to the amount of £30,000."[21] Some of these people with property joined the Elgin Association Settlement at Buxton, purchasing farms, and taking advantage of the opportunities that were provided there for education. A letter to the *Voice of the Fugitive* from Ezekiel C. Cooper, recently arrived at Buxton, says: "Canada is the place where we have our rights."[22] He speaks of having purchased 50 acres of land and praises the school and its teacher at Buxton. Cooper came from Northampton, Massachusetts, driven out by the Fugitive Slave Law. A rather unusual case was that of 12 manumitted [freed] slaves who were brought to Canada from the South. They had been bequeathed $1,000 each by their former owner. They all bought homes in the Niagara district.[23]

While fugitives and free Negroes were being harried in the northern states, slaves continued to run away from their masters and seek liberty. "Slaves are making this a great season for running off to Pennsylvania," said the Cumberland, Virginia *Unionist* in 1851.[24] "A large number have gone in the last week, most of whom were not recaptured." At the beginning of 1851, *The Liberator* had a Buffalo dispatch to the effect that 87 runaways from the South had passed through to Canada since the passing of the bill the previous September.[25] Bibb mentions two runaways from North Carolina who were 101 days reaching Canada.[26] The Detroit *Free Press* reported that 29 runaways crossed to Canada about the end of March 1859, "the first installment of northern emigration from North Carolina."[27] About the same time the Detroit *Advertiser* announced that "70 fugitive slaves arrived in Canada by one train from the interior of Tennessee. A week before a company of 12 arrived. At nearly the same time a party of seven and another of five were safely landed on the free soil of Canada, making 94 in all. The underground railroad was never before doing so flourishing a business."[28] The New Orleans *Commercial Bulletin of December 19, 1860,* asserted that 1,500 slaves had escaped annually for the last 50 years, a loss to the South of at least $40,000,000.

The American Anti-Slavery Society's *Twenty-Seventh Report* said, "Northward migration from slave land during the last year has fully equaled the average of former years."[29]

It is interesting to note that several of the most famous cases that arose under the Fugitive Slave Act had their endings in Canada. Shadrack, Anthony Burns, Jerry McHenry, the Parkers, the Lemmon slaves, and others found refuge across the border after experiencing the terrors of the fugitive slave legislation. The Shadrack incident was one of the earliest to arise under the new law. Shadrack, a Negro employee in a Boston coffee house, was arrested on February 15, 1851, on the charge of having escaped from slavery in the previous May. As the commissioner before whom he was brought was not ready to proceed the case was adjourned for three days. As Massachusetts had forbidden the use of her jails in fugitive cases, Shadrack was detained in the United States courtroom at the courthouse. A mob of people of colour broke into the building, rescued the prisoner, and he escaped to Canada. The rescue caused great excitement in Washington, and five of the rescuers were indicted and tried, but the jury disagreed. The incident showed that the new law would be enforced with difficulty in Massachusetts in view of the fact that the mob had been supported by a vigilance committee made up of most respectable citizens.[30]

A few months later, at Syracuse, a respectable man of colour named Jerry McHenry was arrested as a fugitive on the complaint of a slaver from Missouri. He made an attempt to escape and failed. The town, however, was crowded with people who had come to a meeting of the County Agricultural Society, and to attend the annual convention of the Liberty Party. On the evening of October 1, 1851, descent was made upon the jail by a party led by Gerrit Smith and Samuel J. May, both well-known abolitionists. The Negro was rescued, concealed for a few days, and then sent on to Canada, where he died at Kingston in 1853.[31]

A more tragic incident was that known as the Gorsuch case. A slaver named Gorsuch, with his son and some others, all armed, came to Lancaster, Pennsylvania, in search of two fugitives. In a house two miles from Lancaster was a Negro family named Parker, and they were besieged by the Gorsuchs. The Negroes blew a horn and brought others to their aid. Two Quakers who were present were called upon to render help in arresting the Negroes, as they were required to do under the Fugitive Slave Act, but they refused to aid. In the fighting that took place, the elder Gorsuch was killed and his son wounded. The Negroes escaped to Canada, where they spent the winter in Toronto and in the spring joined the Elgin Association Settlement at Buxton in Kent County.[32]

The Anthony Burns case attracted more attention than any other arising in the execution of the Fugitive Slave Law. Burns, who was a fugitive from Virginia living in Boston, betrayed his hiding place in a letter that fell into the hands of a Southern slaver and was communicated to a slave hunter. The slaveowner tried to coax Burns to go back into bondage peaceably, but failing in this he had him arrested and brought before a commissioner, who, on June 2, 1854, decided that Burns was a fugitive and must be sent back to slavery. Boston showed its feelings on the day that the Negro was removed from jail to be sent South. Stores were closed and draped in black, bells tolled, and across State Street a coffin was suspended bearing the legend: THE DEATH OF LIBERTY. The streets were crowded, and a large military force, with a field piece in front, furnished an escort for the lone Black. Hisses and cries of "shame" came from the crowd as the procession passed. Burns was soon released from bondage, Boston people and others subscribing to purchase his liberty. He was brought North, educated, and later entered the ministry. For several years he was a missionary at St. Catharines, Canada, and died there in the 1860s.[33]

Along the international boundary there were exciting incidents at times, fugitives being chased to the border and often having narrow escapes from recapture. The Monroe family, a mother and several daughters, escaped from slavery in Kentucky in 1856 and was carried by the Underground Railroad to Ann Arbor [Michigan], and on to Detroit, their master in hot pursuit. So close was the chase that, as the runaways pulled out from the wharf on the ferry for Windsor, Canada, the master came running down the street crying out: "Stop them! Stop them!" He was jeered at by the crowd, which sympathized with the Negro woman.[34]

In June 1852, three fugitives arrived in Detroit and, in response to frantic messages from Toledo, were held for their pursuers. In desperation, the Negroes made a savage attack on their jailer, gained their freedom, and got across the border with the assistance of friends in Detroit. Rewards that were offered for their recapture were useless, as the fugitives took care to remain on the Canadian side.[35]

Hiram Wilson tells of an incident that came under his notice at St. Catharines. A beautiful young girl, 14 years of age and almost white, was brought to Buffalo as a maid for a slaveholder's daughter travelling in the North. She was spirited off by some Buffalo abolitionists, transferred to a steamer flying the British flag, and landed in Canada. She was taken to St. Catharines and sheltered in the home of Hiram Wilson. The master came over from Buffalo, bringing a couple of lawyers with him, and tried to secure his property, but his demands were refused. The owner claimed that he valued the girl at $1,000. It was later discovered that she had been sold no less than four times before coming to Canada.[36]

The brutality of the Fugitive Slave Law was shown on more than one occasion along the border. A case that attracted much attention at the time was that of Daniel Davis. He was a cook on the steamer *Buckeye*. One day, while the vessel was in port at Buffalo, he was called up from below. As his head appeared above the deck, he was struck him a heavy blow by a slave catcher named Benjamin Rust, who had a warrant from a United States commissioner for his arrest. The Negro fell back senseless into the hold and landed on top of a stove, being badly burned. He was brought into court at once, and the newspaper accounts relate in detail how he sat during the proceedings "dozing, with blood oozing out of his mouth and nostrils." After a trial that was rushed in a most unseemly way, the Negro was ordered delivered over to Rust, who was really an agent for one George H. Moore, of Louisville. The brutality of the whole proceeding stirred up deep interest in Buffalo, and on a writ of habeas corpus the fugitive was brought before Judge Conkling, of the United States Court at Auburn, and released. Before there could be further steps taken to hold the Negro, he was hurried into Canada, where he remained. He was in attendance at the large Negro convention held in Toronto in September 1851, and with his head still in bandages afforded striking evidence of the effects of the Fugitive Slave Law. Rust, Davis's assailant, was afterward indicted at Buffalo but allowed to go after paying a paltry $50 fine.[37]

Another memorable border incident occurred at Sandusky, Ohio, in October 1852. A party of fugitives, two men, two women, and several children, had been brought from Kentucky and were aboard the steamer *Arrow,* about to sail for Detroit, when they were all arrested by the alleged owner and taken before the mayor of the town. Rush R. Sloane, a local lawyer, offered to act in their defence. The proceedings were so hurried that no warrant or writ was ready to be produced in court, and Sloane signified by a gesture that the Negroes were free. There was an immediate rush for the door on the part of the fugitives and their friends, but even as they fled from the courtroom the claimant entered, calling out: "Here are the papers. I own the slaves. I'll hold you personally responsible for their escape." The fugitives, meanwhile, had gone to the harbour, boarded a sailboat owned by friendly fishermen, and were on their way to Canada. The slaver, frantic at seeing his property vanishing, tried in vain to get other fishermen to pursue them. He then hurried to a neighbouring town trying to secure help, but with no more success. Within a few hours the runaways were landed at Port Stanley, safe from all pursuers. The slaver made good on his threat to hold Sloane responsible for the loss of his property, entering action and securing a judgment for $3,000. It is related as one of the pathetic incidents of this case that when the fugitives were first taken off the steamer *Arrow*, one of the women dropped her infant child on the ground and disowned it, hoping that it, at least, would be free if she were condemned to return to slavery.[38]

With so great an influx of refugees into a country that was sparsely settled, some suffering was inevitable, but contemporary evidence indicates that after all it was but slight. There was probably more distress during the winter of 1850–51 than later on because of the large number who came in during the few months immediately after the passing of the Fugitive Slave Bill. In their haste to find safety, many had left everything behind, entering Canada with little more than the clothes on their backs. A.L. Power, of Farmington, who visited Windsor at the beginning of 1851, found about a score of families living in an old military barracks, most of them in need of both fuel and clothing. At Sandwich, nearby, he also found distress and mentions seeing a family of eight children who were almost nude and were suffering from the cold.[39] Sickness was, in many cases, a result of exposure, to which the Negroes had been subjected in their effort to reach Canada. Later on, the situation improved, and by 1855 the workers of the American Missionary Association reported that "in general, those who have gone there from the United States, even the fugitives, may provide for the wants of their families, after a short residence there; especially if they meet a friendly hand and, more than all, good counsel on their arrival."[40]

Various agencies in both the United States and Canada were active in the work of relieving the distress among the newcomers. The American Anti-Slavery Society addressed itself to this task early on. "Several agents," said Henry Bibb, "have during the past year proceeded to Canada to exert the best influence in their power over the fugitives that have flocked to the province in years past and especially those who have gone the past year. They are supplied with the means of instructing the coloured population, clothing some of the most destitute fugitives and aiding them in various ways to obtain employment, procure and cultivate land and train up their children. Our friends in Canada are exerting a good influence in the same direction."[41]

The fugitives themselves were banded together to aid the newcomers. The Windsor Anti-Slavery Society and the Fugitives'

Union were both organized to relieve distress and assist their fellows in making a living.[42] Supplies were sent in from points at considerable distances in some cases, and included clothing, food, money, and in one case a donation of 2,000 fruit trees, from Henry Willis of Battle Creek, for refugees who were going on the land.[43] Michigan people were exceedingly generous in extending aid, and there is record also of supplies sent from Fall River, Whitestown, New Jersey, Boston, and other places in New England. There was plenty of work for the Negroes, the 1850s being a period of railway building in western Ontario, Writing in 1861, William Troy maintained that nine tenths of the fugitives had gotten along without outside aid of any kind. "The fugitives show a marked disposition to help each other and relieve want," he says. "I could show hundreds of instances of kindheartedness to all persons, irrespective of race."[44]

The organization of the Anti-Slavery Society of Canada came largely as a result of the sudden influx of Negroes after 1850, which, perhaps more than anything else, impressed upon Canadians the great issue that was rapidly dividing the neighbouring republic. Beginning at Toronto, the anti-slavery forces in Canada were organized in the various cities and towns of the province and continued to be active until the Civil War.

There developed in Canada a marked anti-slavery sentiment, which manifested itself, in part, in the very large number of Canadians who enlisted in the Northern armies.[45] The Anti-Slavery Society was also active in extending the helping hand to the fugitives, considerable sums being raised for relief purposes, and support being given to educational and other movements designed to elevate the race.

In Canada, the refugees were absolutely safe from the operations of the Fugitive Slave Law. No loophole could be found in the Canadian law that would permit the rendition of a slave. A famous case arose in the Canadian courts on the eve of the Civil War when a Negro, John Anderson, was arrested and charged with the murder of a slaver named Diggs some years before, the crime having been committed while Anderson was trying to make his escape from slavery. Canadian opinion was much aroused, and though the first decision of the courts was that the Negro must be extradited, this finding was overruled from England, and in the end the prisoner was released on a technicality. It was made quite clear that the British government would view with marked disapproval any decision in Canada that would return a refugee to slavery.

There were doubtless numerous attempts to kidnap Negroes who had escaped to Canada, especially in the border towns, but such attempts must have been rarely successful. An open attempt to induce a Canadian official to act as slave-catcher was exposed in the Montreal *Gazette* of January 13, 1855, when there was published a letter written by John H. Pape, of Frederick, Maryland, to Sheriff Hays, of Montreal, proposing that the latter should use his power to arrest Negroes, who would then be turned over to Pape. The proceeds from the sale of the captured chattels would be divided evenly, according to the plan suggested.

Canadians took a measure of pride in the sense of security with which their Negro immigrants could look back at their pursuers. That the slavery issue in the United States was rapidly coming to a head was also recognized in Canada during the 1850s, and this, too, may have been an influence with the Canadians in doing what they could to assist the great number of more or less helpless people who came among them. Viewed in the light of more than half a century, it can be seen that the influence of Canada in determining the course of the slavery issue was by no means slight.

21

Henry Bibb, a Colonizer

Journal of Negro History, *vol. 5, no. 4 (October 1920), 437–47*

The Underground Railroad has been characterized by one historian of the Negro race as a "safety valve to the institution of slavery," since it tended to remove from the slave states those Negroes whose special abilities and leadership might have involved them in insurrections.[1] Their abilities frequently found an outlet in another land, under different conditions, and in an entirely orderly way. Negroes who fled to Canada were given considerable material aid by the government of Canada, and treated with sympathy by its people. Their own leaders, however, played no small part in the progress that they made in the British provinces, and the names of Josiah Henson, Martin R. Delany, and Henry Bibb stand for intelligence, energy, and high qualities of service on behalf of the race in Canada.

Henry Bibb, born in slavery and without more than the barest rudiments of education, became prominent in the anti-slavery

Henry Bibb, a fugitive born in Shelby County, Kentucky, made several attempts after his initial escape to rescue his still-enslaved wife and daughter. He went on to become a noted anti-slavery lecturer and publisher of the first Black abolitionist paper in Canada, the *Voice of the Fugitive*. From *The Underground Railroad: Next Stop, Toronto!* by Adrienne Shadd et al, 2000.

crusade, and was actively associated with the Liberty Party in the State of Michigan during the 1840s. When the Fugitive Slave Law of 1850 drove thousands of his people out of the North and into Canada, he set himself vigorously to the task of settling them on the land, providing schools and churches, and, through his paper, the *Voice of the Fugitive*, exercised a positive influence on them at a time when their minds might be expected to be unsettled. William Lloyd Garrison and others who were active in the anti-slavery movement paid tribute to his services in that cause.

Bibb's career in slavery is told in his narrative, published in New York in 1849.[2]

He was born in Shelby County, Kentucky, in May 1815, the son of a slave mother and a white father, and he sums up his childhood by saying that he was "educated in the school of adversity, whips, and chains." Of his early life he writes:

> I was a wretched slave, compelled to work under the lash without wages and often without clothes enough to hide my nakedness. I have often worked without half enough to eat, both late and early, by day and by night. I have often laid my wearied limbs down at night to rest upon a dirt floor, or a bench without any covering at all, because I had nowhere else to rest my wearied body, after having worked hard all the day. I have been compelled in early life to go at the bidding of a tyrant through all kinds of weather, hot and cold, wet or dry, and without shoes frequently until the month of December, with my bare feet on the cold frosty ground, cracked open and bleeding as I walked.

From the slaveholder's standpoint he was a most unsatisfactory servant, being an incorrigible runaway, a blemish on his moral character that probably accounted for the frequency with which he changed owners, six separate sales being recorded at prices ranging from $850 to $1,200. The plantation punishments had no effect on him, save to increase his desire for freedom.

As with many other slaves, the very evils of the system served a purpose in Bibb's life. Denied education of a normal kind, he became observant, and his mind was enlightened by what he saw and heard. "Among other good trades," he says, "I learned the art of running away to perfection. I made a regular business of it and never gave it up until I had broken the bonds of slavery and landed myself in Canada where I was regarded as a man and not a thing."

Ill treatment was the incentive for the first attempt of Bibb to secure his freedom. This was in 1835, and the next few years were occupied by repeated unsuccessful efforts to get away, and to take his wife and child with him. He had heard of Canada, and his thoughts ever turned in that direction. On several occasions, his flights led him as far as the Ohio River, the boundary of freedom, but some force seemed always at hand to drag him back. At the end of 1837 he managed to reach Cincinnati, and spent that winter at Perrysburg with a community of Negroes settled there. The next summer he risked his freedom in attempting to bring his wife north, was captured, lodged in jail at Louisville, and managed to escape within a few hours of being locked up. A year later he renewed the attempt, was again captured, and this time was sold, together with his wife, to a trader who dealt in the New Orleans market. It was in the fall of 1839 that the man and wife were exposed for sale in a slaveyard on St. Joseph Street. In the narrative, there is an interesting account of the trade in this southern city. Newly arrived Blacks were taken before a city official who inspected their backs to see if they were scarred and also examined their limbs to see if they were sound. To determine their age, their teeth were examined and the skin pinched on the back of their hands. In the case of old slaves, the pucker would remain for some seconds. There was also rigorous examination as to mental capacity. Slaves who displayed unusual intelligence, who could read or write, or who had been to Canada were not wanted. Bibb notes that practically every buyer asked him if he could read or write and if he had ever run away. Of the slaveyard itself, he writes:

> All classes of slaves were kept there for sale, to be sold
> in private or public — young or old, males or females,
> children or parents, husbands or wives. Every day, at ten

o'clock, they were exposed for sale. They had to be in trim for showing themselves to the public for sale. Everyone's head had to be combed and their faces washed, and those who were inclined to look dark and rough were compelled to wash in greasy dishwater in order to make them look slick and lively. When spectators would come in the yard the slaves were ordered out to form a line. They were made to stand up straight and look as sprightly as they could; and when they were asked a question they had to answer it as promptly as they could and try to induce the spectator to buy them. If they failed to do this they were severely paddled after the spectators were gone. The object for using the paddle in the place of a lash was to conceal the marks, which would be made by a flogging. And the object for flogging under such circumstances is to make the slave anxious to be sold.[3]

The Bibbs were eventually sold to a Red River planter with whom they had a most miserable existence. For attending without leave a religious meeting on a neighbouring plantation, Bibb was ordered to receive five hundred lashes. To avoid this, he took his wife and child and they hid in a swamp. Dogs tracked them down, and every slave on the plantation witnessed the punishment that was given. Shortly afterwards, the planter sold Bibb to a party of southern sportsmen, but refused to sell his wife, whom Bibb never saw again. The new owners quickly resold him to an Indian, from whom he managed to escape, and he successfully made his way through the Indian Territory, Missouri, and Ohio to Michigan and Detroit.[4] He was never returned to the South again.

Bibb's arrival in Detroit came at what proved for him a most opportune time, since it gave scope for his abilities to be utilized in the anti-slavery cause, particularly in the State of Michigan. The Detroit Anti-Slavery Society had been formed in 1837, and by the end of 1840 there were similar societies all over the state. Michigan, at this time, was probably better organized and more united in sentiment than any other of the northwestern states. It was the era of the Liberty Party, whose platform "asserted the over-mastering importance of the one question of the existence of slavery, and the necessity of bringing about a separation of the national government from all connection with the institution." This third party was facing a crisis in 1844 over the question of the annexation of Texas, on which the South was united and on which the political organizations of the North were divided. Bibb had attended a convention of free coloured people held in Detroit in 1843, and the next year he began to give addresses throughout the state in the interests of Liberty Party candidates, a full ticket for both Congress and the state legislature having been nominated. It was a bitter contest in which he engaged.

The Whigs pointed out that they were standing out against the annexation of Texas, a slave empire in itself, and that votes for a third party would pave the way for a Democratic victory. This is exactly what happened. In Michigan, the Liberty Party polled 6.5 percent of the votes, but even this added to the Whig vote would not have brought victory.[5] Bibb continued to work for the Liberty Party during 1844 and 1845, going also into Ohio with Samuel Brooks and Amos Dresser. They were more than once mobbed, and had their meetings broken up by rowdies. Of their work, Bibb writes:

> Our meetings were generally appointed in small log cabins, schoolhouses, among the farmers, which were sometimes crowded full; and where they had no horse teams it was often the case that there would be four or five ox teams come, loaded down with men, women, and children to attend our meetings. The people were generally poor and in many places not able to give us a decent night's lodgings. We generally carried with us a few pounds of candles to light up the houses wherein we held our meetings after night; for in many places they had neither candles nor candlesticks. After the meeting was out we have frequently gone three to eight miles to get lodgings, through the dark forest where there was scarcely any road for a wagon to run on. I have travelled for miles over swamps where the roads were

covered with logs without any dirt over them, which has sometimes shook and jostled the wagon to pieces where we could find no shop or place to mend it. We would have to tie it up with bark, or take the lines to tie it with and lead the horse by the bridle. At other times we were in mud up to the hubs of the wheels.

Bibb found his real work when, with the passing of the Fugitive Slave Law in 1850, there began a trek of coloured people out of the northern states into Canada.[6]

Before the end of 1850, several thousand of these people had crossed the border, and the situation was one that called not only for the aid of generous Canadians, but for all that leaders among their own people could do for them. It was Henry Bibb's belief that the future of the people of colour in Canada depended on getting them settled on the land, and his mind turned to the possibilities of establishing a distinctly Negro colony on the land that might be secured as a grant from the Canadian government, or, if necessary, purchased from the government, as had been done in the case of the Buxton settlement, established by Reverend William King in what is now southwestern Ontario. Bibb succeeded in organizing his colonization society, its object being "to assist the refugees from American slavery to obtain permanent homes and to promote their social, moral, physical, and intellectual development." It was proposed that 50,000 acres of land should be purchased from the government at an estimated cost of about $2 an acre, the purchase money to be derived partly from contributions and partly from the sale of the land. Each family settling was to receive 25 acres, with five acres to be free of cost provided they cleared and cultivated it within three years from the time of occupation. The remaining 20 acres was to be paid for in nine annual installments. Only landless refugees were to receive grants, transfer, except after 15 years occupation, was forbidden and all lands vacated by removal or extinction of families were to revert to the parent society. Money returned to the society was to be spent on schools, for the payment of teachers, and for the purchase of new land. The whole business of the organization was to be in the hands of a board of trustees.[7]

At the beginning of 1851, Bibb established a little newspaper, published bi-monthly and known as the *Voice of the Fugitive*. In the issue of March 12, 1851, he raises the question as to what the fugitives stand most in need, and holds that charity is but a handicap to their progress, and that they must work for their own support, preferably on the land. The recommendation of a recent convention at Sandwich is quoted to the effect that the refugees should go into agriculture, and that to this end an effort should be made to secure a grant of land from the Canadian government, to be disposed of in 25-acre plots. Bibb suggested that there should be at least 20,000 acres secured at once.

To aid in forwarding the plans, Bibb enlisted the support of a number of Michigan people, and at a meeting held in Detroit on May 21, 1851, the Refugee's Home Society was organized, with the following officers: president, Deacon E. Fish, Birmingham; vice-president, Robert Garner; secretary, Reverend E.E. Kirkland, Colchester; assistant secretary, William Newman. It was decided that an effort should be made to secure 50,000 acres of land. New officers appear to have been elected almost immediately after the society had started operations; the new executives being as follows: president, J. Stone, Detroit; vice-president, A.L. Power, Farmington; secretary, E.P. Benham, Farmington; treasurer, Horace Hallock, Detroit.[8] The whole movement was heartily approved at a convention of coloured people held at Sandwich on May 26, 1851. The Canada Company offered to sell large blocks of land to the society at from $2 to $4 an acre; but no large purchases were immediately made. Instead, the society began a canvass for funds, sending out Charles C. Foote, of Commerce, and E.P. Benham, of Farmington, for this purpose. A letter from Foote in the *Voice of the Fugitive* of July 30, 1851, says: "The plan seems popular and he [Charles C. Foote] looks forward to the day when the coloured people will nestle in the mane of the British Lion." In the latter part of 1851, a purchase of land was made from the Canada Company and a contract was entered into for further purchases as soon as the funds should be available.[9]

At the meeting of the society held in Farmington on January 29, 1852, the following officers were elected: president, Nathan Stone, Detroit; vice-president, A.L. Power, Farmington; treasurer, Horace Hallock,

Detroit; recording secretary, E.P. Benham, Livonia; corresponding secretary, Mrs. Mary Bibb, Windsor; executive, William Lolason, Detroit; Coleman Freeman, Windsor; Elisha Vanzant, Detroit; David Hotchkiss, Amherstburg; and Henry Bibb, Windsor. Vanzant and Bibb were appointed trustees, and the latter reported the purchase of 200 acres of land at $3 an acre.

It was decided to reserve 10 acres for school purposes, to send out J.F. Dolbeare as agent to collect funds, and to make Bibb's newspaper the official organ of the society.[10]

The *Second Annual Report of the Anti-Slavery Society of Canada* (1853) reported that at that time the Refugee's Home Society had purchased 1,328 acres of land, of which 600 acres had been taken by settlers. The scheme was considered a good one, but it was emphasized that good management would be needed. The progress of the Elgin or Buxton Settlement showed that success was possible.

When Benjamin Drew visited Canada in 1854, he found that the society had purchased nearly 2,000 acres of land, that 40 of the 25-acre plots had been taken up, and that there were 20 families located. A school was being maintained during three fourths of the year, intoxicating liquors had been completely banned, and a society known as the True Band had been organized to look after the best moral and educational interests of the colony.[11]

The colony was fortunate in the first teacher that was engaged for the school. This was Mrs. Laura S. Haviland who came in the fall of 1852 and began her work in the frame building that had been erected for general meeting purposes. So great was the interest in her Bible classes that even aged people would come many miles to attend. Similar success attended her experiment of a nonsectarian church. In her autobiography, she tells of the conditions in the colony while she was there.

In their clearings the settlers raised corn, potatoes, and other vegetables, while a few had put in two or three acres of wheat. Mrs. Haviland's account of the colony is much more favourable than some of the adverse stories that were sent abroad regarding it.[12] Reverend William M. Mitchell, who was a Negro missionary among his own people in Toronto, makes the following reference to the colony in his *Underground Railroad*:

About ten miles from Windsor there is a settlement
of 5,000 acres which extends over a large part of Essex
County. It is called the Fugitives' Home. Several years
ago a very enterprising and intelligent fugitive slave ...
bought land from the government, divided it into 20-
acre plots and sold it to other fugitives, giving them five
to ten years for payments. Emigrants settled here in such
large numbers that it is called the Fugitives' Home. The
larger portion of the land is still uncultivated, a great
deal is highly cultivated and many are doing well.

The writer goes on to point out the evidence of the material
advancement of the colony. There were two schools, the government
paying half the salary of the teacher and the other half being collected
from the parents. The school, he found, was also used for the church
services, though the spirituality of the people seemed low.[13]

The record of Henry Bibb's activities in Canada shows that he took
a broad view of the refugee question. He associated himself actively
with the Anti-Slavery Society of Canada at its formation in 1851,
and at the first annual meeting, held in Toronto in 1852, was elected
one of the vice-presidents. In the reports of this organization will be
found several references to his work. He was also the first president
of the Windsor branch of the Anti-Slavery Society and made several
tours through the western end of Upper Canada visiting the Negro
communities and speaking on the slavery issue. In his newspaper, the
Voice of the Fugitive, he chronicled every movement that would aid
in the uplift of his people and set forth their needs in an admirable
way. Its columns give a large amount of information concerning the
fugitives in Canada after 1850.

Bibb's colonization plan was a well-meant effort to improve the status
of the Negro in Canada. While it lacked the permanence of the Elgin
Settlement, which even today preserves its character, it opened the way
for a certain number of refugees to provide for their own needs and it
lessened, to some extent, the congestion of refugees in border towns like
Windsor and Sandwich. It is a debatable question whether segregation

of these people was wise or not. At that time it seemed almost the only solution to this very pressing problem. After the Civil War, many of the Negroes in Canada returned to the United States, and those who remained found conditions easier. There was usually work for any man who was willing to labour, and it is a well-recorded fact that many of the fugitives, entering the country under the most adverse of circumstances, succeeded in getting ahead and gathering together property. Benjamin Drew's picture of the Canadian Negroes as he found them in the middle of the 1850s is favourable, and when Dr. Samuel G. Howe investigated the Canadian situation on behalf of the Freedmen's Inquiry Commission in 1863[14] he was able to report: "The refugees in Canada earn a living, and gather property; they marry and respect women; they build churches and send their children to schools; they improve in manners and morals — not because they are picked men but simply because they are free men. Each of them may say, as millions will soon say, 'When I was a slave, I spake as a slave, I understood as a slave, I thought as a slave; but when I became a free man I put away slavish things.'"

22

When Uncle Tom's Cabin Came to Canada

Ontario History, *vol. 44, no. 1 (January 1952), 1–5*

Just one hundred years ago, there appeared on the counters of a few stores in Toronto and Montreal, a new publication written by a little wisp of a woman and the wife of a New England college professor, bearing the curious title *Uncle Tom's Cabin, or Life Among the Lowly*. The Toronto edition was published by Thomas Maclear, of 45 Yonge Street, and printed by Brewer, McPhail & Co., of 46 King Street.[1] The Montreal edition was published, and probably printed also, by B. Dawson, Place d'Armes. Both were reprints of the edition that had just come from the Boston publishers, John P. Jowett & Co.

It may have been with some doubts as to probable sales that these Canadian editions were placed before the public, but, so far as the Toronto firm was concerned, fears were soon dissipated, for within three weeks after the first copies were on sale, a second printing was necessary to meet the public demand. The *Globe* gave immediate publicity to the book. In its issues of April 24 and 27 it printed, in a sort of literary column, two lengthy extracts with some words of appreciation. The first extract was headed by the title of the book and the name of the author, while below were the words "From the New York *Tribune*." Introductory remarks drew attention to the "high moral purpose of the story which has been written with the intention of showing the most fearful aspects of domestic slavery."

In the second portion, appearing three days later, chapter five of the book was reprinted with this comment: "We need not say that these volumes are entitled to a wide perusal, both on account of their intelligence and their humanity. The writer speaks not from rumour, but from observation. Her portraitures of slavery though drawn in deep colours, betray no appearance of being overcharged. She appeals to the imagination through the medium of facts. Her book cannot fail to produce a strong and healthful effect on public opinion." The *Gazette* in Montreal also gave publicity to the book. On April 3, 1832, under the heading "New Books," it printed a review mentioning both the Boston and Montreal editions. The *Gazette's* comment was as follows:

> The authoress whose work is before us is … a leading abolitionist. She has written us a tale of Negro life which has created a regular furor in the capital of New England. No less than 3,000 copies of the book were sold on the day of its publication. Yet her preface speaks moderately and honestly of the Southern slaveholders. She seems to judge charitably of the position in which they are placed. If her preface be a true specimen of the style of the book, it is admirably well written, and on the strength of it, we venture to recommend it to our readers as an interesting work. The book is well got up, nicely printed, bound and illustrated.

Two weeks later the *Gazette* printed a more lengthy review of the book, making these further comments:

> As we are not so far advanced in the march of freedom as to understand the slave holder's logic "that a man may do what he likes with his own" this book may be considered by some to be out of its latitude, but we have so many relations with our friends across the line that the public opinion of one country tells on the other and it becomes apparent that Canadians should feel aright on this great question. Because the stain of slavery no longer embraces our escutcheon, and the cry of suffering millions no longer assails our ears, we should not forget their wrong, and we hail with pleasure the appearance of *Uncle Tom's Cabin*, knowing it will cause many a heart to throb anew in sympathetic feeling with the afflicted sons of Africa.[2]

This is the home in Washington, Kentucky, visited by Cincinnati school-teacher Harriet Beecher Stowe in 1833. At the nearby courthouse she witnessed her first slave auction. Many years later her horror at the sight inspired her to write *Uncle Tom's Cabin*, the most important anti-slavery novel of the antebellum years. *Photo by Karolyn Smardz Frost.*

The appearance of Mrs. Stowe's book coincided with two closely related events that were in the public eye in Canada. The first of these was the large migration of Negroes from the northern states, which followed the signing of the Fugitive Slave Bill by President Fillmore on September 18, 1850. With the passing of this bill, the northern states were no longer a safe refuge for people of colour, whether they were actually free or were runaways from southern plantations. The number of these people migrating to Canada during the winter of 1850–51 has been estimated at a figure as high as 5,000, and the movement continued in the succeeding years, so that the total for the decade may have been four times the above figure.[3]

The second event, arising out of the first, was the organization at Toronto in early 1851 of the Anti-Slavery Society of Canada. The Reverend Michael Willis, principal of Knox Presbyterian College, was the first president, and he continued in that office until the close of the Civil War, when the society ceased to exist. Reverend William McClure, a minister of the New Connexion branch of Methodism, was the secretary, and on the executive committee were George Brown, editor of the *Globe*, and Oliver Mowat, later premier of the Province of Ontario. The corresponding secretary was an interesting figure. This was Captain Charles Stuart, a retired officer from the service of the British East India Company who had already spent 20 years of his life in the anti-slavery cause in England, the United States, and the West Indies. In 1851 he was living in retirement in Canada, his home being on a farm near the shore of Georgian Bay.

George Brown's connection with the society was of material benefit, since he was able to give wide newspaper publicity to the aims and activities of the society. Steps were taken to organize branches in cities and towns throughout the province, and speakers were brought in from England and the United States to arouse public opinion. Much use was made of men such as Fred Douglass, the Negro orator, Reverend Samuel Ringgold Ward, himself a former slave, and others who had known slavery firsthand. The way had thus been paved for a prompt recognition of Mrs. Stowe's book by the constant arrival in Canada of fugitives from slavery, and by the measures already taken on their behalf.

Readers of the book must have been considerably influenced in their sentiments and thoughts by the light it threw on the slavery system. Sir Wilfrid Laurier, late in life, recalled in a public address that as a youth in a Montreal law office he had come to pronounced anti-slavery views by reading *Uncle Tom's Cabin*. His experience was probably that of many another young Canadians of that day, for in Canada, as in the United States, the novel converted, by its emotional appeal, many who had remained quite unmoved by the long debate over the question.

Moreover, it had another effect of some importance. It has often been pointed out that in the United States this book, first appearing in 1852, was read by thousands of young boys in the North who, eight or ten years later, went into the Northern armies. Some similar effect may also have taken place in Canada when we recall the statement of Sir John

A. Macdonald to Goldwin Smith that he had caused careful examination to be made as to the number of Canadians in the armies of the North, and had found that it was 40,000.[4] Regiments raised in states contiguous to the Canadian provinces had hundreds of Canadians on their rolls. Perhaps comparatively few had enlisted as a direct result of reading Mrs. Stowe's novel; far more were drawn by love of adventure or attracted by the money bounties paid to volunteers, but the fact of the large enlistment from Canada remains.

Yet another effect may be noted, namely, the impact of the book on Canadian public opinion during the war years. While there were some Canadians who, like the upper classes in England, sympathized with the South, the mass of Canadian opinion was with the North in its great struggle and with President Lincoln in his determined stand to preserve the Union. Canadians had a far better understanding and appreciation of the American situation than did the upper classes in England, though it must be remembered that by 1863 English opinion of the war had undergone a marked change, and no finer admission of this change of heart was ever made than the beautiful cartoon and accompanying verse that appeared in *Punch* after Lincoln's assassination. And no finer proof of the sincerity of Canadian opinion could be presented than the deep grief and universal mourning over this tragedy in 1865.[5]

Mrs. Stowe's novel first appeared serially between June 5, 1851 and April 1, 1852 in the *National Era* in Washington, a paper that was the organ of the anti-slavery forces in the decade before the war. Publication in book form came almost simultaneously in the United States, England, and Canada, all in 1852. The first English edition appeared on April 16, 1852, and while sales were slow at first, a striking change came in August when *The Times* gave the book a five-column notice and review. Despite the fact that the Vatican placed the book on the *Index Expurgatorius*, it was soon translated into every European tongue, and later into Chinese and Japanese. In almost every country there were pirated editions, and the total sales ran into many millions, though the author received little return. Most of the publishers calmly stole her work and pocketed the profits. Sales in England alone were estimated at 3.5 million copies.

Above: The Ontario Heritage Trust Plaque recognizing the Josiah Henson House at Uncle Tom's Cabin Historic Site, Dresden, Ontario. *Photo by Karolyn Smardz Frost.*

Left: Josiah Henson, in a formal photograph with his second wife, Nancy Gambril. *Courtesy of Uncle Tom's Cabin Historic Site, Dresden, Ontario.*

Playbill for a presentation of *Uncle's Tom's Cabin* at Schomberg, Ontario, date unknown. *Courtesy of the Baldwin Room, TRL, the Broadside Printed Ephemera Collection, #1963 Negroes.*

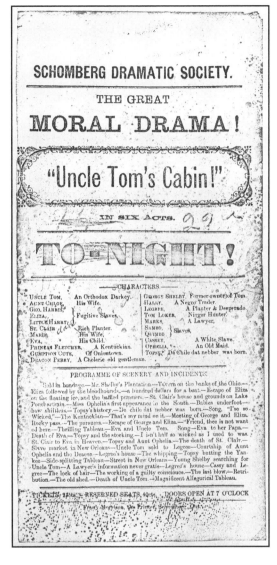

The story was soon dramatized, both in England and in America, and during the next half-century was seen by millions of people. As a play it was often dismissed as worthless, but it never quite ceased to be a part of the American theatre. Theatrical people entered the profession as understudies for the role of Uncle Tom, or Little Eva, or Legree and wound up years later playing the same role. Just as actors and actresses grew old with it, so did audiences. When some religious denominations drew the line at their members attending theatrical performances, an exception was often made for this play because it had a great moral lesson to pass on.

In January 1931, the Toronto *Mail and Empire* drew attention on its editorial page to a report that, for the first time since 1852, there was not a single company in the United States playing *Uncle Tom's Cabin*. Yet only two years later, Otis Skinner was appearing in New York City in the role of the holy slave, Uncle Tom, and playing to capacity audiences. Fay Bainter was a lively Topsy, and Cecilia Loftus was Aunt Chloe. Thomas

Chalmers played Legree, and even got applause when, at the end of the play, the company paraded in, old-fashioned style, across the stage, for his audiences evidently agreed with the sentiment, which was expressed in his own words: "Hard as I am, I have been rocked in the bosom of a mother."

Uncle Tom's Cabin has the same enduring vitality that belongs to the story of old John Brown of Harper's Ferry and the song that carries his name, even though the events with which they are connected take us back to the 1850s. This vitality and enduring quality are the more remarkable because both the book from which the play was taken and the song that followed Brown's execution were propaganda against slavery. Passions were at white heat when they were produced, and it might have been expected that when slavery came to an end, interest in the book and the song would cease in America. But this did not happen, and it is hard to explain the reason.

Van Wyck Brooks [late-nineteenth-century American literary critic] suggests the dramatic impact of the book when he tells us that it appeared in 37 languages; that three Paris newspapers published it all at once; that Macaulay Heine and George Sand reviewed it; that "Uncle Tom's Cabins" rose all over Europe as restaurants, creameries, and bazaars; that it sent Heine back to his Bible; that in far-off Russia, it made such an impression on Tolstoy that when he came to write *What is Art?* he took it as an example of the highest type, with Dostoyevsky's *House of the Dead* and much of Victor Hugo.

"In all the history of the printed book," says Mr. Brooks, "the Bible alone has appeared in so many printed versions. Certainly no play has ever toured so constantly or been seen by so many millions. For years the sun never set on it."[6]

23

1856 Garner Slave Case One of Horror: Missed Escape to Western Ontario, Killed Child

London Free Press *(August 15, 1953), 13*

There is a long record of shocking incidents in connection with the flight of fugitive slaves to Canada in the days of the Underground Railroad, but none are more horrible than the circumstances connected with the Garner fugitive slave case in 1856, really almost the last of the great fugitive slave cases of the 1850s, and one that seemed to overshadow in horror all that had arisen before. For Margaret Garner, a slave after whom the case is named, killed her own little daughter to keep her from being returned to slavery. The affair embarrassed the South, and disturbed the North with more than a hundred arguments from anti-slavery agitators and philosophers. Moreover, the incident has a very real connection to Canada.

The first public word of the case came in a dispatch to the New York *Daily Times* from its Cincinnati correspondent on January 28, 1856. The message advised briefly: "A stampede of slaves from the border counties of Kentucky took place last night.… One slave woman, finding escape impossible, cut the throats of her children, killing one instantly and severely wounding two others. Six of the fugitives were apprehended, but eight are said to have escaped."

The actual facts of the escape were these: Simon Garner Sr. and his wife, Mary; his son, Simon Jr., his wife, Margaret, and their four children fled from their owners on the night of Sunday, January 27, accompanied by nine slave friends from other nearby plantations. Their destination unquestionably was Canada, and the first step on their journey was to cross the Ohio River at Cincinnati. The party of 17 all crowded into a large horse-drawn sleigh and sped over ice-covered roads.

It was a cold winter and the river was frozen over, so they abandoned their sleigh and, as fast as Margaret Garner's pregnant condition would allow, hurried across to Ohio's free ground. By the time they reached the shore it was daylight, and, realizing that 17 strange Negroes would be conspicuous, they separated into two groups, the Garner family in one and the nine others forming a second group. This group of nine successfully reached Canada and joined the thousands of their own people who were already there.

The Garners were less fortunate. They took refuge in the home of a kinsman, Elijah Kite. Kite hurried to the home of Levi Coffin, a rich Cincinnati merchant who was generally known as the "president of the underground" because of his support and continued activity in its work. But before Coffin could act, the fugitives were betrayed, and when Kite returned to his home he found it surrounded by an arresting party.

Inside the cabin, the fugitives hastily barred the doors and windows and Simon Garner Jr. fired two shots from a revolver, but it was clear that nothing could save the party.

Suddenly Margaret Garner seized a butcher knife and turned on her three-year-old daughter, and struck again and again until the child was almost decapitated. Next she turned on one of her little boys, who pleaded piteously with his mother not to kill him. She called to old Mary Garner, "Mother, help me to kill the children." The woman was disarmed by her relatives, sobbing all the while that she would rather kill her children than have them taken back to slavery.

The arresting party finally broke into the house and were met by the horrible sight of a dying child, two others bleeding profusely, and an infant badly bruised. At the station house where the slaves awaited the process of law, Margaret Garner sat as though stupefied, with the surviving children about her. When a compliment was paid her on her fine little boy she replied sadly, "You should have seen my little girl that-that (she did not like to say was killed) that died-that was the bird."

She had a scar on the left side of her forehead running down to her cheekbone. When asked how she came by this mark she replied only, "White man struck me."

The Margaret Garner tragedy threw the cruel nature of American slavery into high relief and newspaper articles appeared across the United States and Britain during her trial. This one was published in the Cincinnati *Enquirer* of January 29, 1856.

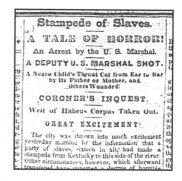

The owners of the Garner family were anxious to secure possession of their slave property as quickly as possible, but abolitionists in the city were determined to resist. They therefore demanded that Margaret Garner be indicted for murder and locked for trial. This would delay matters, while a judgment under the Fugitive Slave Law would send the woman back into slavery immediately.

An involved legal struggle ensued. The inquest into the little girl's death found that the child was "almost white and a little girl of beauty." At the end of February, the fugitives were sent back to Kentucky with the understanding that the mother of the dead child might be recalled for trial. But when requisition was made in March, it was reported that Margaret Garner had been "sent down the river" to the "deep South."

Here there was further tragedy. On the way south, Margaret Garner fell into the river when the steamer on which she was travelling was involved in a collision. She had a child in her arms, which was drowned, though she herself was rescued. The mother, it is said, rejoiced that another child found death rather than slavery.

At a later date, it was reported that the mother had been sent into Ohio and was in jail awaiting trial, but when an officer was sent with a requisition the woman was not found. Thereafter, there is no information on the fate of the woman. Nothing was ever heard of her again.

There is no definite information regarding the nine others who had accompanied the Garner family as far as Cincinnati and then headed for Canada. As they made their way through Ohio, it is probable that they crossed into Canada either at some port on Lake Erie, at Fort Malden (Amherstburg), or elsewhere on the Detroit River, these being the most used channels into the British province.

The Garner case greatly disturbed the people of Ohio. The federal courts had insisted that the Fugitive Slave Law took precedence over the personal liberty and criminal laws of the state. When the second child died by drowning, there was an outburst of indignation and the Fugitive Slave Law was denounced as "repugnant to the plainest principles of justice and humanity."

It was out of such cases as that of Margaret Garner that friction developed between free and slave states, and between the free states and the national government, which at that time was so strongly under the domination of Southern political leaders. And out of this bitter hostility came the Civil War.

24

The Anderson Fugitive Case

Journal of Negro History, *vol. 7, no. 3 (July 1922), 233–42*

The recent decision of the Canadian government not to allow deportation to proceed in the case of Matthew Bullock, a Negro whose return was asked by the State of North Carolina, has served to recall to public attention in Canada certain cases occurring during the period of slavery in the United States, when the Canadian courts were asked to order the return of fugitives. The most famous of these was the Anderson case, tried before the Canadian courts at Toronto in 1860, interest in which stirred the British provinces from end to end.

The Bullock case, recently decided, has some points of similarity to the Anderson case, though the circumstances vary greatly. Bullock was charged with participation in race riots in North Carolina in January 1921. He had made his way to Canada and succeeded in evading immigration authorities in entering the country. It was admitted by the Canadian that he was in the country illegally, but in the final decision it was stated that, as he had conducted himself in an exemplary manner since entering, he would be allowed to remain. On behalf of the fugitive it was freely hinted that, should he be returned to North Carolina, he would risk becoming a victim of mob justice. While this plea doubtless influenced the Canadian immigration authorities, it could not, of course, be stated as their reason for allowing the man his freedom.

The Anderson case of 1860, to which so much newspaper reference was made during the progress of the Bullock case, came just on the eve of the American Civil War. In some respects, it looked to be one of the last efforts of the slaveowners to secure complete enforcement of the Fugitive Slave Law of 1850. That measure, so detested by the North, became a dead letter in many sections by force of public opinion, but

The attempted extradition of John Anderson in 1860 on the eve of the Civil War was a Canadian *cause célèbre* and the last such dispute between Canada and the United States. *Courtesy of the Archives of Ontario E450-A54-T9.*

was also weakened by the fact that the fugitive in the North could soon cross into Canada if threatened by any sudden enforcement of the law. An arrest under the Fugitive Slave Law in any northern city was usually followed by a swift trek into Canada of other Negroes who feared that they might be the next victims. But what if there could be found some means of using British law to secure the return of fugitives from Canada?

This appears to have been on the minds of those who tried to get Anderson out of Canada in 1860. It is difficult to account, otherwise, for the strenuous efforts that were made to secure his extradition. That the Missouri slaveholders felt they were performing something in the nature of a public service by fighting this case in the Canadian courts is evidenced by their request that the state should reimburse them for their outlay.[1]

John Anderson appears to have arrived in Canada in November 1853, crossing over the Detroit River to Windsor where he stayed with Mrs. Bibb, mother of Henry Bibb, who was attempting to organize a refugee settlement not far from that frontier point. Mrs. Laura Haviland, a philanthropic Michigan woman who was doing missionary and educational work among the fugitives, met him soon after his arrival and learned his story. She says that he came to her asking her to write a letter for him. This letter revealed the tragedy in which he had recently figured, and that had caused him to flee to Canada. She had noted the sadness in his face, which indicated the stress through which he had passed. He told her that to satisfy a debt he had been sold by his master, Seneca Diggs, and was to be separated from his wife and four children. Husband and wife pleaded not to be separated, but the reply was that the buyer desired only the man.

Later, however, the master indicated that some other arrangement might be arrived at, but the man was suspicious and armed himself with a dirk. His suspicions were further aroused when he was told to come to the woods, where some trees were to be chopped, and when he noticed that the master had a stout rope under his coat. The slave kept at a distance from the master until the latter finally frankly admitted his purpose. The slave declared that he would never be taken, but at this point another man appeared and Anderson began to run. The slavers followed him for seven miles and finally had him cornered. Anderson flourished his knife and threatened to kill the first man who laid hands on him. All stood back but Diggs, who, with a knife in his hand, rushed at the slave. In the melee, the master was stabbed and the slave escaped into the woods.

That night, Anderson saw his wife and family for the last time. The woman informed him that he had killed his master and that if he were caught he could expect to be burned alive or chopped to pieces. She urged him to flee to Canada, and if he arrived there safely, he was to write to her father, who was free. This is the story as he told it to Mrs. Haviland, and it was the letter to his father-in-law that he wished her to write.

Mrs. Haviland shrewdly suspected that a letter from Canada addressed to a Negro related to Anderson would not likely reach its destination, and would also give a clue as to the fugitive's whereabouts. Accordingly, she dated the letter from Adrian, Michigan, and asked that the reply be sent there. The answer, which came shortly after, said that Anderson's wife and four children were being brought to him. Mrs. Haviland replied to this letter, but warned Anderson not to cross the Detroit River as she suspected a plot.

In her message she asked the party to come to Adrian, Michigan, and inquire for Mrs. Laura Haviland, a widow, from whom information could be had regarding Anderson.

A few days later a white man called, very clearly a southerner, and informed her that Anderson's family was in Detroit, staying in the home of a Negro minister named Williams. The visitor seemed exceedingly anxious to find out where Anderson was, and Mrs. Haviland finally told him that the man was in Chatham and advised that his family should be sent there. At this time, the visitor's face reddened rather noticeably. Mrs. Haviland lost no time in sending a message to Anderson advising him to leave Chatham. He got out none too soon, for within a few days white men were in Chatham inquiring for him. They were told that he had gone to Sault Ste. Marie, and they followed the trail there but without success. Finally, they disappeared after giving the Detroit people power of attorney to arrest Anderson if he should ever be decoyed over the river or should be found there.

Mrs. Haviland, in her memoirs, says that after this effort to capture Anderson as a murderer she wrote a letter to Lord Elgin, the governor of the Canadas, setting forth the facts, and that she received this reply from him: "In the case of a demand for William Anderson, he should require the case to be tried in their British courts; and if twelve freeholders should testify that he had been a man of integrity since his arrival in their dominion it should clear him."[2]

There is a rather curious similarity between the latter part of this statement and the recent decision from Ottawa in the Bullock case, namely, that as the latter had conducted himself well since entering the country he should not be deported.

About three years after the events mentioned above, which would be about 1856, Mrs. Haviland records a meeting with D.L. Ward, a New Orleans attorney, who said to her: "We are going to have Anderson by hook or by crook; we will have him by fair means or foul; the South is determined to have that man."

The whereabouts of Anderson between 1853 and 1859 is not on record. Probably he lived most of that time in southwestern Ontario where his own people were most numerous. It is stated that he had worked in Hamilton and Caledonia. In the spring of 1860 he was working near Brantford when it came to the ears of a magistrate at Brantford, William Matthews by name, that at some time in the past this Negro had committed a crime and was a fugitive from justice in his own state. Matthews had the Negro arrested and locked up. It would appear that he had no evidence of any kind, other than rumor. S.B. Freeman, who defended Anderson later, says that he went to the Brantford magistrate and made inquiries about the prisoner, being told that the fugitive was held pending the receipt of necessary evidence.

According to Freeman's charges, which were made publicly in the Toronto *Globe* on December 11, 1860, Matthews communicated with private detectives in Detroit, who passed the word on to friends of the deceased Diggs in Missouri, and they promptly applied at Washington for extradition papers. The *Hamilton Times* charged that Matthews had subjected his prisoner to most rigorous prison life for two months, keeping him ironed, permitting no Negro friends to see him, not even admitting Reverend Walter Hawkins, the Negro preacher who afterwards became a bishop.[3] It required very much persuasion on the part of Freeman, and apparently some threats as well, to induce the Brantford magistrate to release his prisoner. When let out of jail, Anderson went to Simcoe and was working there when he was again arrested, this time, it would appear, on a warrant sworn out by a Detroit man named Gunning. There are indications in the press reports of the time that the Brantford magistrate was much aggrieved at his prisoner getting into other hands and sought to have the case transferred to Brantford, being aided in this by the county Crown attorney.

In a letter to the *Hamilton Spectator*, Freeman made this charge against the magistrate: "Mr. Matthews arrested him as having been guilty of murder without any legal evidence of a murder having been committed, or, in fact, of anyone having been killed by him. And after he had him in custody he communicated with the authorities for the necessary evidence."[4]

On November 24, Anderson was brought before the Court of Queen's Bench, consisting of Chief Justice Robinson and Justices Burns and McLean. S.B. Freeman appeared for the prisoner, and Henry Eccles and R.A. Harrison for the attorney general. Freeman read the warrant of committal by William Matthews and the two other Brantford magistrates who had been associated with him. The evidence was to the effect that on September 28, 1859 (*sic*) Anderson was on the estate of Seneca T.P. Diggs, in Howard County, Missouri, and that Diggs, while attempting with Negro help to arrest Anderson, was stabbed twice and later died.

The question was whether Canada should administer the slave laws of Missouri. The counsel for the Crown admitted that Anderson's act, if committed in Canada, would not have been murder.

The Anderson case was practically the last important case to come before Chief Justice Sir John Beverly Robinson, and around perhaps no decision of his whole legal career did more excitement centre. While the justices were considering the evidence, public meetings were being held, not only in Toronto but in other Canadian cities. Newspapers were furiously defending the fugitive, and the judgment of the court was being awaited with tense interest.

It was understood on November 30 that the chief justice was ready to give his decision, but that he deferred for his associates. On that date, there were special police on duty all about the court out of fear of an attempt at rescue by the Negroes and others. The *Globe* of that date contended that the question of surrendering the man, being a matter of treaty, should have been dealt with by the executive and not by the courts at all.

"The universal heart and conscience of the people of Canada and of the British nation will say upon the facts of the case that Anderson is not a murderer in the sight of God, or under British law," was a part of its comment editorially on the case. A day or two later, the paper pointed out the significance of this particular case. If Anderson were given up, it maintained, "no fugitive slave in Canada is safe on our soil ... there is not a fugitive in Canada whose extradition may not be demanded upon evidence sufficient to put the accused upon his trial."[5]

The court finally gave its judgment on Saturday, December 15. The papers of the following Monday say that as the decision was being given, police stood about the court with muskets, and that a company of Royal Canadian Rifles were also under arms at the Government House.

In its decision the court was not unanimous. The Chief Justice and Justice Burns favoured extradition, while Justice McLean dissented. The biographer of the Chief Justice says of this judgment: "Their decision was neither in support nor against slavery but was based entirely upon the consideration of the treaty existing between the United States and Canada." The biographer quotes also as follows from an English contemporary: "These judges, proof against unpopularity and unswayed by their own bitter hatred of slavery, as well as unsoftened by their own feelings for a fellow man, in agonizing peril, upheld the law made to their hands and which they are sworn faithfully to administer. *Fiat justitia.* Give them their due. Such men are the ballast of nations."[6]

Gerrit Smith, the famous abolitionist, was one of those who acted on behalf of the fugitive, and his plea made a strong impression. He argued that Anderson was not guilty of murder, but at the worst of homicide, that the Ashburton Treaty did not require the surrender of fugitives, and that in any case Anderson's delivery was a matter for the English courts to decide.

On the evening of December 19, 1860, a huge mass meeting was held in St. Lawrence Hall. The mayor of the city presided, and the chief speaker of the evening was John Scoble, the abolitionist.[7] He was able to throw considerable light on the exact meaning of the extradition treaty, having interviewed both Lord Aberdeen and Lord Brougham on its terms in relation to fugitive slaves at the time that it was passing through the British parliament. He was at that time the secretary of the Anti-Slavery Society of England, which had become alarmed over the possibilities to fugitives in Canada of the extradition clauses.[8]

Ashburton told him, he said, "that the article in question was no more designed to touch the fugitive slave than to affect the case of deserters or parties charged with high treason." Lord Aberdeen stated that instructions would be sent to the governor of Canada that in the case of fugitive slaves, great care was to be taken to see that the treaty did not work toward their ruin. Sir Charles Metcalfe, governor of Canada, was quoted by the speaker as having said that he would never be a party to wronging fugitives.

In the course of his address, Mr. Scoble gave some information about arrest of Anderson. He said that he personally went to Brantford as soon as Anderson was taken up in April and tried to get a writ of habeas corpus, but could get no help from counsel in Brantford. At the Brantford spring assizes, Anderson was released by the judge, since there was no evidence against him, but was rearrested three days later. Other speakers at the St. Lawrence Hall gathering were Reverend William King, M.C. Cameron, Reverend Dr. Willis, Reverend Dr. Burns, Peter Brown, and Reverend

Mr. Marling. At the close of the meeting there were cheers for Anderson and others and groans for Magistrate Matthews.

There was much comment in the Canadian press on the case as a whole, and on the judgment in particular. The *Montreal Herald* of December 19, 1860 said: "We hope that the day will never come when the wretches who traffic in the bodies and souls of their fellow creatures will be able to say to any British subject, 'And thou also art made like unto us.'" The *Quebec Mercury* said: "The judgment of the court in Anderson's case is one of those infamous prostitutions of judicial power to political expediency which in this degenerate age have too frequently polluted the judicial ermine." The Montreal *Witness* said: "Such a gigantic wrong cannot exist on the same continent with us without affecting the people of Canada in one way or another. Slaveholders long looked at Canada with evil eye. If the slavers get Anderson back they will execute him before the slaves. It would be worth hundreds of thousands of dollars to them annually."

Speaking on the evening of December 20 before the St. Patrick's Literary Society of Montreal, the Honourable Thomas D'Arcy McGee condemned the decision in the Anderson case. "As a fugitive slave has never been yielded by this province," he said, "I cannot believe that we are going to take upon ourselves the yoke of that servitude just now. We have no bonds to break or keep with the 'peculiar institution' of the South; and the true voice and spirit of this province is that when the flying slave has once put the roar of Niagara between him and the bay of the bloodhounds of his master — from that hour, no man shall ever dream of recovering him as his chattel property."

As soon as the decision of the Court of Queen's Bench was given, abolitionists in Toronto decided to carry the case to English courts, and did so, securing from the Court of Queen's Bench at Westminster an order to bring Anderson there. In the meantime, the case was carried to the Court of Common Pleas in Toronto, and there, on February 16, 1861, Chief Justice Draper acquitted Anderson for the following reasons, as quoted in the *Toronto Leader*: "In the first place, the magistrate's warrant was defective inasmuch as the words used in the warrant did not imply the charge of murder, though perhaps expressing more than manslaughter; secondly, the warrant of commitment was also defective in not adhering to the words of the treaty."

It would take a long time to list all the meetings, petitions, resolutions, and protests that were brought forth by the Anderson case. The Anti-Slavery Society of Canada, with its headquarters in Toronto, was, of course, active throughout the whole case. Early in January, it was reported that a petition signed by more than 2,500 people had been forwarded from Montreal on behalf of Anderson, and from elsewhere in Canada came similar protests.

With the decision of Chief Justice Draper the Anderson case was closed and the fugitive disappeared from history. As a result, however, of the unseemly actions of the Brantford magistrate, Canadian law was revised so as to take from the control of ordinary magistrates jurisdiction as regards foreign fugitives from justice, leaving such cases with county judges and police justices.

25

Anthony Burns in Canada

Ontario Historical Society, Papers and Records, *vol. 22 (1925)*,
162–66

The most dramatic fugitive slave case ever fought out in the courts of the United States was that of Anthony Burns. His fate interested millions, he was the cause of riots in Boston, and he was returned to slavery in Virginia by the courts of the free state of Massachusetts under circumstances of strikingly sensational character.

The body of Anthony Burns lies buried today in the cemetery at St. Catharines, Ontario, forgotten and neglected save for the attention it gets from one humble coloured family in that city. In the summer of 1924, the tombstone lay in three pieces, as it had fallen over some time before. But the name of Anthony Burns is not forgotten, nor is it likely to be forgotten while men recall the great issue that divided the United States during the first six decades of the nineteenth century, and was settled at last by a long and costly civil war.

The career of Anthony Burns is one well-known to students of American history, though probably few Canadians have heard of it. In the year 1850, there was legislation passed by Congress, known as the Fugitive Slave Act, the purpose of which was to enable the owners of runaway slaves to secure their property, wherever it might be found within the bounds of the republic, and return it to the South. There had been other fugitive slave laws before that of 1850, but none so drastic.[1]

President Millard Fillmore signed the bill on September 18, 1850, and at once consternation reigned among the coloured population in the northern states. Those who were fugitives from the South knew that every effort would be made to track them down, while those who were legally free could not but fear that they might become entangled in the meshes of this new net, and find themselves back in a condition of servitude. The consequence of this double fear was that a movement of Negroes into Canada began immediately, and it is estimated that within three months about 5,000 Black people had entered the British dominions.[2]

More than any other influence of the time, the Fugitive Slave Act stirred the conscience of the free North to a realization of what slavery actually meant. There was an intense, flaming opposition to the legislation. Men and women openly defied its provisions, and some were subjected to imprisonment for so doing. Here and there a whole community would rise in protest against the law, and riots and bloody encounters between abolitionists and slave-catchers marked the years after 1850. The sequel of many such an encounter is found in the brief statement that the escaped slave, the cause of the riot, has "gone to Canada."

Anthony Burns was a runaway slave living in Boston in 1854. He had formerly been the property of a Virginian, and the latter eventually traced him to his place of refuge. The Negro was arrested on the evening of the May 24, 1854, and the next morning was taken, manacled, to the federal courtroom for examination. Proceedings there would have been of a brief character, had not some Boston abolitionists happened to enter the court and there proceeded to set up a defence for the fugitive. The citizens of Boston soon learned by inflammatory handbills and through the newspapers of the court proceedings, and during the following days excitement ran high. A mass meeting of citizens, for the purpose of protesting against the law, was held in Faneuil Hall on the evening of May 26, and speeches of an inflammatory character were delivered by Wendell Phillips and Theodore Parker. These men raised a storm that they found themselves unable to control.[3] An immediate effect of the excitement raised was the rush of a mob to the jail where Burns was confined, 2,000 men being determined to rescue him. The door was broken in, and during the tumult one man was killed and several others injured. Two companies of artillery finally cleared the streets.

On the morning of May 29 the trial of Burns was resumed, with soldiers on guard against further violence. Counsel for the fugitive made a strong defence, but the law was the law, and on the 2nd of June it was decreed by Commissioner Loring that the Negro should be sent back to his former owner in Virginia.

Then came the most dramatic of all the incidents in connection with the case. The public officials were in fear of an attempt at rescue, and a large military force was brought in to guard against any violence. The civic police force was reinforced by no less than 22 companies of state militia, the streets were patrolled by cavalry, artillery was in evidence, and the city as a whole was practically under martial law.

At the appointed hour on the afternoon of June 2, the prisoner was taken from the jail and the parade started in the direction of the harbour, where the fugitive was to be taken aboard ship and returned to slavery. In the guard that marched that day through the streets of Boston, surrounding Burns, there was a regiment of artillery, a platoon of United States Marines, the marshal's civic posse of 125 men close in about the prisoner, two further platoons of Marines immediately behind with a field piece, and yet another platoon of Marines to guard it.

Boston citizens showed quite emphatically what they thought of the whole business. Along the line of march, both store and office windows were draped in black cloth. From a window opposite the old State House was suspended a black coffin on which were the words "The funeral of liberty." Here and there was to be seen the flag of the country reversed as a sign of mourning. It is estimated that 50,000 people stood on the sidewalks and saw the procession pass by. Thousands bared their heads. Hoots and hisses and cries of "Shame" were frequent. And all this military display was for one, lone, friendless Negro who passed along, somewhat as Marie Antoinette had sat in a cart and passed through the crowded streets of Paris 60-odd years before. But this Boston crowd jeered at the guard, while the Paris mob had jeered the royal prisoner. There was a grim spirit abroad in Boston that afternoon. A slight occasion might easily have precipitated a terrible riot. But there was no rioting, no violence, and towards evening the Black man was put aboard a revenue cutter headed for slavery. As the boat passed out of the harbour it met another vessel coming in, a great passenger steamer carrying the Southern members of a commercial convention. They crowded the rail to witness the passing of a boat carrying Anthony Burns, and their band struck up "The Star Spangled Banner." It was a great day for slavery. The *New York Times* said that it cost the federal government more than $40,000 to return Burns to slavery, but the Richmond *Whig* put the cost in another way when it said: "We rejoice at the recapture of Burns, but a few more such victories and the South is undone."

The later history of Anthony Burns has a more special interest for Canadians. Shortly after returning to Virginia, he was sold to go to North Carolina. Within a few months, however, he was purchased with money that was raised by the Twelfth Baptist Church, of Boston, and its pastor, Reverend L.A. Grimes. Burns had been a member of this church. In 1855, through the kindness of a Boston woman, he secured a scholarship at Oberlin College and went there to study. Mr. Azariah S. Root, the librarian of Oberlin College, says that the Oberlin College records show Anthony Burns first enrolled there as a student in 1855, that he continued there during the school year 1885–56, then seems to have been elsewhere for a year. In 1857 he returned, and his name continues on the roll until 1862. Oberlin has no other record of his career. It is stated that he was at Fremont Institute for a time. This may have been during 1856–57. For a short time in 1860 he was in charge of the coloured Baptist church in Indianapolis, but was forced to leave by the threat of enforcement of the Black Laws of the state, which would have meant a fine and imprisonment for him. It was shortly after this that he decided to come to Canada, where he located at St. Catharines and became pastor of Zion Baptist Church. Here he laboured with much zeal until his death on July 27, 1862.

A communication to a St. Catharines paper at the time of his death speaks in warm terms of his work while in that city. The article, in part, reads as follows:

> On Monday last, the mortal remains of the Reverend Anthony Burns, pastor of the coloured Baptist church of this town, were conveyed to their last resting place, the St. Catharines cemetery. It is several months since the deceased was prostrated with disease, but it was not thought that the end was so near or that his labours were to have so abrupt a termination. The best medical aid was procured, but that most uncompromising and wasting disease, consumption, had taken a fast hold of

him and all that human skill could do failed to wrest the sufferer from its grasp.

He had been here only a short time. When he came he saw that there was much for him to do and he set himself to do it with all his heart, and he was prospering in his work, he was getting the affairs of the church in good shape.... Mr. Burns' memory will be cherished long by not a few in this town. His gentle, unassuming and yet manly bearing secured him many friends. His removal is felt to be a great loss and his place will not soon be filled.

Over his grave, a simple stone was raised bearing this inscription:

In Memoriam
REV. ANTHONY BURNS
The fugitive slave of the Boston riots, 1854.
Pastor of Zion Baptist Church.
Born in Virginia, May 31, 1834,
Died in the Triumph of Faith in St. Catharines,
July 27th A.D. 1862.

Reverend R.A. Ball, formerly pastor of the British Methodist Episcopal Church in St. Catharines, but now living in Toronto, has supplied some details of the personal appearance of Anthony Burns. Mr. Ball writes: "He was a fine-looking man, tall and broad-shouldered, but with a slight stoop, indicating a weak chest. His colour was light brown. He was a fine speaker and was considered to be well educated. He was unmarried and very popular with both the white people and the people of his own race."

Mrs. Ball, wife of Reverend Ball, played the organ at the memorial service, which was held in the church of which Anthony Burns had been pastor.

In November 1918, a number of interesting letters and documents connected with the Burns case were sold by the Libbie Book Auction House of Boston. One of these was an offer of $500 from P.T. Barnum, the showman, if Burns would tell his story to the museum* visitors for five weeks. The offer, however, was not accepted. *A Life of Anthony Burns*, by Charles Emery Stevens, was printed in Boston in 1856, too early, of course, to have any details of the later years in Canada. Proceeds from this book appear to have aided Burns in securing his education at Oberlin, for there is a letter written in 1856 in which he says: "I have bought and sold nearly a hundred of these books in Oberlin."

In the same letter, referring to the presidential election of 1856, in which James Buchanan was successful, he says: "I have been waiting to see which way the nation would turn, which seems to have turned together over the left.** I suppose, Sir, that the work of hell will go on in the South."

James Ford Rhodes, the historian, in summarizing the Anthony Burns case says:

> To this complexion had it come at last. In a community celebrated all over the world for the respect it yielded to law, and for obedience to those clothed with authority; in a community where the readiness of all citizens to assist the authorities had struck intelligent Europeans with amazement, it now required to execute a law a large body of deputy marshals, the whole force of the city police, 1,140 soldiers with muskets loaded, supplied with 11 rounds of powder and ball and furnished with a cannon loaded with grapeshot. If anything were needed to heighten the strangeness of the situation, it may be found in the fact that the marshal's deputies were taken from the dregs of society, for no reputable citizens would serve as a slave catcher.
>
> As the men of Boston and the men of New England reflected on what had taken place, they were persuaded,

---

* Editors' Note: This was P.T. Barnum's famous "American Museum" in Lower Manhattan, which stood on Broadway from 1843 to 1865.

** Editors' Note: Possibly he means turning to the left, or sinister, side as in Latin, meaning to turn evil.

as they had never been before, that something was rotten in the United States, and that these events boded some strange eruption to our state. Nor was the significance of the transaction entirely lost upon the South.[4]

"The tables under the Fugitive Slave Law are beginning at last to turn against the law and in favor of humanity," Seward wrote to his wife under the date of May 28, 1854. "There is deep and painful suspense here."[5]

Whittier, the poet, was moved to verse, and his poem, "The Rendition," commemorates the Anthony Burns affair. It may be found in his collected works:

> I heard the train's shrill whistle call,
> I saw an earnest look beseech,
> And rather by that look than speech
> My neighbor told me all.
> And as I thought of Liberty
> Marched handcuffed down that sworded street,
> The solid earth beneath my feet
> Reeled fluid as the sea.
> I felt a sense of bitter loss —
> Shame, tearless grief and stifling wrath,
> And loathing fear, as if my path
> A serpent stretched across.
> All love of home, all pride of place,
> All generous confidence and trust
> Sank smothering in that deep disgust
> And anguish of disgrace.
> Down on my native hills of June,
> And home's green quiet, hiding all,
> Fell sudden darkness like the fall
> Of midnight upon noon.
> And Law, an unloosed maniac, strong,
> Blood-drunken, through the Blackness trod,
> Hoarse-shouting in the ear of God

Anthony Burns in Canada

The blasphemy of wrong.
"O Mother, from thy memories proud,
Thy old renown, dear Commonwealth,
Lend this dead air a breeze of health,
And smite with tears this cloud."
"Mother of Freedom, wise and brave,
Rise awful in thy strength," I said;
Ah me! I spake but to the dead;
I stood upon her grave.

26

Abraham Lincoln a Century Ago

London Free Press *(February 12, 1951)*, 4

Abraham Lincoln must have been in a thoughtful mood a century ago today, when he came to his 42nd birthday. It was usual for him to be thoughtful, but in 1851 there were conditions relating to his own welfare, and conditions relating to the national welfare that could well give him pause for reflection. Life had not hitherto been successful in any material way. He was a small-town lawyer with a reputation for political sense that had led him first to the legislature of his own state, Illinois, and then had given him one none-too-happy term in the House of Representatives at Washington.

He had come away from the capital an unhappy man, disappointed at failing to receive an appointment that he had sought, and with no desire to continue in Congress. He is probably remembered most as a Congressman by the question that he asked: "Where is the spot where the first aggression came from Mexico that led to the war with that country?" The administration did not find it easy to answer that question.

But out of the war that had so recently closed, with Mexico defeated and forced to make vast territorial concessions — California and the great southwestern area — there came a variety of problems that were to vex the country for the next ten years, and then ultimately lead to the election of Abraham Lincoln as president, a great four years of civil war, and the disappearance of that institution of slavery that had so long bedevilled politics.

But on that 42nd birthday in February 1851, slavery had seemed to triumph in the compromise that Henry Clay had brought about in the previous autumn. The whole United States was watching the outcome of the compromise during the year 1850, but opponents of slavery were watching one portion, which provided for the rendition back to slavery of escaped slaves who came into the North. There was nothing new in the idea, but what was new and horrible was the complete lack of humanity in Clay's measure, passage of which had been insisted upon by the South as a condition of supporting other sections of the agreement.

Back in Springfield, Illinois, Lincoln must have read in the newspapers that the Fugitive Slave Act was producing panic among the free Negroes of the North, none of whom were any longer safe from possible apprehension and return to slavery. If he read Garrison's *Liberator*, and no doubt he did, he could find abundant evidence of the panic that had come. Within a month after its passage, the act had been denounced by the Common Council of the City of Chicago, in Lincoln's own state, as a violation of the Constitution of the United States. Charles Sumner had addressed a meeting in Boston in November at which he declared that, though the act might be enforced, even in liberty-loving Massachusetts, he believed that public opinion would make it a dead letter. Yet only three days after Lincoln's birthday, a Negro was to be taken up and charged with being a fugitive. The sequel bore out Sumner's prediction. A mob broke into the jail where the Negro was confined, rescued him, and sent him off to Canada. Violence had begun.

But Lincoln's day had not yet come. There were years ahead, a whole decade, during which he thought over the problems of his country, and particularly the great problem of human slavery. Even the intimate account left for us by [William H.] Herndon, his young law partner, does not reveal clearly the current of Lincoln's thoughts on life generally, or on the political problems that were about him in the early 1850s.

In so far as his thought and study turned to politics, it seems to have led him to the conclusion that there was no immediate place for him. But, as one of his biographers has pointed out, "it does seem that the melancholy sense of some great purpose unachieved or some great destiny awaiting him never quite left him." It was not until 1854, when Stephen Douglas brought forward his bill to open the Nebraska country to settlement, with its ominous clause permitting slavery in this area, that Lincoln was brought to his feet, his whole attitude toward national affairs stirred and his steps planted in the way that was to lead him to the head of the nation, and to ultimate martyrdom.

What a whirl of events followed 1854. The Fugitive Slave Law was no longer the chief centre of abolitionist interest, though in that very year came what was probably the most sensational trial arising out of the legislation, the case of Anthony Burns, which, like that of Shadrack in 1850, originated in Boston and had its termination in Canada.

Lincoln might conceivably have been the Republican candidate for president in 1856, but happily he was not — his time had not yet come. The Supreme Court decision in 1857, by Chief Justice Taney, in the case of the Negro Dred Scott,* gave new life to the defeated Republicans, and by 1858 Abraham Lincoln had become a national figure through his great debate out in Illinois with Douglas. Men began to talk after 1858 of this westerner, whose thinking was so clear and who had such understanding of the country's problems.

By 1859 he was made known to the East, which had not previously encountered him, and in 1860, at the great convention in Chicago, he was the choice of the newly rejuvenated Republican Party that had risen out of the Nebraska issue, but which had behind it the agitation, over decades, of men and women who were opposed to slavery.

The man who thought in 1851, became, in 1861, the man who acted.

---

* Editors' Note: Landon here refers to the case of the enslaved Dred Scott who sued for his freedom in a ten-year court case that began in 1847. When it reached the Supreme Court of the United States, Chief Justice Roger B. Taney brought down a landmark decision, that Black people "had no rights which the white man was bound to respect," and that a Black man was not and could never be a citizen of the United States. He also ruled that the government had no right to prohibit the expansion of slavery into the newly added American territories, a decision that effectively overruled the Missouri Compromise of 1820.

A Bibliography of Fred Landon's
Writings on Black History

This annotated list of Fred Landon's work on Black history is based firstly on the bibliography of his writings that I published in *Ontario History* in March 1970, a bibliography that concentrated on his academic publications and omitted his journalism. Because this book celebrates Landon's contribution to the history of Blacks in Canada, it was important to produce a bibliography that demonstrated the breadth and depth of that rich historiographical vein. Fred Landon reached a broad audience with his newspaper articles, publishing his first one on a Black subject in *The Dawn of Tomorrow* in 1919, and his last in the *London Free Press* in January 1969, the year of his death. I have identified these articles by consulting his voluminous papers deposited in the University of Western Ontario Archives. From his early days as a newspaperman, Landon clipped material on the historical and political subjects that interested him from a variety of published sources, and gathered them into scrapbooks. He did the same with his own journalism. I was able to identify additional articles through indices to the *Free Press* historical page, "Looking Over Western Ontario," consulted both at the University of Western Ontario Archives and the Ivey Family London Room at the London Public Library. I am grateful to the staff of both collections for their advice and assistance. Omissions are regrettably my own, and I would be grateful to be informed of them.

1918

1. "The Buxton Settlement in Canada." *Journal of Negro History* vol. 3, no. 4 (October 1918): 360–67.

2. "The Canadian Anti-Slavery Group." *University Magazine* vol. 17 (1918): 540–47. Reprinted in *The Dawn of Tomorrow* (February 19, 1927): 1, 8; (March 12, 1927): 4, 5.
3. "The History of the Wilberforce Refugee Colony in Middlesex County." *Transactions of the London & Middlesex Historical Society* vol. 19 (1918): 30–44. A paper read before the society on April 16, 1918.

1919

4. "The Anti-Slavery Society of Canada." *Journal of Negro History* vol. 4 (1919): 33–40.
5. "Canada's Part in Freeing the Slave." *Ontario Historical Society, Papers and Records* vol.17 (1919): 74–84.
6. "From Chatham to Harper's Ferry." *Canadian Magazine* vol. 53 (1919): 441–48. Reprinted as: "John Brown Raid Took Place in 1859." *The Dawn of Tomorrow* (September 27, 1924): 1; (October 18, 1924): 1, 6; (October 25, 1924): 1; (November 1, 1924): 1; (November 15, 1924): 1, 4.
7. "The Fugitive Slave in Canada." *University Magazine* vol.18 (1919): 270–79. Reprinted in *The Dawn of Tomorrow* (July 30, 1927): 5; (August 27, 1927): 8; (October 8, 1927): 4, 5.
8. "Fugitive Slaves in London, Before 1860." *London & Middlesex Historical Society* vol. 10 (1919): 25–38. A paper read before the society on January 21, 1919.
9. "The Relation of Canada to the Anti-Slavery and Abolition Movements in the United States." Unpublished M.A. thesis, University of Western Ontario, 1919.

1920

10. "Henry Bibb, a Colonizer." *Journal of Negro History* vol. 5 (October 1920): 437–47.
11. "The Negro Migration to Canada After the Passing of the Fugitive Slave

Act." *Journal of Negro History* vol. 5 (January 1920): 22–36. Reprinted in *The Dawn of Tomorrow* (October 27, 1923): 7; (November 3, 1923): 7; (November 17, 1923): 7; (November 24, 1923): 2; (December 1, 1923): 6; (December 22, 1923): 8; and also (March 12, 1927): 5; (April 8, 1927): 3, 4 [listed incorrectly under "Canadian Anti-Slavery Group"]; (May 6, 1927): 8; and (June 4, 1927): 6.

12. Letter to the editor, *Journal of Negro History* vol. 5 (1920): 462–463. Landon discussed the attitude of Canadians toward Black refugees.

13. Review of W.R. Riddell. *The Slave in Canada. Canadian Historical Review* vol. 1 (1920): 402–03.

1921

14. "Canadian Negroes and the John Brown Raid." *Journal of Negro History* vol. 6, no. 2 (April 1921): 174–82.

15. "A Daring Canadian Abolitionist." *Michigan History Magazine* vol. 5 (1921): 364–73. An abbreviated version was also published as "Dr. Milton Ross Friend of Slaves," *The Dawn of Tomorrow* (July 19, 1924): 1–2; and a second version, "Alexander Milton Ross and the Abolition of Slavery," also in *The Dawn of Tomorrow* (September 29, 1928): 1, 6. Landon told one story from this article again in *The Dawn of Tomorrow* (January 5, 1924): 5. Dr. Alexander Milton Ross helped many Blacks escape slavery on the Underground Railroad.

1922

16. "The Anderson Fugitive Case." *Journal of Negro History* vol. 7, no. 3 (July 1922): 233–42.

17. "Canadian Negroes and the Rebellion of 1837." *Journal of Negro History* vol. 7, no. 4 (October 1922): 377–79.

18. "The Diary of Benjamin Lundy, Written During His Journey Through Upper Canada (January 1832)." Edited and introduced by Fred Landon. *Ontario Historical Society, Papers and Records* vol. 19 (1922): 110–33.

1923

19. "Away to Canada." *The Dawn of Tomorrow* (September 29, 1923): 6. Landon found the lyrics to a fugitive slave song in the *Voice of the Fugitive.*
20. "Canada and the Underground Railroad." *Kingston Historical Society, Reports and Proceedings* (1923): 17–31.

1924

21. "America's Most Famous Fugitive Slave is Buried in Western Ontario Cemetery." *London Free Press* (August 2, 1924): 17, 19. Anthony Burns's grave is in St. Catharines.
22. "John Brown Raid Took Place in 1859." *The Dawn of Tomorrow* (September 27, 1924): 1; (October 18, 1924): 1, 6; (October 25, 1924): 1; (November 1, 1924): 1; (November 15, 1924): 1, 4.
23. "The Negro Refugees in Canada West 1848–1864." *American Missionary* vol. 78 (November 1924): 16–66, 296–97.
24. "Professor Fred Landon Compliments 'Dawn.'" *The Dawn of Tomorrow* (July 12, 1924): 1, 8. On the first anniversary of the publication of *The National Negro Weekly*, Landon drew a parallel between Henry Bibb's *Voice of the Fugitive* and *The Dawn of Tomorrow.*
25. "'We Are Free,' Answer of Slave to 'Old Massa.'" *London Free Press* (August 23, 1924): 18.
26. "The Work of the American Missionary Association Among the Negro Refugees in Canada West, 1848–1864." *Ontario Historical Society, Papers and Records* vol. 21 (1924): 198–205. Printed also in *The Dawn of Tomorrow* (July 14, 1923): 2, 7; (July 21, 1923): 3; (July 28, 1923): 3.

1925

27. "Amherstburg, Terminus of the Underground Railroad." *Journal of Negro History* vol. 10, no. 1 (January 1925): 1–9. Reprinted in *The Dawn of Tomorrow* (February 7, 1925): 1, 6.

28. "Anthony Burns in Canada 1860–62." *Ontario Historical Society, Papers and Records* vol. 22 (1924): 162–66.

29. "The Kidnapping of Dr. Rufus Bratton." *Journal of Negro History* vol. 10 (1925): 330–33. Bratton fled to London, Ontario, after he was involved in a Ku Klux Klan murder in South Carolina. Kidnapped by American detectives, he was returned to Canada after his capture raised issues of extradition and sovereignty between Canada and the United States.

30. "Social Conditions Among the Negroes in Upper Canada Before 1865." *Ontario Historical Society, Papers and Records* vol. 22 (1925): 144–61. Landon included "A Selected Bibliography on the Negro in Canada" at the end of this article. Reprinted in *The Dawn of Tomorrow* (February 6, 1926): 1, 6; (February 20, 1926): 1, 6; (March 6, 1926): 1, 6.

1926

31. "Diary of Anti-Slavery Advocate Furnishes Pen Picture of Early Days." *London Free Press* (February 20, 1926): 10. Benjamin Lundy's travels in Western Ontario.

32. "Elgin Negro Settlement in Kent County Founded by Scottish Minister." *London Free Press* (October 30, 1926): 8. Reverend William King's settlement of fugitive slaves in Buxton.

33. "In an old Ontario Cemetery." *Dalhousie Review* vol. 5 (1926): 523–31. Landon locates the graves of some fugitive slaves in Ontario, especially that of Anthony Burns in St. Catharines.

34. "Wilberforce Colony One of Romantic Chapters in History of This District." *London Free Press* (August 28, 1926): 8.

35. [Fred Landon published an article on the abduction of Dr. Rufus Bratton in 1872 in the *London Free Press* (April 3, 1926). This is mentioned in a letter to the editor, (April 11, 1926), and the article is listed in the indexes to the *Free Press*'s "Looking Over Western Ontario" pages in both the University of Western Ontario Archives and the Ivey Family London Room. It is possible that this article was published in the *Free Press* morning edition, as it could not be found on the microfilm copy of the evening edition.]

1927

36. "Benjamin Lundy, Abolitionist." *Dalhousie Review* vol. 7 (1927): 189–97.
37. "Letters Appearing in *The Fugitive Slave* Over 75 Years Ago." *The Dawn of Tomorrow* (November 5, 1927): 1, 8. These were published in the *Voice of the Fugitive* (January 29, 1852).
38. "The Thames Valley" in Jesse Middleton and Fred Landon, *The Province of Ontario, a History, 1615–1927* vol. 2, chapter 6 (Toronto: Dominion Publishing Company, 1927–28): 1029–1033. In this chapter, Landon traces the movements of fugitive slaves into the province and summarizes the settlements of Wilberforce, Buxton, and Dawn.

1928

39. "Canada before the Civil War." *The Dawn of Tomorrow* (January 26, 1928): 1, 6. Landon recounts the attempted kidnapping of a Black boy, which was foiled by the quick response of Elijah Leonard (and other Good Samaritan actions).
40. "Interesting Report of American Anti-Slavery Society." *The Dawn of Tomorrow* (June 23, 1928): 1, 6. The society's fourth annual report, published in July 1837.
41. "The Origin and Decline of Slavery in the Dominion." *The Dawn of Tomorrow* (October 30, 1928): 1, 6.
42. "Records Illustrating the Condition of Refugees from Slavery in Upper Canada Before 1860." *Journal of Negro History* vol. 13 (April 1928) 199–206. A collection of documents.
43. Review of A.H. Abel and F.J. Klingberg, eds. *A Sidelight on Anglo-American Relations, 1839–1858, Furnished by the Correspondence of Lewis Tappan and Others with the British and Foreign Anti-Slavery Society. Canadian Historical Review* vol. 9 (1928): 72–73.

1929

44. "Negro Colonization Schemes in Upper Canada before 1860." *Transactions of the Royal Society of Canada* 3rd. ser., vol. 23 (1929), section 2, 73–80. A paper read at the annual meeting, May 1929.
45. "Professor William King and North Buxton." *The Dawn of Tomorrow* (December 20, 1929): 1, 2.
46. Review of Ulrich Bonnell Phillips, *Life and Labor in the Old South. Willison's Monthly* vol. 5 (1929): 26.

1930

47. "John Brown and Harper's Ferry." *The Dawn of Tomorrow* (May 21, 1930): 1, 2.
48. "Tablet Unveiled at Windsor, Ontario." *The Dawn of Tomorrow* (October 1, 1930): 1, 7. An account of the commemoration in Windsor by the Historic Sites and Monuments Board of Canada of the part played by that community in the Underground Railway.

1931

49. Letter and editorial note on the work of James F. Jenkins, organizing secretary of the Canadian League for the Advancement of Coloured People and editor of *The Dawn of Tomorrow,* the league's official publication. *Journal of Negro History* vol. 16 (1931): 343.
50. "Richard Realf, Friend of John Brown, Attended Famous Chatham Rally." *London Free Press* (October 17, 1931): 8.

1932

51. "Benjamin Lundy Found London Village Place of Promising Outlook." *London Free Press* (August 13, 1932): 9. Lundy visited London on his

way to the Wilberforce Settlement, north of Lucan.

52. "Canada's Relation to the John Brown Raid." *The Dawn of Tomorrow* (November 30, 1932): 1; (February 28, 1933): 1. An abbreviated version of his article in the *Journal of Negro History,* 1921.

53. "Owned Slaves, Gave Freedom in Homes Here." *London Free Press* (November 12, 1932): 8. Reverend William King and the Elgin Settlement.

54. "Stage Trip to London Revealed Attractions to Pioneer Traveller." *London Free Press* (August 6, 1932): 8. Benjamin Lundy's trip through southwestern Ontario.

55. Review of Ida Greaves. *The Negro in Canada* (McGill University Economic Studies no. 16, National Problems of Canada). *Canadian Historical Review* vol. 13 (1932): 217–18.

1933

56. "Benjamin Lay." *Dictionary of American Biography* vol. 11 (New York: Charles Scribner's Sons, 1933): 63–64. Lay was an abolitionist who influenced Quaker attitudes toward slavery.

57. "Benjamin Lundy." *Dictionary of American Biography* vol. 11 (New York: Charles Scribner's Sons, 1933): 506–07.

1934

58. "Famous Negro Refugee Buried at St. Kitts." *London Free Press* (June 2, 1934): 6. Reverend Anthony Burns.

59. "Ulrich B. Phillips, Southern Historian." *London Free Press* (February 27, 1934): 6. Phillips was a historian of slavery and the plantation system.

60. "Introduction to Everett E. Edwards, a Bibliography of the Writings of Ulrich Bonnell Phillips." *Agricultural History* vol. 8 (1934): 196–99.

61. Review of G.H. Barnes, *The Anti-Slavery Impulse, 1830–1844.* *American Historical Review* vol. 39 (1934): 747–49.

1935

62. "Buxton Negro Colony Most Successful Set up for the Refugees." *London Free Press* (December 21, 1935): 12.

63. "Lundy Close Student of Conditions When Touring West Ontario." *London Free Press* (December 14, 1935): 32.

64. "Richard Realf." *Dictionary of American Biography* vol. 15 (New York: Charles Scribner's Sons, 1935): 434–35. Realf was an American abolitionist who took part in John Brown's convention in Chatham in 1858.

65. Review of G.H. Barnes and D.L. Dumond, eds. *Letters of Theodore Dwight Weld, Angelina Grimké Weld and Sarah Grimké, 1822–1844 American Historical Review* vol. 41 (1935): 162–64. Theodore Dwight Weld was an influential American abolitionist.

1936

66. "Agriculture Among the Negro Refugees in Upper Canada." *Journal of Negro History* vol. 21, no. 3 (July 1936): 304–12.

67. "Fugitive Slaves in Ontario." *Northwest Ohio Historical Society Quarterly Bulletin* vol. 8, no. 2 (1936): 1–12. A digest of two papers read to the London & Middlesex Historical Society.

68. "Henry Bibb was Courageous as Friend of Negro." *London Free Press* (April 25, 1936): 18. In his report on fugitive slaves in Canada in 1851, Reverend Samuel J. May praised Henry Bibb's work in Sandwich, Essex County.

69. "Samuel Ringgold Ward." *Dictionary of American Biography* vol. 19 (New York: Charles Scribner's Sons, 1936): 440. Ward was a Black abolitionist who immigrated to Canada and worked as an agent for the Anti-Slavery Society of Canada.

70. Review of Elizabeth Donnan, ed. *Documents Illustrative of the History of the Slave Trade to America*, 4 vols. *Canadian Historical Review* vol. 17 (1936): 76.

1937

71. "Wilberforce, an Experiment in the Colonization of Freed Negroes in Upper Canada." *Transactions of the Royal Society of Canada*, 3rd ser., vol. 31 (1937), section 2: 69–78. A paper read at the annual meeting, May 1937.

72. Review of H.T. Catterall. *Judicial Cases Concerning American Slavery and the Negro*, 5 vols. *Canadian Historical Review* vol. 18 (1937): 464.

1938

73. "The Fifteenth Anniversary." *The Dawn of Tomorrow* (July 25, 1938): 2. Landon praises this weekly for its leadership in Ontario's Black community.

74. "Henry Bibb Rated High as Director of Flight from Slavery in South." *London Free Press* (March 5, 1938): 15.

75. "Ontario Churches Friends in Need to the Panic-Stricken Fugitives Fleeing from Drastic Slave Laws." *London Free Press,* (April 9, 1938): 15.

1939

76. "Benjamin Lundy, Abolitionist, 1789–1839." [10 pages in] *A Memorial to Benjamin Lundy, Pioneer Quaker Abolitionist, 1789–1839.* A sketch prepared for the centenary of Lundy's death and published by the Lundy Centenary Committee of Illinois in its memorial booklet, 1939.

77. "Benjamin Lundy was Keen Observer on London District Visit in 1832 Seeing Rich Promise for Settlers." *London Free Press* (June 10, 1939): 15.

78. "Coloured People Among First to Settle in City." *London Free Press* (June 21, 1939): 3. Landon's history of Blacks in London for a special issue of the newspaper.

79. "Coloured People Keen to Fight for New Home." *London Free Press* (April 29, 1939): 20. Black refugees who had settled in Upper Canada

helped defend their adopted country against attacks from the United States during the Upper Canadian Rebellion of 1837–38.

80. Review of Dwight Lionel Dumond, ed. *Letters of James Gillespie Birney, 1831–1857. American Historical Review* vol. 44 (1939): 934–35. Birney was a leader in the American anti-slavery movement.

1940

81. "Benjamin Lundy in Illinois." *Journal of the Illinois State Historical Society* vol. 33 (1940): 57–67.

82. "Refugees from Serfdom in South Found to Make Notable Headway as Settlers in Canada in 1850s." *London Free Press* (September 14, 1940): 19. Based on a letter by Reverend Hiram Wilson, missionary in St. Catharines, recounting his observations on Black settlements in the Grand River area.

83. "Ulrich Bonnell Phillips: Historian of the South." *Journal of Southern History* vol. 5 (1940): 364–71. A paper read by Fred Landon at the annual meeting of the Southern Historical Association, November 5, 1938. Landon's biographical note on Phillips demonstrates what he himself valued in the teaching and writing of history.

84. Review of H.A. Turner. *The Settlement of Negroes in Kent County, Ontario, and a Study of Their Mental Capacity*, and Ira De A. Reid, *The Negro Immigrant: His Background Characteristics, and Social Adjustment, 1899–1937. Canadian Historical Review* vol. 21 (1940): 82–83.

1941

85. "The Negro in Canada." *Negro History Bulletin* vol. 4 (1941): 149–50, 158–60, 167.

86. "News Leakage at Chatham Meeting in Brown's Drive Against Slavery Aroused Alarm Among U.S. Friends." *London Free Press* (March 15, 1941): 19.

87. "Paul Brothers were Broken Reeds of Colony." *London Free Press* (February 15, 1941): 18. Reverend Benjamin Paul and Reverend Nathaniel Paul of the Wilberforce Settlement.

1943

88. "Anti-Slavery Advocate Buried in Nearby Thornbury." *Collingwood Enterprise Bulletin* (May 13, 1943): 7. Abolitionist Colonel Charles Stuart spent his last years near Thornbury.
89. Review of R.K. Nuermberger. *The Free Produce Movement, A Quaker Protest Against Slavery. American Historical Review* vol. 49 (1943): 156–57.

1944

90. "Canadian Appreciation of Abraham Lincoln." *Abraham Lincoln Quarterly* vol. 3 (1944): 377.
91. "Coloured Pastor Carried Story of Settlement to London." *London Free Press* (July 29, 1944): 27. Reverend Nathaniel Paul of the Wilberforce settlement spoke to a select committee of the House of Commons, England, on June 11, 1832.

1945

92. "Fred Landon Tells the Story of Escaping Slaves to Canada." *Amherstburg Echo* (September 27, 1945): 1. Landon describes the routes used by fugitive slaves from Ohio and Detroit across Lake Erie and the Detroit River to Canada.
93. "Over Lake Erie to Freedom." *Northwest Ohio Historical Quarterly* vol. 17 (1945): 132–38.
94. "Slaves Entering Canada Termed 'Sublime' Sight." *London Free Press* (September 15, 1945): 6.

1946

95. "University Library Acquires Rare *Liberator* File." *London Free Press* (July 29, 1946): 4. The University of Western Ontario library acquired copies of *The Liberator,* an anti-slavery journal.

1947

96. "American Abolitionist Found Essex Area Likely to Prosper." *London Free Press* (February 8, 1947); 18. Benjamin Lundy's visit to western Ontario in 1832.

97. "Frozen Thames Below Chatham Used as Early Stage Coach Road." *London Free Press* (January 25, 1947): 18. Benjamin Lundy's journey through Kent County.

98. "Negroes Fleeing to Sanctuary in Canada Minus Possessions, Endured Many Hardships." *London Free Press* (December 13, 1947): 20. A report by Reverend Samuel J. May on fugitive slaves in Upper Canada.

99. "Thames Settlements, Fairfield Site in 1832 Described by Lundy Narrative." *London Free Press* (January 18, 1947): 18.

100. "Vivid Pen Picture of District Painted by Pioneer Abolitionist After Trip to Lucan Negro Colony." *London Free Press* (January 11, 1947): 11. Benjamin Lundy's 1832 visit to the Wilberforce settlement.

101. Review of Brion Gysin. *To Master — A Long Goodnight: The Story of Uncle Tom, a Historical Narrative. Canadian Historical Review* vol. 28 (1947): 440.

1948

102. Review of J.H. Franklin. *From Slavery to Freedom: A History of American Negroes. Canadian Historical Review* vol. 29 (1948): 205.

1949

103. "Benjamin Lundy described Pioneer Scene in District in Diary of 1832 Journey." *London Free Press* (June 18, 1949): 22.
104. "Our Joint Historical Heritage." *Michigan History* vol. 33 (1949): 5–21. A paper read before the Historical Society of Michigan at its annual meeting, September 25, 1948. Landon discusses the shared history of Ontario and Michigan, including a description of fugitive slave movements.

1950

105. "The Fugitive Slave Law and the Detroit River Frontier, 1850–61." *Detroit Historical Society Bulletin* vol. 7, no. 2 (1950): 5–9.
106. "Fugitive Slave Law Century Old." *London Free Press* (September 20, 1950): 4.
107. "Seventh of March Plea by Webster." *London Free Press* (March 8, 1950): 4. Senator Daniel Webster's speech regarding the spread of slavery into new western states.

1951

108. "Abraham Lincoln a Century Ago." *London Free Press* (February 12, 1951): 4. The first of a series of columns that Fred Landon wrote on the anniversary of Lincoln's birthday describing what was happening in Lincoln's life a hundred years before.
109. "Evidence is Found of Race Prejudice in Biddulph, 1848." *London Free Press* (July 7, 1951): 11. Barns and crops owned by several families in the Wilberforce Settlement suffered from arson in October 1848.
110. "Uncle Tom." *London Free Press* (September 17, 1951): 4.

1952

111. "Abolitionist Interest in Upper Canada 1830–65." *Ontario History* vol. 44 (1952): 164–72.
112. "Ohio Quaker Made 1859 Visit to Freed Slaves in Western Ontario." *London Free Press* (September 27, 1952): 15. Joseph Morris visited fugitive slave settlements in Chatham, Buxton, and Shrewsbury, and published his impressions in *The Friend,* a Quaker journal.
113. "When Uncle Tom's Cabin Came to Canada." *Ontario History* vol. 44, no. 1 (1952): 1–5.

1953

114. "1856 Garner Slave Case One of Horror: Missed Escape to Western Ontario, Killed Child." *London Free Press* (August 15, 1953): 13. Margaret Garner, a fugitive slave, killed her daughter in Cincinnati rather than have her return to slavery.
115. "A Figure of Importance in Struggle over Slavery." *Amherstburg Echo* (September 3, 1953): l. Captain Charles Stuart was active in assisting fugitive slaves who made their way to Amherstburg (Fort Malden) on the Underground Railroad.
116. "Story of Captain Charles Stuart While Living at Lora Bay Near Town." *Thornbury Review-Herald* (October 1, 1953): 1. Stuart was buried in the Union Cemetery, Thornbury.
117. "Wilberforce Negro Colony in 1832 described to United Kingdom House Session." *London Free Press* (September 19, 1953): 15. Reverend Nathaniel Paul addressed the British House of Commons about the Wilberforce Settlement, thus influencing Parliament's decision to abolish slavery in the British Empire.

1954

118. "Abraham Lincoln a Century Ago." *London Free Press* (February 12,

1954): 4.

119. "Anniversary of Famous Arrest." *London Free Press* (May 24, 1954): 4. The arrest of fugitive slave Anthony Burns in Boston in 1854.

120. "Recall London's Colored Population in Good Position in Civil War Time." *London Free Press* (April 12, 1954). [Copy in Fred Landon Fonds, University of Western Ontario Archives, but could not locate on microfilm copy of *Free Press* for pagination. Possibly published in morning edition.]

121. "Slaves' Church." *London Free Press* (June 24, 1954): 4. Reverend Marmaduke Dillon's work with the Free Coloured Mission in London, Ontario.

1955

122. "The Negroes in Upper Canada." *The Dawn of Tomorrow* (June 1955): 1. (Excerpts from an article.)

123. "The Underground Railway Along the Detroit River." *Michigan History* vol. 39 (1955): 63–68. Originally a broadcast on radio station CKLW, the 13th in a series commemorating the centennial of Windsor.

124. "Whole World Honors Lincoln." *London Free Press* (February 12, 1955): 4.

125. "When Lincoln Became a National Figure," being the substance of an address delivered before the Lincoln Fellowship of Hamilton, Canada, at McMaster University, on the evening of Saturday, February 12, 1955. (12-page pamphlet, n.p., 1955). Landon describes Lincoln's career after he had completed his term in Congress in 1849, how his political awareness developed through the Missouri Compromise of 1850, its repeal in 1854, the spread of slavery into Kansas Territory, the Dred Scott affair, and how he emerged as a national figure.

1956

126. "The Anti-Slavery Society of Canada." *Ontario History* vol. 48, no. 3

(1956): 125–31.

127. "Captain Charles Stuart, Abolitionist." *Western Ontario Historical Nuggets* 24 (1956) [19 pages]. A paper presented to the Royal Society of Canada in 1952. Reprinted in *Profiles of a Province* (Toronto: Ontario Historical Society, 1967): 205–14, without original footnotes.

128. "Crime, Violence Ushered in the Civil War." *London Free Press* (December 14, 1956): 6. The Dred Scott case and its influence on James Buchanan's presidency.

129. "Strange Sequence in Lincoln's Story." *London Free Press* (February 13: 1956): 4. Lincoln's understanding, reflected in his early political speeches, that the United States would soon be forced to confront the divisive issue of slavery.

1957

130. "Lincoln Crusader for Brotherhood." *London Free Press* (February 13, 1957): 6. Lincoln challenged the theory of white racial superiority articulated in Chief Justice Roger B. Taney's judgment in the Dred Scott case.

131. "Josiah Henson, the Black Moses." *London Free Press* (November 28, 1957): 6. A review of Jessie L. Beattie's biography, *Black Moses, the Real Uncle Tom*.

1958

132. "Abe Lincoln's Decisive Year." *London Free Press* (February 12, 1958): 6. One hundred years after Lincoln's 49th birthday, Landon describes Lincoln's return to politics and his senatorial race against Stephen Douglas.

133. "Fugitive Slave Provides Focal Point for Change in Canadian Law." *London Free Press* (August 23, 1958): 24. Nelson Hackett was followed to Chatham in 1841 by his former owner and charged with theft.

134. "Runaway Slaves in Canada Stirred Mixed Feelings." *London Free*

Press (January 4, 1958): 12. Describes the visits of several abolitionists to fugitive slave settlements in Canada West.

1959

135. "Abraham Lincoln Back in 1859." *London Free Press* (February 12, 1959): 6. In 1859, Lincoln had recently been defeated in his race to become a senator of Illinois. During the campaign he had spoken on the slavery issue, but the events of Harper's Ferry and the execution of John Brown had blocked his political ambitions.
136. "Early Fugitive Journal." *London Free Press* (August 17, 1959): 6. Landon describes the founding of *The Voice of the Fugitive* by Henry Bibb, in Windsor, Ontario.
137. "John Brown's Last Coup Took Slaves to Windsor." *London Free Press* (March 14, 1959): 22. This visit of John Brown in 1859 was commemorated by a plaque erected by the Historic Sites and Monuments Board of Canada. Landon was a member of the board from 1932–58.
138. "Unique Journal Discovered." *London Free Press* (August 6, 1959): 6. Landon reports on the acquisition of microfilm copies of *The Provincial Freeman*, 1853–57, by the University of Western Ontario library. Edited by Mary Ann Shadd Carey and Samuel Ringgold Ward, this newspaper advocated equality for Blacks.

1960

139. "A Pioneer Abolitionist in Upper Canada." *Ontario History* vol. 52 no. 2 (June 1960): 77–83. Benjamin Lundy visited Upper Canada in 1832 to report on the lives of Black refugee settlers from the United States.
140. "Coloured Settlers Found a Haven Near Elginfield." *London Free Press* (January 2, 1960): 36. Benjamin Lundy's visit to the Wilberforce Settlement.

141. "Lincoln 100 Years Ago." *London Free Press* (February 12, 1960): 6. The steps of Lincoln's progress to the Republican nomination for president of the United States.
142. "Lincoln's Nomination, 1860." *London Free Press* (May 18, 1960): 6. Landon describes the 1860 Republican Party convention.

1961

143. "1861 Choice: Cotton or Slavery." *London Free Press* (December 1, 1961): 6. Landon analyzes the intimate relationship between the market demand for cotton in Britain and that country's views on slavery in America.

1962

144. "Lincoln Among the Minority." *London Free Press* (September 21, 1962): 6. Lincoln's Republican Party still controlled the House of Representatives after the election of 1862, but his stand against slavery had weakened his political support.
145. "Lincoln's Birthday." *London Free Press* (February 12, 1962): 6. One hundred years after Lincoln's 53rd birthday, Landon describes the state of the Civil War and the steps toward the eventual issuance of the Emancipation Proclamation.

1963

146. "A Tribute to James F. Jenkins." *Dawn of Tomorrow* (December 1963): 2. Jenkins was the founder of the Canadian League for the Advancement of Coloured People and editor of its official newspaper, *The Dawn of Tomorrow*.
147. "Negroes in the Civil War." *London Free Press* (September 28, 1963): 6. History of the enlistment and service of Blacks in the Union army.

148. "Slavery and the Underground Railroad." *CC Outlook* (April 1963): 3. [A one-page article located in Fred Landon Fonds, University of Western Ontario Archives.]

1965

149. "Death Rattle of Despair Begins for the Confederacy." *London Free Press* (February 12, 1965): 6.

1967

150. Review of Merton L. Dillon. *Benjamin Lundy and the Struggle for Negro Freedom. Canadian Historical Review* vol. 48 (1967): 170–71.
151. "Captain Charles Stuart, Abolitionist." *Profiles of a Province: Studies in the History of Ontario* (Toronto: Ontario Historical Society, 1967), 205–14.

1969

152. "Book Battled Slavery." *London Free Press* (January 18, 1969): section M, 10. Harriet Beecher Stowe's *Uncle Tom's Cabin.*

No date

153. "Plans of More Than a Century Ago to Place Seminary at Wilberforce Wrecked On Financial Misfortune." *London Free Press* [Newspaper article in Fred Landon Fonds, University of Western Ontario Archives, no date given.]

Hilary Bates Neary

Ontario's African-Canadian Heritage:
Sources and Resources

This is by no means intended to be a complete bibliography of every article, book, and dissertation on the subject of Ontario's African-Canadian heritage. Rather, it is a selection of resources that scholars of Black Canada dealing with the periods of Fred Landon's major interests, and that researchers, as well as the more general public, have found useful over the years. It is interesting, in light of the purpose and sponsorship of this book, that so many of the articles noted below were first published by The Ontario Historical Society in the pages of *Ontario History*, or in earlier incarnations of the same journal.

In order to conserve space, there has been no attempt to cite all reprints, later editions, and edited versions of the works mentioned below. Rather, the original editions are referenced in most cases, although many of the earlier works are available in more up-to-date forms. For the same reasons, the literally hundreds, if not thousands of websites dealing with North American Black history have been omitted. Their ephemeral nature, and in many cases uneven quality, would require a level of analysis far outside the boundaries of this essay. I have made passing mention to the importance of certain primary sources, including important archival collections, newspapers, and the almost untapped resource provided by historical archaeology, for the study of African-Canadian life and culture in the nineteenth century.

There is actually very little in print in the form of books or extensive monographs on the history of Black Ontario. James W. St. George Walker's *A History of the Blacks in Canada: Study Guide for Teachers and Students* (Ottawa: Minister of State for Multiculturalism, 1980), now unfortunately long out of print, and his more recent article, "African Canadians," in Paul R. Magocsi, ed. *Encyclopedia of Canada's Peoples* (Toronto: Published for the Multicultural History Society of Ontario by the University of Toronto Press, 1999), 139–176 remain the authoritative works. Robin W. Winks's sweeping study, *The Blacks in Canada: A History* (Montreal: McGill-Queen's University Press, 1971 and 2005), and Daniel G. Hill's richly illustrated and very readable *The Freedom-Seekers: Blacks in Early Canada* (Agincourt, Ontario: Book Society of Canada, 1981), both much in need of revision in light of recent scholarship, round out the available general works. Jason Silverman's *Unwelcome Guests: Canada West's Response to American Fugitive Slaves, 1800–1865, Series in Comparative Studies in Race and Ethnicity* (Millwood, N.Y.: Associated Faculty Press, 1985), offers much useful detail, particularly in respect to the racial discrimination that incoming African-Americans experienced in early nineteenth-century Canada.

Amongst several important theses now published in book form is that of Donald George Simpson, with Paul E. Lovejoy, ed. as *Under the North Star: Black Communities in Upper Canada* (Trenton, NJ: African World Press, 2005): 161. Jonathan Walton's thesis, "Blacks in Buxton and Chatham, Ontario, 1830–1890: Did the 49th Parallel Make a Difference?" (unpublished Ph.D. dissertation, Princeton University, 1979) is also helpful, as is Sharon A. Hepburn's work on Buxton, recently published, entitled, *Crossing the Border: A Free Black Community in Canada* (Champaign, IL: University of Illinois Press, 2007).

A considerable number of very good early articles exist. These include the writings of the incredibly prolific Fred Landon, as well as those of Judge William Renwick Riddell in two journals, *Ontario History* and the *Journal of Negro History* (now the *Journal of African American History*). Mainly written early in the last century, Landon and Riddell's research regarding several different aspects of Canadian Black history has been neither replicated nor surpassed. Interestingly, neither betrays the perhaps unconscious bias of some later writers. Riddell's work is particularly valuable for studying the legal history of slavery in Upper and Lower Canada: "Notes on Slavery in Canada," *Journal of Negro History* vol. 4 (January 1919): 396–408; "The Slave in Upper Canada," *Journal of Negro History* vol. 4 (October 1919): 372–95; "The Slave in Canada," *Journal of Negro History* vol. 5 (1920): 261–375; and "Some References to Negroes in Upper Canada," *Ontario Historical Society Papers and Records* vol. 19 (1922): 144–46, to name only a few of his articles. Much more recently, Afua Cooper's *Hanging of Angelique: The Untold Story of Canadian Slavery and the Burning of Old Montreal* (Toronto: Harper Collins, 2006) tells a gripping true story demonstrating Canada's role in slavery and the part that the economies of the Atlantic world played in human trafficking in the seventeenth and eighteenth centuries.

First-person accounts by those who lived the Black experience in Canada include the works of Henry Bibb, *The Life and Adventures of Henry Bibb: An American Slave* in *Wisconsin Studies in Autobiography* (Madison: University of Wisconsin Press, 2001). In 1852, Mary Ann Shadd Cary published her landmark *A Plea for Emigration; or, Notes of Canada West, In Its Moral, Social, and Political Aspect* (Detroit: George W. Pattison, 1852), recently edited and reprinted by Richard Almonte. Josiah Henson, founder of the Dawn Settlement, wrote several versions of his own autobiography, starting with *The Life of Josiah Henson, Formerly a Slave, Now an Inhabitant of Canada, as Narrated by Himself* (Boston: Arthur D. Phelps, 1849). A clergyman named William M. Mitchell wrote *The Underground Railroad from Slavery to Freedom*, 2nd ed. (London: W. Tweedie, 1860), and another, the Reverend William Troy, produced *Hair-Breadth Escapes from Slavery to Freedom* (Manchester: W. Bremner, 1861). Samuel Ringgold Ward, a brilliantly eloquent Congregationalist minister who became the travelling agent for the Anti-Slavery Society of Canada, provides unique insights into Canadian racism in *Autobiography of a Fugitive Negro* (London: John Snow, 1855), and his even more pointed "Canadian Negro Hate." *Voice of the Fugitive* (October 12, 1852). See Thomas Smallwood and Richard Almonte, ed., *A Narrative of Thomas Smallwood (Coloured Man)* (Toronto: Mercury Press, 2000) for a vivid firsthand account of Underground Railroad operations in Washington, D.C. and how they led to a precipitous resettlement of the Black conductor's own family in Toronto.

Very interesting insights into the Black Canadian experience in the years before the American Civil War can be found in the writings of contemporary observers who visited Canada for the express purpose of documenting the conditions under which fugitive slaves were living. These included abolitionists like Benjamin Lundy, who visited Canada and published a long series of articles in his own newspaper, *The Genius of Universal Emancipation*, from January through April, 1839; Levi Coffin, the "President of the Underground Railroad" at Cincinnati, who gives helpful details about Canada and the Underground Railroad in his own *Reminiscences* (Cincinnati: Western Tract Society, 1876); and Benjamin Drew, who interviewed more than 100 refugees from bondage and wrote down their stories, as well as his own observations, in *The Refugee, or A North-Side View of Slavery* (Boston: J.P. Jewett and Co., 1856). The remarkable Laura Haviland provides a woman's perspective in *A Woman's Life-Work* (Cincinnati: Printed by Walden & Stowe for the author, 1882). Former slave and prominent author, playwright, and poet William Wells Brown visited in 1861 and published his insightful "The Coloured People of Canada," in his paper, the *Pine and Palm*, while Samuel Gridley Howe travelled to Canada at Abraham Lincoln's behest near the end of the Civil War to find ways to assist the enslaved people of the South once they were freed. His observations of African Canada reflect the prejudices held by Northerners, even of the abolitionist persuasion, but his report is an invaluable overview of fugitive slave life in Ontario nonetheless: Samuel Gridley Howe, *The Refugees from Slavery in Canada West: Report to the Freedmen's Inquiry Commission* (Boston: Wright and Potter, 1864).

A very good overview of national attempts to commemorate the historic sites relating of Ontario's African-Canadian past is provided by Shannon Ricketts, "Commemorating the Underground Railroad in Canada," *CRM* vol. 5 (1999), 33–34. The settlements, which were largely centred in southwestern Ontario, are detailed in William H. Pease and Jane H. Pease's *Black Utopia: Negro Communal Experiments in America* (Madison, WI: State Historical Society of Wisconsin, 1963), and *They Who Would Be Free: Blacks' Search for Freedom, 1830–1861* (Urbana and Chicago, IL: University of Illinois Press, 1974. Reprint, 1990). For the Wilberforce settlement, the main resource is Austin Steward's autobiography, *Twenty-Two Years a Slave and Forty Years a Freeman,* 2nd ed. (Rochester, NY: Allings & Cory, 1859). The story of the Elgin Association fugitive slave colony at Buxton and the man who first paved the way for its establishment are told in three volumes: Arlie C. Robbins, *Legacy to Buxton* (Chatham, NY: Ideal Printing, 1983); Victor Ullman, *Look to the North Star: a Life of William King* (Boston: Beacon Press, 1969); and Annie Straith Jamieson, who was King's niece, *William King, Friend and Champion of Slaves* (Toronto: Missions in Evangelism,

1925). Researchers should also consult Howard Law, "'Self-Reliance is the True Road to Independence': Ideology and the Ex-Slaves in Buxton and Chatham." *Ontario History* vol. 77, no. 2 (June 1985): 107–21 and the much more recent book by Patricia Lorraine Neely, *The Houses of Buxton: A Legacy of African Influences in Architecture* (P. Designs Publishing, 2005).

Dr. Bryan Walls's *The Place that Led to Somewhere* (Windsor: Olive Publishing Co., 1980) is a documented novel about his own family's experiences on the Underground Railroad, and provides rich detail about the settlement at the Refuge Home Society. A new book by Joyce A. Pettigrew adds much to our understanding of the lesser-known settlements around Norwich, *A Safe Haven: The Story of the Black Settlers in Oxford County* (Otterville, ON: South Norwich Historical Society, 2006). For the scattered farms that lay in the wilderness north of Guelph, see Linda Brown-Kubisch, *The Queen's Bush Settlement: Black Pioneers, 1839–1865* (Toronto: Natural Heritage Books, 2004). The Oro settlement, north of Lake Simcoe, is described in Gary French, *Men of Colour: An Historical Account of the Black Settlement on Wilberforce Street and in Oro Township, 1819–1949* (Stroud, ON: Kaste Books, 1978). For the Niagara Region, see Michael Power and Nancy Butler, *Slavery and Freedom in Niagara* (Niagara-on-the-Lake, ON: Niagara Historical Society, 1993) and Owen Thomas, *Niagara's Freedom Trail: A Guide to African-Canadian History on the Niagara Peninsula* (Niagara Falls, ON: The Region of Niagara Tourist Council, 1995). On Black Chatham there is Gwendolyn and John Robinson's fascinating *Seek the Truth: The Story of Chatham's Black Community,* (Chatham, ON: privately published, 1989). See also John Farrell, "The History of the Negro Community in Chatham, Ontario, 1787–1865," (doctoral dissertation, Ottawa University, 1955); and "Schemes for the Transplanting of Refugee American Negroes from Upper Canada in the 1840s," *Ontario History* vol. 52 (1960): 245–49. While not a book on African-Canadian history per se, there is much new research on Amherstburg's long history of Black settlement in a recent book by the Amherstburg Bicentennial Committee, entitled *Amherstburg, 1796–1996: A New Town on the Garrison Grounds* (Amherstburg, ON: The Marsh Collection, 1996).

On the lives of interesting individuals, see Peter Meyler and David Meyler's *A Stolen Life: Searching for Richard Pierpoint* (Toronto: Natural

Heritage Books, 1999); Glenelg. Peter Meyler ed., *Broken Shackles: Old Man Henson from Slavery to Freedom* (Toronto: Natural Heritage Books, 2001). Reprinted January 2007. Kate Clifford Larson, *Bound for the Promised Land: Harriet Tubman, Portrait of An American Hero* (New York: Ballantine, 2003); Stephen L. Hubbard's *Against All Odds: The Story of William Peyton Hubbard, Black Leader and Municipal Reformer* (Toronto and Reading: Dundurn Press, 1987); Dalyce Newby, *Anderson Ruffin Abbott: First Afro-Canadian Doctor, Canadian Medical Lives* (Markham, ON: Associated Medical Services and Fitzhenry & Whiteside, 1998); Hilary Dawson, "The Life and Times of Alfred Lafferty: A Black Educator and Lawyer." *North Toronto Historical Society Newsletter* vol. 29, no. 1 (April 2005): 4–5; and "From Immigrant to Establishment: A Black Family's Journey," *Ontario History* vol. 99, no. 1 (Spring 2007), 31–43; Bryan Prince, "The Case of Isaac Brown, Fugitive Slave," *Ontario History* vol. 99, no. 1 (Spring 2007): 18–30; Patrick Brode, *The Odyssey of John Anderson* (Toronto: University of Toronto Press for the Osgoode Society, 1989). For more on the John Anderson case, see Robert Reinders, "The John Anderson Case, 1860–61: A Study in Anglo-Canadian Imperial Relations," *Canadian Historical Review* vol. 56 (1975): 393–415. The Abbott family of Toronto and Buxton is the subject of Cathy Slaney's *Family Secrets: Crossing the Colour Line* (Toronto: Natural Heritage Books, 2003).

Topical volumes include the excellent and far-reaching Peggy Bristow et al., *We're Rooted Here and They Can't Pull Us Up: Essays in African Canadian Women's History* (Toronto: University of Toronto Press, 1994), which includes the seminal article by Adrienne Shadd, "The Lord Seemed to Say 'Go': Women and the Underground Railroad Movement," (41–68). Also on the lives of women is Maureen Elgersman, *Unyielding Spirits: Black Women and Slavery in Early Canada and Jamaica* (New York: Garland, 1999) and Shirley J. Yee's important article, "Gender Ideology and Black Women as Community Builders in Ontario, 1850–1870," *Canadian Historical Review* vol. 75, no. 1 (March 1994): 53–73. Rella Braithwaite deals with both historical and more modern women's history in *Some Black Women: Profiles of Black Women in Canada* (Toronto: Sister Vision Press, 1993).

For specific women in African-Canadian history, see Shirley J. Yee, *Black Women Abolitionists: A Study in Activism, 1828–1860* (Knoxville, TN: University of Tennessee Press, 1992) and "Finding a Place: Mary Ann

Shadd Cary and the Dilemmas of Black Migration to Canada," *Frontiers: A Journal of Women Studies,* vol. 18, no. 3 (1997): 1–16; Jane Rhodes, *Mary Ann Shadd Cary: The Black Press and Protest in the Nineteenth Century* (Bloomington, IN: Indiana University Press, 1998), and the classic Jim Bearden and Linda Jean Butler, *Shadd: The Life and Times of Mary Shadd Cary* (Toronto: NC Press, 1977).

On education, see Afua Cooper, "The Search for Mary Bibb, Black Woman Teacher in Nineteenth-Century Canada West," *Ontario History* vol. 83, no. 1 (March 1991): 39–54; Adrienne Shadd, "No 'Back Alley Clique': the Campaign to Desegregate Chatham's public schools, 1891–1893," *Ontario History* vol. 99, no. 1 (Spring 2007), 77–95; and the earlier Jason H. Silverman and Donna J. Gillie, "'The Pursuit of Knowledge Under Difficulties': Education and the Fugitive Slave in Canada," *Ontario History* vol. 74 (June 1982): 95–112. On the numbers of fugitive slaves in Canada, see Michael Wayne, "The Black Population of Canada West on the Eve of the American Civil War: A Reassessment Based on the Manuscript Census of 1861," *Histoire Social/Social History* vols. 28/56 (November 1995), as well as the excellent Appendix in Winks's *Black in Canada*, 484–96.

The most recent work on the subject of fugitive slave extradition is that included in Karolyn Smardz Frost's Governor General's Award–winning biography of Toronto fugitive slave couple Lucie and Thornton Blackburn, *I've Got a Home in Glory Land: A Lost Tale of the Underground Railroad* (Toronto: Thomas Allen Ltd. and New York: Farrar Straus & Giroux, 2007). The scholarly and detailed book by David Murray, *Colonial Justice: Justice, Morality, and Crime In the Niagara District, 1791–1849* (Osgoode Society for Canadian Legal History, Toronto: University of Toronto Press, 2002) contains much new information, as do two of his articles: "Hands Across the Border: The Abortive Extradition of Solomon Moseby," *Canadian Review of American Studies* vol. 30, no. 2 (2000): 187–209; "Criminal Boundaries: The Frontier and the Contours of Upper Canadian Justice, 1792–1840," *Canadian Review of American Studies/American Review of Canadian Studies* vol. 26, no. 3 (Autumn 1996): 341–66. Alexander Lovell Murray's dissertation on the same topic is earlier but still very useful: "Canada and the Anglo-American Anti-Slavery Movement; A Study in International Philanthropy," (doctoral dissertation, University of Western Ontario, 1960). An excellent account of

Solomon Moseby's rescue from the Niagara jail remains Janet Carnochan's "A Slave Rescue in Niagara Sixty Years Ago," *Niagara Historical Society, Paper No. 2* (1897): 8–17. Another case is that described by J. Mackenzie Leaske in "Jesse Happy, A Fugitive Slave from Kentucky," *Ontario Historical Society Papers and Records* vol. 54 (June 1962): 85–98. For the single case where a fugitive was returned to his Arkansas owner, see Roman J. Zorn, "An Arkansas Fugitive Slave Incident and Its International Repercussions," *Arkansas Historical Quarterly* (Fayetteville) vol. 16 (1957): 140–49. Important publications include Roman J. Zorn, "Criminal Extradition Menaces the Canadian Haven for Fugitive Slaves, 1841–1861," *Canadian Historical Review* vol. 38 (1957): 284–94, and Alexander Lovell Murray, "Extradition of Fugitive Slaves from Canada," *Canadian Historical Review* vol. 43 (1962): 298–313. More recently is Donald V. Macdougall, "Habeas Corpus, Extradition and a Fugitive Slave in Canada," *Slavery and Abolition* (Great Britain) vol. 7 (1986): 118–28.

For the role Black Canadians played in the War of 1812 and the Rebellion of 1837, see Ernest Green, "Upper Canada's Black Defenders," *Ontario History* vol. 37 (1931): 365–91; Wayne Kelly, "Canada's Black Defenders, Former Slaves Answered the Call to Arms," *Beaver* vol. 77 (April-May 1977): 31–34; and "Race and Segregation in the Upper Canada Militia," *Journal of the Society of Army Historical Research* vol. 78 (2000): 264–77. For the activities of fiery white abolitionist John Brown in what is now Ontario, see Frederick Benjamin Sanborne, *Life and Letters of John Brown* (Boston: Roberts Brothers, 1885). Sanborne was one of the "Secret Six" that funded the raid on the military arsenal at Harper's Ferry. For a new take on John Brown's life, consult the excellent biography by David S. Reynolds, *John Brown, Abolitionist: The Man Who Killed Slavery, Sparked the Civil War, and Seeded Civil Rights*, (New York: Knopf/Vintage Books, 2006).

There are a number of interesting sources on the Canadian Black church, including James K. Lewis's dissertation on the "Religious Life of Fugitive Slaves and Rise of Coloured Baptist Churches, 1820–65," completed at the McMaster School of Divinity in 1965, and his "Religious Nature of the Early Negro Migration to Canada and the Amherstburg Baptist Association," *Ontario History* vol. 58, no. 2 (1966): 117–32, as well as Dorothy Shadd Shreve's two privately published volumes on Black church history, *The Africanadian Church: A Stabilizer* (Jordan Station, ON: Paideia Press, 1983) and *Pathfinders of Liberty and Truth: A Century with the Amherstburg Regular Missionary Baptist Association* (privately published, 1940). For the very important role freemasonry plays in Canada's Black communities, see Arlie C. Robbins, *Prince Hall Masonry in Ontario, 1852–1933* (Chatham: privately published, 1980).

On Black life in Toronto, there is a single doctoral dissertation, that of former ombudsman Daniel G. Hill, entitled, "Negroes in Toronto: A Sociological Study of a Minority Group," (unpublished Ph.D. dissertation, University of Toronto, 1960). He also wrote the two main articles on Toronto Black history: "The Blacks in Toronto," in Robert F. Harney, ed. *Gathering Place: Peoples and Neighbourhoods of Toronto, 1834–1945, Studies in Ethnic and Immigration History* (Toronto: Multicultural History Society of Ontario, 1985): 75–105, and "Negroes in Toronto, 1793–1856," *Ontario History* vol. 55, no. 2 (1983): 73–91. Frederick H. Armstrong's article, "The Toronto Directories and the Negro Community in the Late 1840s," *Ontario History* vol. 61 (1969): 111–19 is very helpful for researching the urban context for the lives of both fugitive slave and free African-American immigrants to the urban centre. Armstrong was the first to note that the community's residential patterning demonstrates a clustering around the several Black churches that had grown up in Toronto by the mid-nineteenth century. For African-American abolitionist influence in the city, see Hilary Russell, "Frederick Douglass in Toronto," *CRM* vol. 4 (1998): 23–7. Also useful for understanding political activism in Toronto's large and flourishing nineteenth-century Black community is Karolyn Smardz Frost's "Communities of Resistance: African Canadians and African Americans in Antebellum Toronto," *Ontario History* vol. 99, no. 1 (Spring 2007): 44–63, and for the racial discrimination they faced, see Colin McFarquhar's "Blacks in 1880's Toronto: The Search for Equality," *Ontario History* vol. 99, no. 1 (Spring 2007): 77–95.

For an analysis of abolitionist sentiment in Canada, see Afua Cooper, "Acts of Resistance: Black Men and Women Engage Slavery in Upper Canada, 1793–1803," *Ontario History* vol. 99, no. 1 (Spring 2007): 5–17; and Robin W. Winks, "'A Sacred Animosity,' Abolitionism in Canada," in Martin Duberman's *The Antislavery Vanguard: New Essays on the*

Abolitionists, (Princeton, NJ: Princeton University Press, 1965): 301–42. Allen Stouffer's opus on white abolitionism, *The Light of Nature and the Law of God* (Baton Rouge, LA: Louisiana State University Press, 1992) is an extremely important resource focusing largely on anti-slavery activities that took place in Toronto and highlighting the pivotal role played by George Brown, publisher of Canada's largest newspaper, the *Globe*, in encouraging anti-slavery activism. See also his "Michael Willis and the British Roots of Canadian Antislavery," *Slavery and Abolition* (Great Britain) vol. 8 (1987): 294–312. More recent is the paper for the 2008 annual meeting of the American Studies Association by Ikuko Asaka, "The Malleable Fugitive Slave Subject: Race and Gender in the Nineteenth-Century Canadian-U.S. Abolitionism," www.allacademic.com/meta/p103604_index.html. Afua Cooper's extraordinary dissertation, "'Doing Battle in Freedom's Cause,' Henry Bibb, Abolitionism, Race Uplift, and Black Manhood, 1842–1854," (University of Toronto, unpublished Ph.D. dissertation, 2000) goes a very long way toward filling the gaps in earlier discussions of Canadian anti-slavery activities. Her work demonstrates how both noted African-American and African-Canadian abolitionists, and ordinary Black men and women, were fundamental to the anti-slavery cause.

For twentieth-century Black history in Ontario, of particular interest is Dionne Brand's *No Burden to Carry: Narratives of Black Working Women in Ontario, 1920s–1950s* (Toronto: University of Toronto Press, 1989) and James W. St. G. Walker's *Racial Discrimination in Canada: The Black Experience* (Ottawa: Canadian Historical Association, 1985.) Walker's article, "On the Record: The Testimony of Canada's Black Pioneers," first published in A.W. Bonnett and G.L. Watson, eds., *Emerging Perspectives on the Black Diaspora* is republished in a revised edition in 2008, entitled *Continuing Perspectives on the Black Diaspora*, edited by A.W. Bonnett and C.B. Holder, from University Press of America.

The *Annual Reports of the Anti-Slavery Society of Canada* and the *Annual Reports of the Elgin Association* provide much useful contemporary information, as do the papers of the American Missionary Society and the Colonial Church and School Society of Britain, both of which supported schools for Black children in Ontario. The single key resource for annotated primary materials was edited by Peter C. Ripley and Roy

Finkenbine, with the help of a host of scholars and graduate students in the early 1980s. It is entitled *The Black Abolitionist Papers* (Chapel Hill, NC: University of North Carolina Press, 1985). Comprising some 17 reels of microfilm (more than 17,000 documents in all) and accompanied by a series of superb regional guides, it includes papers, correspondence, speeches, tracts, and an enormous range of publications produced by Black abolitionists. Volume 2 is confined to the work of Black Canadian abolitionists. It contains superbly researched short biographies of people who were engaged in resistance and who lived in or visited Canada.

American volumes about the Underground Railroad bear witness to Canada's crucial role as the northern terminus of fugitive slave routes. Most recently, Fergus Bordewich, in *Bound for Canaan, The Underground Railroad and the War for the Soul of America* (New York: Amistad/Harper Collins, 2005) uses animated storytelling to enliven the results of solid research. Of the contemporary writings, William Still's *The Underground Railroad from Slavery to Freedom* (Philadelphia: Porter & Coates, 1872) is especially useful. Still was the secretary of the Pennsylvania Anti-Slavery Society and operated a very active Underground Railroad station in Philadelphia. He not only recorded the stories, names, and often earlier homes of refugees who passed through, but also kept up a vivid correspondence with those he assisted. His book, published soon after the Civil War, contains numerous letters written by former slaves living in what is now Ontario and details the conditions of life after such individuals reached the city, their relative prosperity, and family circumstances. Wilbur H. Siebert's exhaustive research included interviews with many former Underground Railroad "conductors" and their children, as well as refugees from slavery living on both sides of the border, and resulted in the authoritative *Underground Railroad* (New York: The Macmillan Company, 1898).

It must be noted that the modern historian's perspective on African-Canadian history, including Fred Landon's, is irremediably skewed. In any assessment of antebellum Black resistance, one is limited to two major sources of information. The first is the papers original to the Black community. These include important groups of papers such as the Alvin McCurdy Collection at the Archives of Ontario; the Anderson Ruffin Abbott Papers at the Baldwin Room of the Toronto Public Library; the Daniel G. Hill Papers at both the

Archives of Ontario and at Library and Archives Canada in Ottawa; and the collections of the Ontario Black History Society. There are also important collections held in local African-Canadian heritage sites such as the John Freeman Walls Historic Site, the Buxton National Historic Site and Museum, Uncle Tom's Cabin Historic Site, Collingwood's Sheffield Park Black History Museum, and Amherstburg's North American Black Historical Museum.

For the abolitionist press, the two papers of Black abolitionist Canada, the *Voice of the Fugitive* and the *Provincial Freedman,* contain information available nowhere else about events, activities, concerns, and, above all, resistance to both slavery and racial oppression on the part of African Canadians. A second source, subjected to various forms of bias, lies in what members of the dominant North American culture, including white journalists, had to say *about* Black life and culture. The Toronto *Globe* regularly published anti-slavery articles and announcements of events of interest to the Black community, and the slightly scurrilous Toronto *World* is full of fascinating details for the latter half of the nineteenth century. Across the province, the *Amherstburg Echo,* Chatham *Planet,* and other local newspapers contain much useful information, including the ways local whites viewed their Black neighbours.

The most objective resources are in the public record. These include census documents, tax rolls, land registry data, court records, government documents, and the like. These are particularly important for the study of illiterate individuals, and of those who could write but whose words have not survived. As a final note on sources, and for the same reason, the historical archaeology, as conducted at the Thornton and Lucie Blackburn Site in 1985, and without which their story would likely have remained a "lost tale of the Underground Railroad," must be mentioned. On one level, it can be perceived as social historical data collection, and at its most basic it is "pots and pans history," with an emphasis on cookware. Archaeological excavations have been conducted at the home of African-American refugees Enerals and Priscilla Griffin, who arrived in Ancaster, Ontario, in 1829; at the Old Durham Road Pioneer Cemetery near Flesherton, Ontario; and in the graveyard of the North Buxton Community Church.

The long history of Blacks in Ontario is also a focus of Joseph Mensah's *Black Canadians: History, Experience, Social Conditions* (Halifax: Fernwood

Publishing, 2002). For further information on sources, see Hilary Russell's "A Bibliography Relating to African Canadian History," Historical Research Branch, National Historic Sites Directorate, Parks Canada (rev. ed., 1990). Newer still is David C. Estes' in-depth analysis of the literature and the historians that produced it, "Black Canadian Historical Writing, 1970–2006: An Assessment," *Journal of Black Studies* vol. 38 (2008), 388–406.

There are a number of popular books, most of them quite recent. Standing out among them is Lawrence Hill's profoundly moving and extremely well-researched Commonwealth Award–winning historical novel on the Black Loyalist migration to Canada, *The Book of Negroes* (Toronto: HarperCollins, 2006). Much earlier, Hill published a book suitable for young people, *Trials and Triumphs: The Story of African Canadians* (Toronto: Umbrella Press, 1993). There is also Bryan Prince's beautifully written *I Came as a Stranger* (Toronto and New York: Tundra Books, 2004), which won the Nebula Award in 2005; it is based on excellent research and is of interest to readers of all ages.

There is not yet a scholarly volume on antebellum African-Canadian Toronto; the only book on the subject is aimed at a popular audience, Adrienne Shadd, Afua Cooper, and Karolyn Smardz Frost, *The Underground Railroad: Next Stop, Toronto!* (Toronto: Natural Heritage Books, 2002). Others suitable for young people are Rosemary Sadlier's award-winning volumes, which include *Mary Ann Shadd Cary, Publisher, Editor, Teacher, Lawyer, Suffragette* (Toronto: Umbrella Press, 1995); *The Kids' Book of Black Canadian History* (Toronto: Kids Can Press, 2003); *Leading the Way: Black Women in Canada* (Toronto: Umbrella Press, 1995), and *Harriet Tubman and the Underground Railroad: Her Life in the United States and Canada* (Toronto: Umbrella Press, 1994). *Towards Freedom: The African-Canadian Experience* (Toronto: Umbrella Press, 1996), by Ken Alexander and Avis Glaze, has an accompanying curriculum guide for use by teachers.

It is of considerable note that nearly all of the secondary sources published on the subject of Ontario's African-Canadian heritage since the 1920s cite articles by Fred Landon. What a tribute to a life spent focusing on this very worthy — and at his time of writing, almost entirely neglected — field of study.

Dr. Karolyn Smardz Frost

Notes

Editors' Note: These are Fred Landon's own endnotes as they were written for each article included in this book. Publication information has been added for the sources, based on the edition of each book and article that Landon himself used. We have not attempted to bring this up to date with the inclusion of subsequent editions of the same volumes. However, the title and other information regarding a published version of a document Landon used in manuscript form are provided, in order to enhance accessibility. Editorial notes and additions are included below in square brackets. There, we have added more modern sources to assist the reader. The full citation for each work is only included the first time it appears in the endnotes for this entire book.

One: Canada's Part in Freeing the Slaves

1. Benjamin Drew, *The Refugee; or the Narratives of Fugitive Slaves in Canada Related by Themselves, with an Account of the History and Condition of the Coloured Population of Upper Canada* (Boston: J.P. Jewett and Company; New York: Sheldon, Lamport and Blakeman, 1856), 244–45 [available online at http://docsouth.unc.edu].
2. William M. Mitchell, *Underground Railroad*, 2nd ed. (London: W. Tweedie, 1860), 150–51.
3. Wilbur H. Siebert, *The Underground Railroad from Slavery to Freedom* (New York: The Macmillan Company, 1898). This is best account of the workings of the underground system. Professor Siebert has an excellent chapter on the life of the Negro refugees in Canada before the outbreak of the Civil War.
4. Siebert, *The Underground Railroad*, 194.
5. A. Judd Northrup, "Slavery in New York," *New York State Library Report* (1900) 258–59.
6. James Birney, *James G. Birney and His Times* (New York: D. Appleton and Company, 1890), 435.
7. Samuel Gridley Howe, *Refugees from Slavery in Canada West, Report to the Freedmen's Inquiry Commission* (Boston: Wright & Potter, printers,

1864), 11–12. [This has been reprinted as *Report to the Freedmen's Inquiry Commission, 1864: The Refugees from Slavery in Canada West* (New York: Arno Press, 1969)].

8. In a speech in the United States Senate on May 5, 1858, Senator Mason, of Virginia, said of the fugitives: "They perish with the cold in Canada." See also Samuel Ringgold Ward, *Autobiography of a Fugitive Negro* (London: John Snow, 1855), 161.

9. James Redpath, *Public Life of Captain John Brown* (Sandusky, OH: Kinney Brothers, 1872), 229.

10. *Independent* (January 18, 1855). Quoted in Siebert's *The Underground Railroad*, 194.

11. John F.H. Claiborne, *Life and Correspondence of John A. Quitman*, vol. 2 (New York: Harper & Brothers, Publishers, 1860), 28.

12. *Cong. Globe*, XXXVI Cong., 2nd Session, 356.

13. Quoted in *American Anti-Slavery Society Annual Report* (1861), 158.

14. Mitchell, *Underground Railroad*, 113.

15. Alexander Milton Ross, *Recollections and Experiences of an Abolitionist from 1855 to 1865* (Toronto: Rowsell and Hutchison, 1875).

16. Josiah Henson, *Father Henson's Story of His Own Life* (Boston: J.P. Jewett; Cleveland: H.P. B. Jewett, 1858), 149–50. [Henson published several versions of his autobiography.]

17. William Wells Brown, *Narrative of William Wells Brown, an American Slave* (London: Charles Gilpin, Billingsgate, 1849), 109.

18. Sarah H. Bradford, *Harriet, the Moses of Her People* (New York: G.R. Lockwood & Son, 1886), 88. For a well-researched new biography of Harriet Tubman, see Kate Clifford Larson, *Bound for the Promised Land: Harriet Tubman, Portrait of an American Hero* (New York: Ballantine, 2003).

19. Levi Coffin, *Reminiscences* (Cincinnati: Western Tract Society, 1876), 249–50.

20. Howe, *Refugees from Slavery in Canada West*, iv. For Howe's general conclusions with regard to the improvement of the race in Canada, see 101–10 of his report.

21. For a more detailed account of the Anti-Slavery Society of Canada, see Fred Landon, "The Anti-Slavery Society of Canada," *Journal of Negro History* vol. 4, no. 1 (January 1919), 33–40. [Allen P. Stouffer's excellent work should be consulted, *The Light of Nature and the Law of God* (Baton Rouge, Louisiana: Louisiana State University Press, 1992).]

22. Henson, *An Autobiography*, 176. [As noted earlier, Henson published several versions of his autobiography.]

23. Howe, *Refugees from Slavery in Canada West*, 77–78; also, Carter G. Woodson, *Education of the Negro Prior to 1861*, 2nd ed. (Washington, DC: Associated Publishers, 1919), 248–55.

24. Howe, *Refugees from Slavery in Canada West*, 79–81.

25. The Consolidated Statutes of Canada … (Toronto: S. Derbishire and G. Desbarats, 1859) cap. XXIV.

26. For a more detailed account of the Buxton colony, see Fred Landon, "The Buxton Settlement in Canada," *Journal of Negro History* vol. 3, no. 4 (October 1918): 360–67. Mrs. Annie Straith Jamieson, of Montreal, wrote an unpublished history of the colony, based on the papers of Reverend William King. [This manuscript was published in 1925 as: Annie Straith Jamieson, *William King, Friend and Champion of Slaves* (Toronto: Missions in Evangelism, 1925), and again in 1969 under the same title in New York by the Negro Universities Press].

Two: A Pioneer Abolitionist in Upper Canada

1. Benjamin Lundy, *The Diary of Benjamin Lundy, Written During His Journey Through Upper Canada* (Published in *The Genius of Universal Emancipation*, January 1832).

2. *The Genius of Universal Emancipation*, March 1832.

3. Reprinted with introduction and notes by Fred Landon in *Ontario Historical Society, Papers and Records* vol.19 (1922) 110–33. *Ontario History* vol. 52, no.2 (1960).

4. See: *Laws of Ohio* vol. 2, 63 and vol. 5, 53.

5. See Drew, *North-Side View of Slavery*, 244–45, for Brown's report of his reception. Also, Colonial Office Records, series Q, vol. 386, part 1, no. 37: a letter from Sir John Colborne in which he writes of the original Negro settlers that they possessed sufficient means to be able to establish themselves on the land and that at the time of their first appearance they were favourably received.

6. Fred Landon, "Benjamin Lundy in Illinois," *Journal of the Illinois State Historical Society* vol.33, no. 1 (March 1940).

7. Merton L. Dillon, "Benjamin Lundy in Texas," *Southwestern Historical Quarterly* vol. 63, no. 1 (July 1959): 46–62.

8. Austin Steward, *Twenty-Two Years a Slave and Forty Years a Freeman*, 2nd ed. (Rochester, NY: Allings & Cory, 1859).

9. Copies of all of these 12 issues except the first are preserved in the library of the Chicago Historical Society. [*The Genius of Universal Emancipation* is available in most university libraries: American periodical series, 1800–1850; 1272–1273, 2 reels (Ann Arbor, MI: University Microfilms, 1972).

Three: Amherstburg, Terminus of the Underground Railroad

1. Mitchell, *Underground Railroad*, 149.

2. Drew, *North-Side View of Slavery*, 348.

3. *Liberator*, November 23, 1849.

4. *Liberator*, August 23, 1850.

5. Siebert, *The Underground Railroad*, 194.

6. Brown, *Narrative of William W. Brown*, 109–10.

7. *Chicago Western Citizen*, September 23, 1842. [The *Western Citizen* was published in Chicago from 1842–52 as the official media outlet for the Illinois Liberty Party, and contains much of the abolitionist writing of the period for the mid-western states.]

8. Mitchell, *Underground Railroad*, 55–60.

9. Howe, *Refugees from Slavery in Canada West*, 50 ff.

10. Drew, *North-Side View of Slavery*, 348.

11. This organization had already opened a school for Negro children in London. The work was under the superintendence of Reverend Dr. Hellmuth, afterwards bishop of the Diocese of Huron.

12. Howe, *Refugees from Slavery in Canada West*, 67.

13. Coffin, *Reminiscences*, 249–50.

14. The resolution goes on to say: "The increased immigration of foreign Negroes into this part of the province is truly alarming. We cannot omit mentioning some facts for the corroboration of what we have stated. The Negroes, who form at least one-third of the inhabitants of the township of Colchester, attended the township meeting for the election of parish and township officer, and insisted upon their right to vote, which was denied them by every individual white man at the meeting — the consequences of which was that the chairman of the meeting was prosecuted and thrown into heavy costs, which costs were paid by subscription from the white inhabitants, as well as many others. In the same township of Colchester the inhabitants have not been able to get schools in many school sections in consequence of the Negroes insisting on their right of sending their children to such schools. No white man will even act with them in any capacity; this fact is so glaring that no sheriff in this province would dare to summon colored men to do jury duty. That such things have been done in other parts of the British Dominions we are well aware of but we are convinced that the Canadians will never tolerate such conduct."
(The above extreme views fail to present the true situation. Negroes did occasionally do jury duty and held some minor offices. The justice of Canadian law is indicated by the punishment that fell upon the individual mentioned in the above resolution, who discriminated against Negro voters.)

The *Amherstburg Courier* (January 12, 1850) says that "the white inhabitants are fast leaving the vicinity of the proposed colored settlement (the Elgin settlement) for the United States" and adds: "The coloured company is about to be disbanded at Thorold. The western district will, no doubt, be their future place of abode should the Elgin Association carry out their designs. It appears from the advertisement that Raleigh is to be settled by darkies of good moral and religious character already actual settlers, thus leaving the runaway, worthless majority as well as all newcomers to prey upon the community at large."

15. Howe, *Refugees from Slavery in Canada West*, 58.
16. Howe, *Refugees from Slavery in Canada West*, 58, 75–77.
17. Drew, *North-Side View of Slavery*, 349.
18. Drew, *North-Side View of Slavery*, 61.
19. Drew, *North-Side View of Slavery*, 63–64.
20. Patrick Shirreff, *A Tour Through North America* (Edinburgh: Oliver & Boyd, 1835), 207. "The soil of Malden seems superior to that of Colchester and improves, on approaching Amherstburg, to the finest quality. In both townships there are a good many people of colour who generally rent the farms on which they reside or obtain so many years' possession on condition of clearing a certain extent of wood. A considerable amount of tobacco is here grown, chiefly by the Black population."

Six: The Buxton Settlement in Canada

1. Drew, *North-Side View of Slavery*, 292.
2. Documents in Library and Archives Canada. [The original is in the King Papers, "Memorial of the Inhabitants of Raleigh Township and Vicinity to the Presbyterian Synod at Toronto, June 1849." For a more detailed discussion, see William H. and Jane H. Pease, "Opposition to the Founding of the Elgin Settlement," *Canadian Historical Review* vol. 38 (1957), 202–18; Robin W. Winks, *The Blacks in Canada: A History*, 1st ed. (Montreal: McGill-Queen's University Press, 1971), 212–15. The petition is cited in Donald G. Simpson, with Paul E. Lovejoy, ed., *Under the North Star: Black Communities in Upper Canada* (Trenton, NJ: African World Press, 2005), 161.]
3. Toronto *Weekly Globe*, January 1, 1858.
4. Drew, *North-Side View of Slavery*, 292–93.
5. Drew, *North-Side View of Slavery*, 293–97. The slaves who had been freed by Mr. King formed the nucleus of the colony, but others came as soon as the land was thrown open. The advances made by this colony during the

first years of its existence were remarkable. The *Third Annual Report* (1852) showed a population of 75 families or 400 inhabitants, with 350 acres of land cleared and 204 acres under cultivation. A year later, the *Fourth Annual Report* (1853) showed 130 families or 520 persons, with 500 acres of land cleared and 135 partially cleared, with 415 acres under cultivation. The livestock was given as 128 cattle, 15 horses, 30 sheep, and 250 hogs. The day school had 112 children enrolled and the Sabbath School, 80.

The *Fifth Annual Report* (1854), showed 150 families in the colony or immediately adjoining it, 726 acres of land cleared, 174 acres partially cleared, and 577 acres under cultivation. During the year, there had been an increase of cleared land amounting to 226 acres, and of land under cultivation of 162 acres.

The livestock consisted of 150 cattle and oxen, 38 horses, 25 sheep, and 700 hogs. The day school had 147 on the roll and the Sabbath School, 120. A second day school was opened that year.

The *Sixth Annual Report* (1855) shows 827 acres of land cleared and fenced, and 216 acres chopped and to go under cultivation in 1856. There were 810 acres cultivated that year, while the livestock consisted of 190 cattle and oxen, 40 horses, 38 sheep, and 600 hogs. The day school had an enrolment of 150. Among the advances this year was the erection of a saw- and gristmill, which supplied the colony with lumber and with flour and feed. The building of the sawmill meant added prosperity, for an estimate made in 1854 placed the value of standing timber at $127,000.

A representative of the New York *Tribune* visited the colony in 1857, and his description of what he saw was reprinted in the Toronto *Globe* (November 20, 1857). The colony was then seven years old and had a population of about 200 families or 800 souls. More than 1,000 acres had been completely cleared, while on 200 acres more the trees had been felled and the land would be put under cultivation the next spring. The acreage under cultivation in the season of 1857 he gives as follows: corn, 354 acres; wheat, 200 acres; oats, 70 acres; potatoes, 80 acres; other crops, 120 acres. The livestock consisted of 200 cows, 80 oxen, 300 hogs, 52 horses, and a small number of sheep. The industries included a steam sawmill, a brickyard, pearl-ash factory, blacksmith, carpenter, and shoe shops, as well as a good general store. There were two schools, one male and one female. The latter, which had been open only about a year, taught plain sewing and other domestic subjects. The two schools had a combined enrolment of 140 with average attendance of 58. In order to make the schools self-supporting, a small payment was being proposed. The Sabbath School had an enrolment of 112 and an average attendance of 52.

6. New York *Tribune* reprinted in the Toronto *Globe*, November 20, 1857.

7. Ward, *Autobiography of a Fugitive Negro*, 214.
8. Howe, *Refugees from Slavery in Canada West*, 70–71.
9. Toronto *Globe*, November 4, 1859.

Seven: Agriculture among the Negro Refugees in Upper Canada

1. Howe, *Refugees from Slavery in Canada West*, 70–71.
2. Jamieson, *William King, Friend and Champion of Slaves*. A history of the Buxton settlement. Mrs. Jamieson, who was a niece of Reverend William King, has deposited his papers at the Library and Archives Canada, Ottawa. [There is also an extensive collection of her papers for this book, including illustrations, in the Special Collections at the D.B. Weldon Library, University of Western Ontario.]
3. "The Diary of Benjamin Lundy Written During His Journey Through Upper Canada," (January 1832). Reprinted from *The Genius of Universal Emancipation* (March, April, May 1832) *Ontario Historical Society, Papers and Records* vol.19 (1922) 110–33.
4. Steward, *Twenty-Two Years a Slave*.
5. Shirreff, *Tour Through North America*, 178.
6. Files of this paper are in the library of the University of Michigan and in the Burton Library, Detroit. [The *Voice of the Fugitive* is contained in the Baptist Church Archives at McMaster University, Hamilton. It is now widely available on microfilm in university libraries, and online at *Paper of Record*, http://www.paperofrecord.com, which is a subscription service available through university and public libraries.]
7. Reprinted in the *Voice of the Fugitive*, January 1, 1852.

Nine: The Work of the American Missionary Association Among the Negro Refugees in Canada West 1848–64

1. The American Missionary Association was organized at Albany, New York, on September 3, 1846, and openly opposed slavery in its policies. Its official organ, *The American Missionary*, has been published continuously since 1856. A complete file of the magazine and of the annual reports is preserved at the association's head office, 287 Fourth Avenue, New York. The New York Public Library has copies of the third to fifteenth annual reports (covering the period of work in Canada) with the exception of the ninth. [The American Missionary Association Archives up to 1861 are on microfilm and are

available at the Robarts Library, University of Toronto, and the Wellington County Archives in Fergus, Ontario.]

2. *American Missionary Association, Eighth Annual Report* (1854), 48.

3. *American Missionary Association, Eleventh Annual Report* (1857), 36–37.

4. *American Missionary Association, Fifteenth Annual Report* (1861), 28–29.

5. *American Missionary Association, Fifth Annual Report* (1851), 34–35. "We were told of instances in which three or four men would club together, call themselves a society, make one of their number their agent, and divide up what he collected."

   American Missionary Association, Sixth Annual Report (1852), 34. "The missionary in Canada finds many whom he labours to bless who regard his efforts with great disfavour. There is a class of preachers and self-constituted collecting agents who, to retain their own influence, are labouring, some of them avowedly, to drive every white missionary from the colony. The influence of this class of men has been very extensive."

6. See Fred Landon, "Henry Bibb, a Colonizer," *Journal of Negro History* vol. 5, no. 4 (October 1920), 437–47, reprinted in this book.

7. Fred Landon, "The Buxton Settlement in Canada," *Journal of Negro History* vol. 3, no. 4 (October 1918), 360–67, reprinted in this book.

8. Howe, *Refugees from Slavery in Canada West*, 70–71; *American Missionary Association Fourteenth Annual Report* (1860), 30. Dr. Samuel Howe, who visited Canada representing the Freedmen's Inquiry Committee, had the following to say with regard to the Elgin Association Settlement: "This settlement is a perfect success. Here are men who were bred in slavery, who came here and purchased land at the government price, cleared it, bought their own implements, built their own houses after a model and have supported themselves in all material circumstances and now support their schools in part.... I consider this settlement has done as well as a white settlement would have done under the same circumstances."

9. *American Missionary Association Third Annual Report* (1849), 21–22.

10. As many as 30 a day crossed into Canada at this point after the passing of the Fugitive Slave Law in 1850. See Siebert, *The Underground Railroad*, 194. The Negro population of Amherstburg on the eve of the Civil War was placed at 800 out of a total population of 2,000. See Mitchell, *Underground Railroad*, 149. Five years earlier, it was estimated to be between 400 and 500. See Drew, *North-Side View of Slavery*, 348.

11. Coffin, *Reminiscences*, 249–50.

12. Chicago *Western Citizen*, September 27, 1849, quoted in *Transactions of the Illinois Historical Society* (1917), 95.

13. Mitchell, *Underground Railroad*, 55–60.

14. Howe, *Refugees from Slavery in Canada West*, 50.

15. Drew, *North-Side View of Slavery*, 348.

16. Howe, *Refugees from Slavery in Canada West*, 67.

17. William Troy, *Hair-Breadth Escapes from Slavery to Freedom* (Manchester: W. Bremner, 1861): "The fugitives in Amherstburg have a society for the relief of those who are continually coming in from slavery.... The True Band Society.... This society has been the means of relieving many very destitute cases." A copy of this interesting book is in the Princeton University library. It has a portrait of the author, who is described as being from Windsor, Canada West, and is dedicated to William Howard Day, M.A., of Chatham, Canada West. [Troy's entire book is available online at http://docsouth.unc.edu/neh/troy/troy.html.]

18. The work at Dawn appears to have been the responsibility of a committee or board of trustees, of which the famous Josiah Henson was the agent. A sketch of Henson appeared in the *Journal of Negro History* vol. 3, no. 1 (January 1918), 1–21. This article is based on Henson's own account of his life, which appeared in several editions under varying titles. He claimed to have been the inspiration of Harriet Beecher Stowe's "Uncle Tom." He is buried near the Village of Dresden, in Kent County, Ontario.

19. *American Missionary Association Fourth Annual Report* (1850), 14. "After the departure of Mr. and Mrs. Brooks the work at this point seems to have been continued by a Miss Susan Teall, who taught the school. She reported in August of 1849 that she had over 100 [students] in her school. Mr. Brooks left Canada for Africa and died at sea, being buried at York, Sierra Leone." [This account of Brooks's life is slightly inaccurate; he survived the voyage, but his wife died soon after her arrival in Sierra Leone. Brooks later returned to the Queen's Bush to sell all of his remaining property, then spent the rest of his life in Sierra Leone. See Linda Brown-Kubisch, *The Queen's Bush Settlement: Black Pioneers, 1839–1865* (Toronto: Natural Heritage Books, 2004), 148–49.]

20. *American Missionary Association Fourth Annual Report* (1850), 27–30.

21. See Fred Landon, "The Negro Migration to Canada After the Passing of the Fugitive Slave Act," *Journal of Negro History* vol. 5, no.1 (January 1920), 22–36, for an estimate of the effect of the Fugitive Slave Law on the movement of refugees to Canada. The migration of Negroes into Canada in the year after this act passed into law was very large. [Landon's article is reprinted in this book.]

22. Mary Shadd's school in Windsor was partly supported by the American Missionary Association, which paid $120 a year to assist it. The pupils paid 37 1/2 cents each. These figures are given in the *Voice of the Fugitive* (June 17, 1852), published by Henry Bibb. In the June 3, 1852 issue, it is announced that Mrs. Mary Shadd was issuing a little book of 30 or 40 pages on Canada West. I have been unable to trace a copy of this. She does not appear to have had a

lengthy connection with the work of the American Missionary Association, as the sixth annual report, issued in 1852, reports that she has left and gone back to the United States. She was coloured and had taught school in New York State and elsewhere before coming to Canada. At one time she lived in Chatham and was associated with a little paper issued there in the interest of the refugees. [Landon's notes on Mary Ann Shadd's life (1823–93) are inaccurate. A famous figure in North American Black history, Mary Ann Shadd was the first woman to publish a newspaper in Canada, the only woman recruiting officer for the Union army, and later the first woman to graduate with a law degree from Howard University. She had been educated in Quaker schools in Pennsylvania before migrating to Canada in 1852, followed by her family, which was headed by her father, the noted Black abolitionist Abraham D. Shadd. All but Mary Ann moved to the district of the Elgin Settlement at Buxton soon after the passing of the Fugitive Slave Law; Mary Ann had already gone to Windsor to open her school. Mary Ann Shadd was an ardent opponent of slavery and lectured widely, as well as editing the *Provincial Freeman.* This, with the *Voice of the Fugitive,* was one of the two African-Canadian abolitionist papers published during the 1850s in what is now Ontario. She married Thomas Cary of Toronto in 1856. The book to which Landon refers has recently been republished. See Mary Ann Shadd Cary, *A Plea for Emigration, or, Notes of Canada West/Mary Shadd*, edited, annotated, and with an introduction by Richard Almonte (Toronto: Mercury Press, 1998). For more details on the life of Mary Ann Shadd Cary, see Jim Beardon and Linda Jean Butler, *Shadd: The Life and Times of Mary Shadd Cary* (Toronto: NC Press Ltd., 1977); Jane Rhodes, *Mary Ann Shadd Cary: The Black Press and Protest in the Nineteenth Century* (Bloomington: IN University Press, 1998); and Shirley J. Yee, *Black Women Abolitionists: A Study in Activism, 1828–1860* (Knoxville, TN: University of Tennessee Press, 1992). A children's book on Shadd's life was written by Rosemary Sadlier, *Mary Ann Shadd Cary, Publisher, Editor, Teacher, Lawyer, Suffragette* (Toronto: Umbrella Press, 1995).]

23. *American Missionary Association, Sixth Annual Report* (1852), 34. "There has been a large increase of the colored population during the past year."

24. Reverend Hiram Wilson's contract with the American Missionary Association expired in 1851 and was not renewed, but he continued his work at St. Catharines, apparently on friendly terms with the association. He writes that he can use all the clothing that may be sent to him. [See James W. St. G. Walker, "African Canadians," in Paul R. Magosci, ed. *Encyclopedia of Canada's Peoples* (Toronto: University of Toronto Press, 1989), 139–76; and Winks, *Blacks in Canada*, 179–83 and 197–200. Wilson's papers are in the Special Collections of Oberlin College, Ohio.]

25. During 1860 there were 30 members added at London, bringing the total there to 100, and 16 added at Ingersoll, for a total of 61 there. The building of the railroads attracted the large Negro population to Ingersoll. The wood for the engines was cut and stored there, as well. The work was done almost entirely by Negroes.

26. Estimates of the Negro population of Upper Canada on the eve of the Civil War range from 20,000 to more than 40,000. Probably a figure between these two extremes would be about correct. [A thorough analysis of sources for the numbers of people of African descent living in Canada during the antebellum period is found in Winks, *Blacks in Canada*, 484–96.]

Thirteen: Records Illustrating the Condition of Refugees from Slavery in Upper Canada Before 1860

1. Collected by Fred Landon of the University of Western Ontario, *Journal of Negro History* vol. 13, no. 2 (April, 1928), 199–207.

2. Robert Graham Dunlop, born in 1789, died near Goderich, in Upper Canada, in 1841. His early life was spent in the British naval service, which he entered at the age of 13. He was the first representative of Huron County in the legislature of the province.

3. William Lyon Mackenzie (1795–1861) was prominent in the reform agitations in Upper Canada before 1837 and was at the head of the armed outbreak in the province in that year. His criticism of the coloured population is that their gratitude for British protection makes them blind to the government's ills, which others are seeking to remedy.

4. Toronto, the capital of the province, was more generally known in this period as York.

5. John Henry Dunn came to Canada in 1820 from England and died in London in 1854. He was receiver general and member of Executive and Legislative Councils of Upper Canada.

6. Malcolm Cameron (1808–1876) was elected to the Assembly of Upper Canada for Lanark in 1836. A persistent advocate of the Family Compact, he held various offices in the La Fontaine-Baldwin and Hincks administrations. Appointed Queen's Printer in 1863. Represented South Lanark in the Canadian House of Commons, 1874–76.

7. The Elgin Association Settlement was founded in the late 1840s by Reverend William King. [For a sketch of its history, see Landon, "Buxton," in this book.]

8. Published at Sandwich, Upper Canada, by Henry Bibb. [See Landon, "Henry Bibb," in this book.]

9. Misprint for Reverend Jermain W. Loguen.

Fourteen: Social Conditions Among the Negroes in Upper Canada Before 1865

1. Howe, *Refugees from Slavery in Canada West.*
2. Howe, *Report to the Freedmen's Inquiry Commission* (Boston 1864), 17.
3. Ward, *Autobiography of a Fugitive Negro,* 154.
4. Richard J. Hinton, *John Brown and His Men* (New York: Funk & Wagnalls Co., 1894), 171.
5. Mitchell, *Underground Railroad,* 127, 166.
6. Siebert, *The Underground Railroad,* 221.
7. Coffin, *Reminiscences,* 253.
8. Ward, *Autobiography of a Fugitive Negro,* 154. That was following the passing of the Fugitive Slave Act of 1850.
9. Josiah Henson, *Life of Josiah Henson Narrated by Himself* (London: Charles Gilpin, 1852), 97.
10. James B. Brown, *Views of Canada and the Colonists* (Edinburgh: 1851), 353.
11. *Voice of the Fugitive,* June 4, 1851. This paper was published by Henry Bibb, himself a fugitive at Sandwich.
12. *Voice of the Fugitive,* May 20, 1852.
13. Drew, *North-Side View of Slavery.* The author gathered his narratives from persons whom he met in the course of a tour through the western part of the province.
14. The Colonial Church and School Society had a school in London in the 1850s, which Benjamin Drew noted in 1855 as caring for the bulk of the Negro children.
15. Shirreff, *Tour Through North America,* 207.
16. Troy, *Hair-Breadth Escapes from Slavery to Freedom,* 26.
17. Quoted in the *Voice of the Fugitive,* October 21, 1852. This resolution also suggested that the government consider the propriety of laying a poll tax on American Negroes coming into the province, together with an enactment against amalgamation [meaning intermarriage between Black and white couples], and the introduction of regulations thereby. All foreign Negroes should be compelled to furnish good security that they would not become a burden on the community. The question of further allowing the suffrage to Negroes was also mentioned.
18. *Voice of the Fugitive,* September 9, 1852.
19. Quoted in the *National Anti-Slavery Standard,* February 21, 1850. A reflection

of the annexation movement of 1849 can be seen in the *Pilot*'s comments. One of the chief fomenters of prejudice against the Negroes was Edwin Larwill, of Chatham, a tinsmith by trade and a typical brawling Tory politician.

20. *Voice of the Fugitive*, November 4, 1852.

21. *Voice of the Fugitive*, May 21, 1851. In his letter, Fisher makes open protest to the Chief Justice of the Court of Common Pleas. His charge is that Thomas Tilly, a coloured man, was dismissed from jury service because of his colour. On the other hand, the *Voice of the Fugitive* (July 2, 1851) noted that a Negro was the foreman of a jury three times in one day in a Toronto court. The incident was quoted from the Toronto *Patriot*.

22. Toronto correspondence of the New York *Tribune*, quoted in the *Voice of the Fugitive* (July 29, 1852).

23. *Liberator*, July 13, 1849.

24. *American Anti-Slavery Society, Twenty-Eighth Annual Report* (New York 1861), 171.

25. Quoted in the *Voice of the Fugitive*, November 5, 1851. These visitors made the vastly exaggerated estimate of 80,000 as the Negro population.

26. An account of the history of this society can be found in Fred Landon, "The Anti-Slavery Society of Canada," *Journal of Negro History* vol. 4 (1919), 33–40. [The version printed in *Ontario History* (1956) is reprinted in this book. Reverend Michael Willis was principal of Knox College, Toronto.]

27. *American Anti-Slavery Society, Twenty-Eighth Annual Report* (1859), and *Eleventh Annual Report* (1851), 100.

28. *American Anti-Slavery Society, Ninth Annual Report* (1855), 47. For an account of the work of this missionary organization among the Negroes in Canada, see Fred Landon, "The Work of the American Missionary Association Among the Negro Refugees in Canada West 1848–64," *Ontario Historical Society, Papers and Records* vol. 21 (1924), 198–205. [Reprinted in this book.]

29. Troy, *Hair-Breadth Escapes*, 108, 122.

30. Reprinted in the *Voice of the Fugitive*, May 20, 1852. John Scoble was the secretary of the British and Foreign Anti-Slavery Society and had visited Canada in 1851 to see the condition of the refugees. He later advocated emigration from Canada and the United States to the West Indies as the best opportunity for the Negro.

31. *Voice of the Fugitive*, January 1, 1852.

32. Francis Bond Head, *A Narrative* (London: J. Murray, 1839), 392.

33. Jermain W. Loguen, *Reverend Jermain W. Loguen as a Slave and as a Freeman* (Syracuse: J.G.K. Truair & Co., printers, 1859), 344–45.

34. Josiah Henson, *An Autobiography of the Reverend Josiah Henson, "Uncle Tom," from 1789 to 1881* (London, ON: Schuyler, Smith, & Co., 1881) 176.

35. Reprinted in the *Quarterly Anti-Slavery Magazine* vol. 2, no. 4 (July 1837), 350–51

36. F. Severance, "Old Trails at Niagara," published by Niagara Historical Society, *Transactions No. 2*, 190–91. Head, *A Narrative*, 200–204. Also: Mrs. Anna Jameson's *Winter Studies and Summer Rambles* vol. 1 (New York: Wiley and Putnam, 1839), 246–50. Sir Francis Bond Head says that two men were killed and others were wounded in the riot in which the prisoner Moseby escaped. [For a full analysis of the Moseby affair, see David Murray, *Colonial Justice: Justice, Morality and Crime in the Niagara District* (Toronto: University of Toronto Press, 2002); also Michael Power and Nancy Butler, *Slavery and Freedom in Niagara* (Niagara-on-the-Lake, ON: Niagara Historical Society, 1993); Owen Thomas, *Niagara's Freedom Trail: A Guide to African-Canadian History on the Niagara Peninsula* (Niagara Falls, ON: The Region of Niagara Tourist Council, 1995).]

37. Head, *Narrative*, 200–04.

38. Library and Archives Canada, *Colonial Office Records*, series Q, vol. 430, part 3, 415.

39. Toronto *Globe*, December 24, 1860.

40. *Ibid.*

41. For a more detailed account of the Anderson case, see Fred Landon, "The Anderson Fugitive Case," *Journal of Negro History* vol. 7, no. 3 (July 1922), 233–42. [Reprinted in this book.] Also Paul Finkelman, "International Extradition and Fugitive Slaves — The John Anderson Case," *Brooklyn Journal of International Law* vol. 18, no. 765 (1992); William Teatro, *John Anderson, Fugitive Slave* (Toronto: Treasure Island Books, 1986), 765–810; Harper Twelvetrees, *The Story of John Anderson: The Fugitive Slave* (London: W. Tweedie, 1863) [online at http://docsouth.unc.edu/neh/twelvetr/menu.html].

42. Toronto *Globe*, December 20, 1860.

43. Chicago *Western Citizen*, August 10, 1843 and December 18, 1843, quoted in *Transactions of the Illinois State Historical Society* (1917), 93–94.

44. *Voice of the Fugitive*, February 26, 1852. The Toronto *Globe* (December 27, 1861) reports a mass meeting of coloured people at Chatham protesting against begging for refugees and institutions. Mary Ann Shadd Cary is denounced, in particular, for begging on behalf of a mission school.

45. *Voice of the Fugitive*, July 30, 1851.

46. Laura S. Haviland, *A Woman's Life Work* (Cincinnati: Printed by Walden & Stowe for the author, 1881), 193.

Fifteen: Canadian Negroes and the Rebellion of 1837

1. A convention of Hunters' Lodges of Ohio and Michigan, held at Cleveland, September 16–22, 1838, was attended by 70 delegates.
2. Head, *A Narrative*, 392.
3. Loguen, *The Reverend Jermain W. Loguen*, 343–45.
4. Henson, *An Autobiography*, 177.
5. John MacMullen, *History of Canada from its First Discovery to the Present Times* (Brockville, ON: J. McMullen, Publisher, 1868), 459–60. He gives Radcliff's dispatch of January 10, 1838 as his authority.
6. The Rebellion Losses Bill proposed compensation for those who had sustained losses in Lower Canada (Quebec) during the troubles of 1837. It was fiercely opposed in Upper Canada (Ontario) by the element that regarded the French as "aliens" and "rebels." When Lord Elgin, the governor, gave his assent to the bill in 1849, there were riots in Montreal in which the Parliament Buildings were burned.
7. Colonel Prince was one of the leaders in the defence of the Canadian frontier along the Detroit River during 1838, and afterwards a member of the Canadian Parliament. During the troubles of 1838, he ordered the shooting of four prisoners without a trial. The act was condemned with great severity by Lord Brougham and others, and is one dark spot on the records of the Canadian forces during this trying period.

Sixteen: Canadian Negroes and the John Brown Raid

1. Samuel Longfellow, *Life of Henry Wadsworth Longfellow* vol. 2 (Boston and New York: Houghton, Mifflin and Co., 1891), 347.
2. Henry David Thoreau, "A Plea for Captain John Brown" (Read at Concord, Maine, October 30, 1859). [For a more detailed account of the Canadian connection, see James Cleland Hamilton, "John Brown in Canada," *The Canadian Magazine* vol. 4 (December 1894), 133–34; David S. Reynolds, *John Brown, Abolitionist: The Man Who Killed Slavery, Sparked the Civil War, and Seeded Civil Rights* (New York: Alfred A. Knopf. Distributed by Random House, 2005); Winks, *The Blacks in Canada*, 267–68).]
3. Toronto *Globe*, November 25, 1859.
4. Toronto *Globe*, December 9, 1859 and December 16, 1859.
5. Toronto *Globe*, December 12, 1859.
6. Ward, *Autobiography of a Fugitive Negro*, 158: "There is no country in the world so much hated by slaveholders as Canada."

7. *Journal of the Senate of Virginia* (1859), 9–25.
8. The Toronto *Globe*, December 6, 1859 reported Governor Wise as saying: "One most irritating feature of this predatory war is that it has its seat in the British provinces which furnish asylum for our fugitives and send them and their hired outlaws upon us from depots and rendezvous in the bordering states."
9. Toronto *Globe*, December 28, 1859.
10. *Ibid.*
11. Toronto *Globe*, December 23, 1859.
12. Toronto *Globe*, July 20, 1860.
13. *Report of the Select Committee on the Invasion of Harper's Ferry.* U.S. government publication, serial set 1040, doc. no. 278: 2, 7.
14. Harper's Ferry Invasion, *Report of Senatorial Committee*, 99.
15. Hinton, *John Brown and His Men*, 504–07.
16. Hinton, *John Brown and His Men*, Appendix, 704. See also *Report of Senatorial Committee*, 97.
17. Hinton, *John Brown and His Men*, 171–72.
18. Hinton, *John Brown and His Men*, 175.
19. *Report of Senatorial Committee*, 97.
20. Franklin B. Sanborn ed., *Life and Letters of John Brown* (Boston: Roberts Brothers, 1885), 457–58.
21. Sanborn, *Life and Letters of John Brown*, 536–38, 547.
22. Hinton, *John Brown and His Men*, 261–63.

Seventeen: Abolitionist Interest in Upper Canada

1. Charles Stuart, *The West India Question* (New Haven, Connecticut: Hezekiah Howe & Co., 1833), 18. [See also Fred Landon, "Abolitionist Interest in Upper Canada," *Ontario History* vol. 44, no. 4 (1952), 165–72, reprinted in this book.]
2. Fred Landon, "The Diary of Benjamin Lundy, Written During his Journey Through Upper Canada," (January 1832), *Ontario Historical Society, Papers and Records* vol.19 (1922), 110–33.
3. Steward, *Twenty-Two Years a Slave and Forty Years a Freeman*. Steward's self-sacrificing but unhappy experiences in the Wilberforce Settlement are recorded in his autobiography. He and Benjamin Lundy are our chief authorities, but there are references to the colony in a number of early works of Canadian travel. Reverend Nathaniel Paul, a Negro Baptist minister from Wilberforce, was called as a witness before a select committee of the British House of Commons when he was in England in 1832 and gave testimony concerning the condition of his people in Upper Canada. His brother, Reverend Benjamin

Paul, died at Wilberforce and his grave is one of the few existing reminders of this early colony. [The best account of Wilberforce is by Austin Steward in *Twenty-Two Years a Slave and Forty Years a Freeman*. See also William H. Pease and Jane Pease, *Black Utopia: Negro Communal Experiments in America* (Madison, WI: State Historical Society of Wisconsin, 1963), 46–62; Simpson, *Under the North Star*, 172–80; Winks, *The Blacks in Canada*, 156–62.]

4. Coffin, *Reminiscences*, 247–53.

5. Coffin, *Reminiscences*, 150–51.

6. This former slave was forcibly taken from the courtroom at Syracuse to Kingston, Upper Canada, by abolitionists and sympathizers. He resided in Kingston until his death.

7. John Hope Franklin, *From Slavery to Freedom: A History of American Negroes* (New York: A.A. Knopf, 1947), 249–50. Douglass was a close friend of John Brown and sought to dissuade him from the ill-fated Harper's Ferry raid. Their final conference, at which Douglass declined to participate in the enterprise, took place in a stone quarry near Chambersburg, Pennsylvania, in August 1859. After the Harper's Ferry Raid, Douglass, like several other abolitionist leaders, took refuge in Canada for a time, fearing arrest.

8. See *News of the Week,* (Toronto, March 13, 1857). His speech was printed in the *Gospel Tribune* (Toronto, April 1857), 328–29, a Baptist publication edited by Reverend Robert Dick.

9. The Canadian Library Association has reproduced the first volume of this newspaper on film, and it may be consulted in a number of Canadian libraries today. It was well-edited and provides much information that cannot be found elsewhere. [The *Voice of the Fugitive* is contained in the Baptist Church Archives at McMaster University, Hamilton. It is now widely available on microfilm in university libraries and online at *Paper of Record*, http://www.paperofrecord.com, which is a subscription service available through university and public libraries.]

10. Howe, *Refugees from Slavery in Canada West*.

11. Howe, *Refugees from Slavery in Canada West*, 104.

Nineteen: The Anti-Slavery Society of Canada

1. The only Canadian reference to this that I have found is in the Toronto *Constitution* of November 16, 1837. This is the report of a meeting held at Toronto City Hall, at which the mayor of the city presided and the speaker was Hiram Wilson, agent of the American Anti-Slavery Society. Resolutions relating to the slavery question were passed. One of these was moved by

Reverend Ephraim Evans, a Methodist minister. In the Burton Library [Burton Historical Collection, Main Branch of the Detroit Public Library] in Detroit there is a list of anti-slavery societies existing in 1837. The Upper Canada Society is included in this, Ephraim Evans is listed as secretary, and the membership is reported as 106 in January 1837.

2. William McClure, *Life and Labours of Rev. Wm. McClure, for More than Forty Years a Minister of the Methodist New Connexion, Chiefly an Autobiography.* Edited by Reverend David Savage (Toronto: James Campbell & Son, 1872).

Twenty: The Negro Migration to Canada After the Passing of the Fugitive Slave Act

1. James Ford Rhodes, *History of the United States from the Compromise of 1850 to the McKinley-Bryan Campaign of 1896*, 4 vols., vol.1 (New York: Harper & Brothers, 1893–99, 1920), 185: "One of the most assailable laws ever passed by the Congress of the United States ... Under this act ... the Negro had no chance; the meshes of the law were artfully contrived to aid the master and entrap the slave."

2. *American Anti-Slavery Society, Annual Report* (1851), 31. "A large proportion of the coloured persons who have fled from the free states have sought refuge in Canada where they have been received with remarkable kindness and have testified the grateful sense of their reception by their exemplary conduct."

3. *Liberator*, October 18, 1850.

4. *American Anti-Slavery Society, Annual Report* (1851), 30.

5. *Voice of the Fugitive.*

6. *American Missionary Association, Sixth Annual Report* (1852), 34.

7. Mitchell, *Underground Railroad*, 113.

8. *Liberator*, October 4, 1850.

9. *Liberator*, October 18, 1850.

10. *Liberator*, October 4, 1850.

11. *Liberator*, April 25, 1851.

12. *Liberator*, May 2, 1851.

13. Siebert, *The Underground Railroad*, 249.

14. *Ibid.*

15. Charles Emery Stevens, *Anthony Burns, a History* (Boston: John P. Jewett & Co., 1856), 208. [See also Albert J. Von Frank, *The Trials of Anthony Burns: Freedom and Slavery in Emerson's Boston* (Cambridge: Harvard University Press, 1998), and James Brewer Stewart, *Holy Warriors: The Abolitionists and American Slavery* (New York: Hill and Wang, 1997), 157–58. An excellent

book for young people is Virginia Hamilton's *Anthony Burns: The Defeat and Triumph of a Fugitive Slave* (New York: A.A. Knopf, 1988).]

16. *American Anti-Slavery Society, Eleventh Annual Report* (1851), 31.

17. *Voice of the Fugitive*, April 9, 1851.

18. *Congressional Herald*, (May 13, 1861), quoted in *American Missionary Association Fifteenth Annual Report* (1861), 28. There is evidence that the Fugitive Slave Law was used in some cases to strike fear into the hearts of Negroes in order to cause them to abandon their property. *The Liberator* (October 25, 1850) quotes the Detroit *Free Press* to the effect that land speculators had been scaring the Negroes in some places in the North in order to get possession of their properties. [See also Reverend Samuel J. May, *The Fugitive Slave Law and its Victims* (New York: American Anti-Slavery Society, 1861).]

19. *American Anti-Slavery Society Twenty-Seventh Annual Report* (1861), 49.

20. In *The Liberator* (July 30, 1852), a letter from Hiram Wilson, at St. Catharines, says: "Arrivals from slavery are frequent."

21. *Voice of the Fugitive*, July 29, 1852.

22. *Voice of the Fugitive*, July 1, 1852.

23. St. Catharines Journal, quoted in the *Voice of the Fugitive* (September 23, 1852).

24. Quoted in *The Liberator*, September 12, 1851.

25. *Liberator*, February 14, 1851.

26. *Voice of the Fugitive*, August 27, 1851.

27. Quoted in *American Anti-Slavery Society, Twenty-Seventh Report* (1861).

28. *American Anti-Slavery Society, Twenty-Seventh Annual Report* (1861), 48–49.

29. *American Anti-Slavery Society, Twenty-Seventh Report* (1861), 157.

30. Rhodes, *History of the United States* vol.1 (1920), 210.

31. Rhodes, *History of the United States* vol.1 (1920), 224–25. See also Ward, *Autobiography of a Fugitive Negro*, 127.

32. Rhodes, *History of the United States* vol.1 (1920), 222–23. See also the *Voice of the Fugitive*, June 3 and July 1, 1852.

33. Schauler, *History of the United States* vol. 5, 290–91.

34. Troy, *Hair-Breadth Escapes from Slavery to Freedom*, 39–43.

35. *Liberator*, June 11, 1852. See also the *Voice of the Fugitive*, June 17, 1852.

36. *Liberator*, July 30, 1852.

37. *Liberator*, September 12, 1851; *Voice of the Fugitive*, September 24, 1851; *Anti-Slavery Tracts, New Series*, no.15, no. 19 (New York: Anti-Slavery Society).

38. *Sandusky Commercial Register*, October 21,1852; *Liberator*, October 29, 1852), *Anti-Slavery Tracts, New Series*, no.15, no. 24.

39. *Voice of the Fugitive*, February 12, 1851.

40. *American Missionary Association, Ninth Annual Report* (1855).

41. *American Anti-Slavery Society, Eleventh Annual Report* (1851), 100.

42. *Voice of the Fugitive*, January 15, 1851, and November 18, 1852.

43. *Voice of the Fugitive*, January 1 and May 20, 1852.

44. Troy, *Hair-Breadth Escapes*, 108, 122.

45. "The Canadian government reckoned that there had been not less than 40,000 Canadian enlistments in the American Army during the Civil War," in Arnold Haultain, ed., *A Selection from Goldwin Smith's Correspondence* (Toronto: McClelland & Stewart, n.d.), 377. Collected by his literary executor. Letter to Moberly Bell, 377.

Twenty-one: Henry Bibb, a Colonizer

1. George W. Williams, *History of the Negro Race in America*, 2 vols, vol. 2 (New York: Putnam, 1883), 58.

2. Henry Bibb, *The Narrative of the Life and Adventures of Henry Bibb, an American Slave, Written by Himself, with an Introduction by Lucius Matlack* (New York: privately published, 1849). I am indebted to the Brooklyn Public Library for loaning me this book. [The authoritative source on Henry Bibb in Canada is Afua Cooper, "Henry Bibb and the Underground Railroad." Annual meeting of the Association for the Study of Afro-American Life and History, Buffalo, October 2005; "'Doing Battle in Freedom's Cause': Henry Bibb, Abolitionism, Race Uplift, and Black Manhood, 1842–1854" (unpublished Ph.D. dissertation, University of Toronto, 2000).]

3. Compare this with the description of a New Orleans slave pen in descriptions of Richmond auctions by William H. Russell, *My Diary North and South* (New York: T.O.H.P. Burnham, 1863), 68, and William Chambers, *Things as They Are in America* (London and Edinburgh: W. & R. Chambers, 1854), 273–86.

4. He says that his object in going to Detroit was to get some schooling. He was unable to meet the expense, however, and as he puts it: "I graduated in three weeks and this was all the schooling I ever had in my life." His teacher for this brief period was W.C. Monroe, who afterward presided at John Brown's Chatham Convention in May 1858.

5. Theodore C. Smith, *Liberty and Free Soil Parties in the Northwest* (New York: Longmans, Green & Co., 1897).

6. Fred Landon, "The Negro Migration to Canada After the Passing of the Fugitive Slave Act," *Journal of Negro History* vol. 5, no.1 (January 1920), 22–36. [Reprinted in this book.]

7. This plan was recommended by a convention of coloured people held at Sandwich, Canada West, in early 1851. See *Voice of the Fugitive*, March 12, 1851.
8. *Voice of the Fugitive*, June 4, 1851.
9. *Voice of the Fugitive*, November 19, 1851.
10. *Voice of the Fugitive*, January 29, 1852. See also *Liberator*, June 11, 1852.
11. Drew, *North-Side View of Slavery*, 323–26.
12. Haviland, *A Woman's Life Work*, 192.
13. Mitchell, *Underground Railroad*, 142–49.
14. Howe, *Refugees from Slavery in Canada West*. The Freedmen's Inquiry Commission was instituted by Secretary of War Stanton in 1863 to consider what should be done for slaves who had already been freed. The members of the commission were Dr. Samuel Gridley Howe, Robert Dale Owen, and James McKaye. [See also "An Act to Establish a Bureau for the Relief of Freedmen and Refugees," *U.S. Statutes at Large, Treaties, and Proclamations of the United States of America* vol. 13 (Boston, 1866), 507–59.]

Twenty-two: When Uncle Tom's Cabin Came to Canada

1. A copy of the first printing of the Toronto edition is in the Toronto Reference Library, and one of the second printing is in the library of the University of Western Ontario.
2. No copy of this Montreal edition is reported by the Montreal libraries. [See Charles T. Davis and Henry Louis Gates, *The Slave's Narrative: Texts and Contexts* (New York: Oxford University Press, 1985), 121.]
3. Fred Landon, "The Negro Migration to Canada After the Passing of the Fugitive Slave Act," *Journal of Negro History* vol.5, no. 1 (January 1920), 22–36.
4. Haultain, *A Selection from Goldwin Smith's Correspondence*, 377.
5. Fred Landon, "Canadian Appreciation of Abraham Lincoln," *Abraham Lincoln Quarterly* vol. 3, no. 4 (December 1944), 159–77.
6. *Saturday Review of Literature* (October 6, 1945), 24.

Twenty-four: The Anderson Fugitive Case

1. On March 27, 1861, certain Howard County citizens petitioned for they had advanced to prosecute Anderson in the Canadian Courts, *Missouri Session Laws* (1860), 534.
2. Haviland, *A Woman's Life Work*, 197–98.
3. Toronto *Globe*, November 14, 1860.

4. Toronto *Globe*, November 29, 1860.

5. Toronto *Globe*, December 3 1860.

6. C.W. Robinson, *Life of Sir John Beverly Robinson, Bart., C.B., D.C.L.: Chief Justice of Upper Canada* (Toronto: Morang & Co., 1904), 326–27. [A far more recent biography is Patrick Brode, *Sir John Beverly Robinson: Bone and Sinew of the Compact* (Toronto: University of Toronto Press, 1984).]

7. The proceedings of this meeting are reported at length in the *Globe* of the following day.

8. Article X of the Ashburton Treaty, dealing with extradition, reads as follows: "It is agreed that the United States and Her Britannic Majesty shall, upon mutual requisition by them, or their ministers, officers, or authorities, respectively made, deliver up to justice all persons who, being charged with the crime of murder, or assault with intent to commit murder, or piracy, or arson, or robbery, or forgery, or the utterance of forged paper, shall seek an asylum, or shall be found within the territories of the other; provided that this shall only be done upon such evidence of criminality as, according to the laws of the place where the fugitive or person so charged shall be found, would justify his apprehension and commitment for trial, if the crime or offence had there been committed, etc." [The full text of the treaty is online at http://www.yale.edu/lawweb/avalon/diplomacy/britain/br-1842.htm; see also Howard Jones, *To the Webster-Ashburton Treaty: A Study in Anglo-American Relations, 1783–1843* (Chapel Hill, NC: University of North Carolina Press, 1977).]

Twenty-five: Anthony Burns in Canada 1860–62

1. Rhodes, *History of the United States* vol. 1, 185–86. Rhodes, chief American historian of this period, describes the act as one of the most assailable laws ever passed by the Congress of the United States. "Under this Act of ours, the Negro had no chance: the meshes of the law were artfully contrived to aid the master and entrap the slave." [The full text of the Fugitive Slave Act of 1850 is online at http://www.yale.edu/lawweb/avalon/fugitive.htm.]

2. No jury trial was allowed to the Negro claimed as a fugitive. Master or agent simply had to present an affidavit before a United States judge or commissioner, whose fee was doubled if he decided in favour of the claimant. The whole community was bound by the law to come to the aid of the commissioner as a *posse comitatus* to prevent the rescue or escape of the condemned fugitive, and the United States marshal was liable to a fine of $1,000 and a civil lawsuit for the value of the slave in case the latter got away or was rescued. Finally,

the law was *ex pas facto* (and therefore unconstitutional) in that it applied to slaves who had fled from their master at any time — even years before.

3. Fred Landon, "The Negro Migration to Canada after the Passing of the Fugitive Slave Act," *Journal of Negro History* vol. 5, no.1 (January 1920), 22–36. [Reprinted in this book.] For a special study of this movement to Canada, Phillips, says Rhodes, had the manner of Brutus, but his words were like those of Mark Anthony, fitted to stir up mutiny. "See to it," he said, "that tomorrow, in the streets of Boston, you ratify the verdict of Faneuil Hall, that Anthony Burns has no master but his God … Nebraska I call knocking a man down, and this spitting in his face after he is down."

4. Rhodes, *History of the United States* vol.1, 505–06.

5. Rhodes, "Life of Seward," *History of the United States* vol. 2, 230.

Acknowledgements

Permission to reprint the articles by Fred Landon in this book has been given by the following publications and organizations:

Association for the Study of African American Life and History (*Journal of Negro History*): "Agriculture Among the Negro Refugees in Upper Canada," "Amherstburg, Terminus of the Underground Railroad," "The Anderson Fugitive Case," "The Buxton Settlement in Canada," "Canadian Negroes and the John Brown Raid," "Canadian Negroes and the Rebellion of 1837," "Henry Bibb, A Colonizer," "The Negro Migration to Canada After the Passing of the Fugitive Slave Act," "Records Illustrating the Condition of Refugees from Slavery in Upper Canada Before 1860."

London Free Press: "Abraham Lincoln a Century Ago," "Evidence is Found of Race Prejudice in Biddulph, 1848," "Fugitive Slave Provides Focal Point for Change in Canadian Law," "Slaves' Church," "'We Are Free,' Answer of Slave to 'Old Massa,'" "1856 Garner Slave Case One of Horror: Missed Escape to Western Ontario, Killed Child."

Ontario Historical Society, Papers and Records: "Anthony Burns in Canada," "Canada's Part in Freeing the Slave," "Social Conditions Among the Negroes in Upper Canada Before 1865," "The Work of the American Missionary Association Among the Negro Refugees in Canada West, 1848–64."

Ontario History: "Abolitionist Interest in Upper Canada, 1830–65," "The Anti-Slavery Society of Canada," "A Pioneer Abolitionist in Upper Canada," "When Uncle Tom's Cabin Came to Canada."

Profiles of a Province: Studies in the History of Ontario: "Captain Charles Stuart, Abolitionist."

Transactions of London & Middlesex Historical Society: "Fugitive Slaves in London Before 1860," "The History of the Wilberforce Refugee Colony in Middlesex County."

Index

Index

The Editorial Board

Frederick H. Armstrong

A Toronto native, Fred Armstrong attended the University of Toronto, obtaining his M.A. in 1949. In 1960, after some years in business, he returned to take his Ph.D. Following a brief stint of teaching at Toronto, he joined the History Department at the University of Western Ontario. His specializations, both in writing and teaching,

were pre-Confederation Ontario and urban history. He has written histories of Toronto and London, Ontario, and many *Ontario History* articles. Active in the preservation movement, he has been the chair of London's heritage committee, and also president of both the Champlain Society and The Ontario Historical Society.

Frederick H. Armstrong *Photo by Sheila Creighton.*

Hilary Bates Neary

Hilary Bates Neary has been a librarian and library trustee, as well as a researcher, editor, and writer of Ontario history. In the 1970s, she contributed to *Ontario History*'s "Book Notes," and edited, along with Robert Sherman, the *Index to the Publications of the Ontario Historical Society, 1899–1972*. More recently, she co-edited

Hilary Bates Neary *Photo by Renée Silberman.*

with Michael Baker both *London Street Names* (2003) and *100 Fascinating Londoners* (2005) for James Lorimer & Company. She is the chair of the Historic Sites Committee of the London Public Library Board.

Karolyn Smardz Frost

Karolyn Smardz Frost is an archaeologist, educator, and author with a doctorate in the History of Race and Slavery. A former executive director of The Ontario Historical Society and vice-chair of Toronto's Historical Board, Karolyn teaches community history and primary research techniques at York University's Atkinson College. She is internationally recognized for her work in multiculturalism and anti-racism education using public history and public

Karolyn Smardz Frost *Photo by Eric Lundsted.*

archaeology. Karolyn's volume, *I've Got a Home in Glory Land: A Lost Tale of the Underground Railroad*, was awarded the Governor General's Award for Non-fiction in 2007, the first book detailing the proud heritage of Canada's people of African descent to be so honoured.

Bryan Walls

Bryan Walls, C.M., O.Ont., a dental surgeon, historian, and author, was born on a farm near Puce, Ontario, just outside of Windsor. His ancestors date back to a time before the end of enslavement. Raised with a belief in education as an avenue for freedom and achievement, Bryan has received

the University of Toronto Faculty of Dentistry Honouree of Distinction Alumni Award of Merit, 2005; Order of Canada (C.M.) 2003; Chancellor's Award, Iona College, University of Windsor 2002; and the Order of Ontario (O.Ont.) 1994, among other honours. Bryan is a committee member of the Metropolitan Toronto Police Services Recruiting Unit; board member of the National Alliance of Faith and Justice out of Washington D.C.; deacon of the historic First Baptist Church, Puce, Ontario ; and a past president of The Ontario Historical Society, founded in 1888.

Bryan Walls Photo by Carlos Ferguson.

Of Related Interest

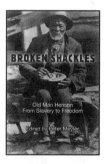

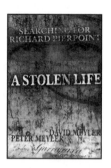

Broken Shackles
Old Man Henson from
Slavery to Freedom
by John Frost
978-1-89621-957-8
$22.95

In 1889, *Broken Shackles* was published in Toronto under the pseudonym of Glenelg. This unique book, containing the recollections of a resident of Owen Sound, Ontario, an African American known as Old Man Henson, was one of the very few books that documented the journey to Canada from the perspective of a person of African descent.

A Stolen Life
Searching for Richard Pierpoint
by Peter Meyler
978-1-89621-955-4
$19.95

An African warrior, Richard Pierpoint, or Captain Dick as he was commonly known, was captured at about the age of sixteen. From his birth in Bundu (now part of Senegal) around 1744 until his death in rural Ontario in the 1830s, Pierpoint allows us to glimpse the activity of an African involved in some of the world's great events, including the American Revolution and the War of 1812.

The Underground Railroad:
Next Stop, Toronto!
by Adrienne Shadd, Afua Cooper,
and Karolyn Smardz Frost
978-1-89621-986-8
$14.95

Not only does this book trace the story of the Underground Railroad itself and how people courageously made the trip north to Canada and freedom, it explores what happened after they arrived. This exciting book will interest readers both young and old who want to learn about this unexplored chapter in Toronto's history.

Tell us your story! What did you think of this book? Join the conversation at www.definingcanada.ca/tell-your-story by telling us what you think.

Available at your
favourite bookseller

DUNDURN PRESS
www.dundurn.com